THE NEW MIDDLE AGES

BONNIE WHEELER, *Series Editor*

The New Middle Ages is a series dedicated to transdisciplinary studies of medieval cultures, with particular emphasis on recuperating women's history and on feminist and gender analyses. This peer-reviewed series includes both scholarly monographs and essay collections. The following books have all been published by Palgrave:

Encountering Medieval Textiles and Dress: Objects, Texts, Images
edited by Désirée G. Koslin and Janet Snyder

Eleanor of Aquitaine: Lord and Lady
edited by Bonnie Wheeler and John Carmi Parsons

Isabel La Católica, Queen of Castile: Critical Essays
edited by David A. Boruchoff

Homoeroticism and Chivalry: Discourses of Male Same-Sex Desire in the Fourteenth Century
by Richard Zeikowitz

Portraits of Medieval Women: Family, Marriage, and Politics in England 1225–1350
by Linda E. Mitchell

Eloquent Virgins: From Thecla to Joan of Arc
by Maud Burnett McInerney

The Persistence of Medievalism: Narrative Adventures in Contemporary Culture
by Angela Jane Weisl

Capetian Women
edited by Kathleen Nolan

Joan of Arc and Spirituality
edited by Ann W. Astell and Bonnie Wheeler

The Texture of Society: Medieval Women in the Southern Low Countries
edited by Ellen E. Kittell and Mary A. Suydam

Charlemagne's Mustache: And Other Cultural Clusters of a Dark Age
by Paul Edward Dutton

Troubled Vision: Gender, Sexuality, and Sight in Medieval Text and Image
edited by Emma Campbell and Robert Mills

Queering Medieval Genres
by Tison Pugh

Sacred Place in Early Medieval Neoplatonism
by L. Michael Harrington

The Middle Ages at Work
edited by Kellie Robertson and Michael Uebel

Chaucer's Jobs
by David R. Carlson

Medievalism and Orientalism: Three Essays on Literature, Architecture and Cultural Identity
by John M. Ganim

Queer Love in the Middle Ages
by Anna Klosowska Roberts

Performing Women: Sex, Gender and the Medieval Iberian Lyric
by Denise K. Filios

Necessary Conjunctions: The Social Self in Medieval England
by David Gary Shaw

Visual Culture and the German Middle Ages
edited by Kathryn Starkey and Horst Wenzel

Medieval Paradigms: Essays in Honor of Jeremy duQuesnay Adams, Volumes 1 and 2
edited by Stephanie Hayes-Healy

False Fables and Exemplary Truth: Poetics and Reception of a Medieval Mode
by Elizabeth Allen

Ecstatic Transformation
by Michael Uebel

Sacred and Secular in Medieval and Early Modern Cultures
edited by Lawrence Besserman

Tolkein's Modern Middle Ages
edited by Jane Chance and Alfred Siewers

Representing Righteous Heathens in Late Medieval England
by Frank Grady

Byzantine Dress
by Jennifer Ball

The Laborer's Two Bodies
by Kellie Robertson

The Dogaressa of Venice, 1200–1500: Wife and Icon
by Holly S. Hurlburt

Medieval Theology of Work: The Contributions of Peter Damian and the Medieval Movement
by Patricia Ranft

On the Purification of Women: Churching in Northern France, 1100–1500
Paula Rieder

Logic, Theology, and Poetry in Boethius, Abelard, and Alan of Lille: Words in the Absence of Things
by Eileen C. Sweeney

LOGIC, THEOLOGY, AND POETRY IN BOETHIUS, ABELARD, AND ALAN OF LILLE

WORDS IN THE ABSENCE OF THINGS

Eileen C. Sweeney

First published in 2006 by
PALGRAVE MACMILLAN™
175 Fifth Avenue, New York, N.Y. 10010 and
Houndmills, Basingstoke, Hampshire, England RG21 6XS
Companies and representatives throughout the world.

PALGRAVE MACMILLAN is the global academic imprint of the Palgrave Macmillan division of St. Martin's Press, LLC and of Palgrave Macmillan Ltd. Macmillan® is a registered trademark in the United States, United Kingdom and other countries. Palgrave is a registered trademark in the European Union and other countries.

ISBN 1–4039–6972–8

Library of Congress Cataloging-in-Publication Data

Sweeney, Eileen.
    Logic, theology, and poetry in Boethius, Abelard, and Alan of Lille : words in the absence of things / by Eileen Sweeney.
        p. cm.—(New Middle Ages)
    Includes bibliographical references and index.
    ISBN 1–4039–6972–8 (alk. paper)
        1. Latin poetry, Medieval and modern—History and criticism—Theory, etc. 2. Christian poetry, Latin (Medieval and modern)—History and criticism. 3. Alanus, de Insulis, d. 1202—Criticism and interpretation. 4. Abelard, Peter, 1079–1142—Criticism and interpretation. 5. Boethius, d. 524. De consolatione philosophiae. 6. Christianity and literature—History—To 1500. 7. Boethius, d. 524—Poetic works. 8. Boethius, d. 524—Influence. 9. Logic, Medieval, in literature. 10. Theology in literature. I. Title. II. New Middle Ages (Palgrave Macmillan (Firm))

PA8056.S94 2006
871'.03093822—dc22   2005051334

A catalogue record for this book is available from the British Library.

Design by Newgen Imaging Systems (P) Ltd., Chennai, India.

First edition: March 2006

10 9 8 7 6 5 4 3 2 1

Printed in the United States of America.

For my father,
J. Vincent Sweeney

CONTENTS

ABBREVIATIONS

For full bibliographical information, consult the bibliography. Translations are my own unless otherwise noted here or in the text.

AC	Alan of Lille, *Anticlaudianus* (Cited by the book number; page numbers from Sheridan's English translation, and line numbers from Bossuat's Latin text. I have used Sheridan's translation unless otherwise noted in the text.)
ADLMA	*Archives doctrinale et littéraire du moyen âge*
ALGCJG	*Alain de Lille, Gautier de Châtillon, Jakemart Giélée, et leur temps*
AST	*Abélard et son temps*
B-FG	*Boethius*, edited by Manfred Fuhrmann and Joachim Gruber
CCCM	*Corpus christianorum continuatio mediaevalis*
CCSL	*Corpus christianorum series latina*
CSEL	*Corpus scriptorum ecclesiasticorum latinorum*
Comm Is	Boethius, *Commentaria in Porphyrium*
Comm PH	Boethius, *Commentarium in librum Peri hermeneias*
Conf.	Abelard, "Confessio fidei ad Heloisam"
Consol.	Boethius, *Philosophiae Consolatio* in *The Theological Tractates and The Consolation of Philosophy*
De Heb	Boethius, *De hebdomadibus* in *The Theological Tractates and The Consolation of Philosophy*
DP	Alan of Lille, *De planctu naturae.* (Cited by the book number, page numbers from Sheridan's English translation, and line numbers from Häring's Latin text. I have used Sheridan's translation unless otherwise noted in the text.)
De Trin	Boethius, *De trinitate* in *The Theological Tractates and The Consolation of Philosophy*
Dict.	Alan of Lille, Liber in *distinctionibus dictionum theologicalium*
Eth.	Abelard, *Ethica sive Scito teipsum*
EN	Boethius, *Contra Eutychen et Nestorium* in *The Theological Tractates and The Consolation of Philosophy*
Ep. 1–4	Abelard and Heloise, "The Personal Letters between Abelard and Heloise"

Ep. 5–6	Abelard and Heloise, "The Letter of Heloise on Religious Life and Abelard's first Reply"
Ep. 7	Abelard, "Abelard's Rule for Religious Women"
Exp Hex	Abelard, *Expositio in hexaemeron*
Gl Por	Abelard, *Glossae super Porphyrium*
Gl PH	Abelard, *Glossae super Peri ermeneias*
GPC	*Gilbert de Poitiers et ses contemporains: Aux origines de la "Logica Modernorum"*
HC	Abelard, *Historia calamitatum*
Hym Par	Abelard, *Hymnarius paraclitensis*
LH	*Listening to Heloise: The Voice of a Twelfth Century Woman*
LNPS	Abelard, *Logica nostrorum petitioni sociorum*
PA	*Peter Abelard*
PAPV	*Pierre Abélard—Pierre le Vénérable: Les courants philosophiques, littéraires et artistiques en occident au milieu de XIIe siècle*
PAPWW	*Petrus Abaelardus (1079–1142): Person, Werk, und Wirkung,*
PG	*Patrologiae cursus completes, series graeca*
PL	*Patrologiae cursus completes, series latina*
Pl Din	Abelard, "Planctus Dinae filiae Jacob" in *Petri Abaelardi Planctus*
Pl Jac	Abelard, "Planctus Jacob super filios suos" in *Petri Abaelardi Planctus*
Pl vir Is	Abelard, "Planctus virginum Israel super filia Jephthe Galadite"
Pl Sans	Abelard, "Planctus Israel super Sanson" (I have used Dronke's translation unless otherwise noted in the text.)
Pl Ab	Abelard, "Planctus David super Abner filio Ner quem Joab occidit" in *Petri Abaelardi Planctus*
Pl Saul/Jon	Abelard, "Planctus David super Saul et Jonathan" (I have used Stevens's translation unless otherwise noted in the text.)
Reg.	Alan of Lille, *Regulae caelestis iuris* (Cited by the rule number.)
SN	Abelard, *Sic et non*
Solil.	Abelard, *Soliloquium*
SQH	Alan of Lille, *Summa quoniam homines* (Cited by the section divisions in the text.)
TChr	Abelard, *Theologia christiana* in *Petri Abaelardi opera theologica*, CCCM, vol. 12
TSch	Abelard, *Theologia 'scholarium'* in *Petri Abaelardi opera theologica*, CCCM, vol. 13
TSum	Abelard, *Theologia 'summi boni'* in *Petri Abaelardi opera theologica*, CCCM, vol. 13

ACKNOWLEDGMENTS

I wish to thank Sebnem Yavuz for permission to reprint portions of chapter one on Boethius' logic which appeared as "Connecting Boethius's Logic and Theology," in *Neue Prozesse um Boethius, Schriften zur Gregorianik-Forschung*, Vol. 2, Köln: Verlag der Gesellschaft für Gregorianik-Forschung e.V. A very early version of my interpretation of Alan of Lille's *Anticlaudianus* appeared as "The *Anticlaudianus* and the 'Proper' Language of Theology," *Essays in Medieval Studies*, Vol. 4 (Fall, 1987): 45–54, some parts of which are reprinted in chapter three with permission.

Early research for this volume was supported by a grant from the Alexander von Humboldt Foundation, by a summer grant from the Bradley Foundation, as well as by a sabbatical leave from Boston College. I especially want to thank Klaus Jacobi of the University of Freiburg for serving as my sponsor and mentor while I was a Humboldt fellow and member of the seminar, Mündlichkeit und Schriftlichkeit im Mittelalter. I thank Prof. Jacobi for his great hospitality during my stay in Germany, his unwavering support for the project, ungainly as it seemed, and helpful direction as I began my research. I wish also to thank Steve Brown for his advice on many aspects of this project, from early grant proposals to composing a prospectus; Steve has been most generous with his time, expertise, and friendship, for which I am most grateful. The most important influence on my thinking was my teacher and mentor, Louis Mackey, who died in 2004. I miss him deeply and can think of no higher compliment than to be called his student.

I am grateful to Jane McIntosh Snyder for looking over my translations of Abelard's laments, Robert Crouse and Jaroslav Pelikan for reading the Boethius chapter, Klaus Jacobi for his reading of the Abelard chapter, and my colleague Richard Cobb-Stevens who read various parts of the manuscript at different stages. I wish to also thank Marcia Colish for her very careful reading of the manuscript and for her suggestions and corrections which have improved it. My graduate assistants over the past few years,

David Bollert, Tedmun Chan, John Burmeister, Susan Bencomo, Maggie Labinski and Matthew Robinson also worked hard gathering sources, checking and correcting footnotes and bibliography and proofreading; my mistakes made their work harder.

I am especially grateful to Boston College and my colleagues in the Philosophy Department. They have allowed me to take a somewhat indirect and extra-philosophical path in my research and writing, given me great freedom in my teaching, and in many ways provided a community that has fostered my work. Lastly, I wish to thank to my husband, Ira Kronitz, and my two daughters, Mariel and Eliana, born during the composition of this book, for the many sacrifices they made so that I might write. One can, as many others have, give birth to both books and babies, but not alone.

INTRODUCTION: WORDS IN THE
ABSENCE OF THINGS

It was not an arbitrary choice when Peter Lombard ordered the subjects of theology in his *Sentences* according to Augustine's distinction between signs and things. "All teaching," Augustine writes in the opening lines of *De doctrina christiana*, "has to do with signs or things."[1] But since, as Augustine notes, "things are learned by signs," the knowledge of signs is the first and most crucial of the academic disciplines.[2] Peter Lombard simply renders canonical the centrality of signs and language that had already occurred in practice in the Latin west. Before the dissemination of the complete Aristotelian corpus, language was for the medieval world its technology and its science, and God its most important and problematic object. The threefold function of the redeemed language Augustine struggles to create in the *Confessions*, *De doctrina christiana*, and other works is to express the nature of God as ultimate reality, to persuade God to bring about union with him, and to move others to accept that reality and to convert their lives accordingly. In *De doctrina*, Augustine "transcends his own classical education," completely reforming the education program for Christians by laying out the legitimate uses of a redeemed language.[3] Hence, the sciences of words—logic, grammar, and rhetoric—are developed and their power harnessed in order to name God, interpret scripture, argue in support of Christian doctrine, and ultimately reach God in prayer and meditation.

Since for Augustine all the things of this world are also signs signifying God, everything except God is a sign to be interpreted.[4] The consequences of this are two-fold. First, all problems become problems of interpretation, the misreading of signs or the taking of signs for things.[5] Second, since God is the thing which cannot be expressed, we are confined within the realm of signs trying (and always to some degree failing) to reach the signified, inhabiting a world of words/signs in the absence of things.[6] That failure does not result in silence, because of the obligation to speak, though imperfectly, and the possibility of doing so through the redemption of words by the Word.[7] In this way, Augustine lays out the parameters for the importance, promise, and limits of language which form the foundation of work in the Latin West for almost a millennium.

In this volume, I assume Augustine's well-documented and accepted place as the source of the nature and importance given to the language arts and look instead at the theory and theme of language in Boethius, and two twelfth-century figures influenced by him, Abelard and Alan of Lille.[8] While Augustine is the source of what has aptly been called "the semiological consciousness of the Christian West," Boethius is the source of its technical vocabulary and academic form.[9] For the twelfth century as a whole, Boethius's logical commentaries and theological tractates are the standard works of reference and provide the technical vocabulary for new work. As we shall see, Abelard and Alan take up not just Boethius's vocabulary but his questions and issues in their accounts of language and theology. Moreover, they take up not just the logical and theological parts of Boethius's project but also the questions and themes of the *Consolation* in their poetry.

Boethius's project was to translate, comment on, and transfer the language of philosophy into theology, to incorporate secular disciplines and texts into his own philosophical/theological vision. Boethius's imaginative world is one populated largely by other texts, and is notably different from Augustine's appropriation of secular texts in the more positive and autonomous place given to Aristotelian logic and pagan literature. The voices of these texts speak themselves in the work of Boethius. They are not, as in Augustine's *Confessions*, translated into the language of scripture and made part of an ordered narrative of the author's development, divided firmly into those that speak the same, although impoverished, truth of scripture and those that contradict that truth.

Moreover, there is in Augustine a seamless synthesis between the technical, analytic problems of language and theology and the spiritual/existential project of mapping a journey to God both for himself and as a model to others. By the twelfth century this unity has broken down to some degree, parts of it appearing in different authors and genres. These projects, intellectual/analytic and imaginative/existential are linked in the authorships of Boethius, Abelard, and Alan but have been divided into different works— Boethius's logical commentaries, tractates and *Consolation*; Abelard's logical and theological works, his poetry, autobiography, and letters; Alan's theological disputations, axioms, dictionary, and allegories.

These formal and rhetorical differences in the treatment of texts and sources in Augustine and Boethius point to a substantive, philosophical difference. Augustine's rejection of Aristotle is based on the rejection of the view that the world makes sense on its own terms, as classified in terms of the categories or as analyzed into matter and form, act and potency.

Boethius, by contrast, we shall see, is committed to the partial truth and relative utility of understanding the world on its own terms, that is, as Aristotle, the Stoics, the poets, and even ordinary opinion grasp it. Thus these voices are less assimilated in the Boethian corpus than in Augustine's and, as a result, they create interesting tensions in the stories within which Boethius incorporates them. This is true not only of the *Consolation* but also the tractates, not just of the plays of Seneca but also the logic of Aristotle.

The continuation of this project—the independent pursuit of secular disciplines but as ultimately rejoining the project of union with God—is one way we might characterize twelfth-century humanism.[10] Abelard and Alan, unlike other important twelfth-century figures, Bernard Sylvestris or Gilbert of Poitiers, for example, take up both the pursuit of secular knowledge and its ultimate unity with the theological goal in forms and projects derived from Boethius. As we shall see, they both endorse the project at the same time as they point to its fragility, even its ultimate failure. In Abelard the ultimate unity of these different perspectives found in Boethius almost breaks down into contradiction, and in Alan the possibility of separating different perspectives even provisionally is shown to limp.

In what follows, I offer an interpretation of each of these thinkers by following the theme of language and the shape of the relationship between word and thing. I read across logical, theological, and literary writings from each author, tracing the ways in which conclusions and distinctions taken from their logical or grammatical positions both form and are formed by their speculative, poetic, and spiritual concerns. In this way, I attempt to place the logic and philosophy of language of these thinkers within the context of their work as a whole. In these authors and in the medieval west as a whole, at least until the independence of the arts faculties in the fourteenth century, logic and philosophy of language were embedded in metaphysical, theological, and spiritual projects: for example, to describe the nature of God and the Trinity, to interpret scripture as well as the tradition of commentary on it, and to serve as instruments of prayer and teaching. Thus, while it may be important to study their views on logic and language in abstraction, it is imperative that these elements be replaced in the larger intellectual context which gave birth to them.

What I have found by tracing the theme of language through their speculative theological work as well as literary and poetic works is not only that their theories of language turn up in the other areas of their corpus but also that there are structural, rhetorical, and narrative connections and similarities between the problems of how words illuminate things, how the mind comprehends God, and how an individual reaches beatitude. Throughout the works of Boethius, Abelard, and Alan, the relationship of sign to signified and the position of language as mediator between thought and thing become models for describing separation and the desire for union, for effecting reintegration and reparation in the moral, interpersonal, metaphysical, and theological realms. The narrative about both words and human life as a project of unsatisfied desire and postponed union—of creatures for God, of words for their objects—is shared, though shaped differently, by all three. Thus I have worked to show the linguistic/logical elements of the theology and poetry but also the poetic/narrative elements of the logical and theological works. For me, the most surprising and rewarding part of this study has been to see the ways in which the narrative of estrangement and longing explicitly laid out in the literary works is adumbrated in their logical and speculative works. But finding those connections was only possible by crossing over the usual disciplinary boundaries between philosophy, theology, and literature of the Middle Ages.

In recent years there has been an explosion of work on medieval texts that were overlooked because of the emphasis on theological work of the high culture; these studies of vernacular, pastoral, and mystical theologies have immeasurably enriched our sense of the depth and richness of medieval culture and religion. What I offer here is an installment on the project of reconnecting more traditional, canonical authors, and questions to this now more richly understood background. Boethius, Abelard, and Alan are a good place to start because their work can be characterized as scholastic and poetic, analytical and mystical, speculative and pastoral. A look at the range of the work of Boethius, Abelard, and Alan of Lille shows us some ways in which the high academic and more popular, accessible forms might be linked. Thus, Boethian and twelfth–century forms of theological reflection are not just, as earlier intellectual history had it, that which is overcome in the story of the progress of the formation of theology in high scholasticism.[11] Nor are they (or parts of their authorship) something to be ignored because they are too scholastic or theological to be relevant to the larger culture, as some more recent studies might imply.

Two very recent volumes also work to re-knit some of these pieces of medieval thought in ways that overlap this volume, studying works which are as literary as they are philosophical/theological: Barbara Newman's *God and the Goddesses* and Willemien Otten's *From Paradise to Paradigm*.[12] Willemien Otten describes the work of twelfth–century authors as "theologizing" (rather than doing theology) because of the "mixture of rhetorical and grammatical commonplaces interspersed with moments of sharp reflection of a broadly theological and philosophical nature," which is markedly different from scholastic theology. The term "theologizing" works not just because, as Otten argues, it captures the fluidity of philosophical/theological boundaries of the period, but also, I would argue, because it captures the sense that all their work is suffused with theological motifs and aspirations.

Newman's study develops a new category of "imaginative theology," which she describes as "the pursuit of serious religious and theological thought through the techniques of imaginative literature, especially vision, dialogue, and personification."[13] The genre would include not just Alan's allegories (which form part of Newman's study) but also Boethius's *Consolation* as the model and inspiration for the others, as well as Abelard's poetry. While Newman makes the convincing case that in these literary works, writers were allowed a kind of freedom to explore what might otherwise have been seen as heterodox themes if explored using the forms of academic theology, I would like to make the case that in Boethius, Abelard, and Alan at least, their imaginative visions portraying God and the understanding of God also inform their speculative theologies and accounts of language. Moreover, the latter provide the theory that justifies their own and others' more daring literary work: because there is no proper language of God, we are left only with various types of improper language, including those constructed by the imagination as well as reason, those composed of images as well as arguments.

Because these writers use a number of different literary forms—commentary, disputation, poetry, axiom, and allegory—my analysis is as much literary as logical, as much about their metaphors, style, and rhetoric as about the substance of their positions and arguments. I do not argue that these formal literary elements contradict the content of these works, but I do try to show how they support, complement, and complicate that content. And because my conclusions rest as much on the dialectical and rhetorical structure of the arguments as on their logic, they require some fairly close reading of these texts. As a way into and around those readings, I have provided an introduction to each chapter which sketches the conclusions I then attempt to show through a reading of that author's logical, philosophical/theological, and literary works.

CHAPTER 1

BOETHIUS: TRANSLATION, TRANSFER, AND TRANSPORT

Integrating Multiple Perspectives

Many scholars over the years, confronting the heterogeneous group of texts attributed to Boethius, argued that they were written by different authors or were written by one author whose views have undergone a fairly radical transformation between the writing of the tractates and the *Consolation*.[1] Since it has become widely accepted that Boethius is the author of all the works of logic, theology, and philosophy traditionally attributed to him, the debates about Boethius that have been the most lively are about his religion and ultimate philosophical sources and allegiances. For some he is an Augustinian,[2] for others a Christian adapting his Platonism to Christianity;[3] for still others he is an Alexandrian Platonist,[4] a Stoic,[5] or stoicized Platonist.[6] In a way all these debates about Boethius's originality, the unity of his authorship, his ultimate sources, and commitments are about the same thing: how do we read across this collection of very different texts?

Although I do not pretend to have found the definitive solution to the problem of interpreting Boethius, following the theme of language through the main parts of the corpus has yielded a stronger sense of the unity, autonomy, and originality of Boethius. One way to express it is in visual terms, terms suggested, I will show below, by the *Consolation* itself.[7] My contention is that Boethius's innovation is the construction in some detail of multiple and correct, though limited, perspectives from which human understanding can view itself and the nature of reality. As we will see, the method of the Boethian project is linguistic: different perspectives are constructed by developing different vocabularies and different senses of the same terms. Then, the perspectives are arranged hierarchically, the lower encompassed by the higher.[8]

The themes to which Boethius returns again and again in the logical commentaries are the distinction between the order of words and things and the conventionality of language. From this fundamental distinction between what is the case and what we say, it is only a short step to the elaboration and amelioration of this gap in terms of multiple senses of terms, multiple disciplines with distinct methods and terminologies, and even multiple ontologies which either describe the same reality in different terms and/or are true descriptions of different strata of reality. The conviction that motivates a good portion of the tractates is the view that disagreement and contradiction can be mediated by the creation of or the distinction between different vocabularies. And while it is true that the *Consolation* attempts to hierarchize the different perspectives on Boethius's fate, it still gives voice to those "lower" perspectives through the voice of Boethius, the prisoner.

Boethius's own use of language mirrors this multiplicity of meanings, methods, and rhetorics. He goes from close, careful translation, paraphrase, and commentary designed to provide an introduction to the greenest of beginners, to the terse, esoteric, and technical language of the tractates, to the complex interweaving of poetic and philosophical language and allusions in the *Consolation*.

Boethius surely had important models for such multileveled and synthetic views in his Neoplatonic masters and contemporaries, who would have seen his stated plan to translate, comment on, and show the agreement between Plato and Aristotle as an understandable if bold undertaking.[9] Boethius's vision differs from theirs both in being Christian and in being worked out in almost exclusively textual terms—in the mediation of texts in the translation and commentary, in the self-conscious production of new textual forms, and in the development of new vocabularies. Boethius both creates his own vocabulary in his translations and transfers it from its "proper" and original location to theological topics where it is radically reworked in the theological tractates. The same project continues in the *Consolation*'s attempt to ascend from the prisoner's worldly perspective to that of Lady Philosophy by means of the language and arguments of different philosophical schools.

I will trace the construction of this peculiarly Boethian textuality in Boethius's *Isagoge* and *Peri hermeneias* commentaries, theological tractates and *Consolation*. In all these texts, Boethius's most common methods are, first, the division or distinction, and second, the construction and relating of different perspectives. Following Boethius's own pedagogical plan, then, I begin with the logic commentaries.

Logic: Distinguishing Words and Things

Boethius's logic texts share two things. The first I have already mentioned: a special care to distinguish between the order of words and things. The second is a strategy of mediating the non-identity of words and things by inserting distinctions and narrative relationships between them, following and extending Porphyry's example of adding the layer of the predicamentals between Aristotle's categories and things.

The paradox is that the strategy of mediation and distinction aimed at bringing together different perspectives puts *more* rather than *less* distance between reader and the text being interpreted. For the new terminology is an extra layer between the reader and the things described by the text; it thus separates and creates a replacement for the two things it wishes to join. Logical categories are already "second intentions," words about words meant to mediate the understanding and application of words to reality. The Boethian logical corpus is, then, a tissue of "third intentions" on "second intentions."

This motive (to join) and this effect (to separate) can also be read off the nature of the logical corpus Boethius left us. Almost every aspect of Boethius's logical work is doubled. The *Isagoge* is a double for the *Categories*, and Boethius's own task as translator is to produce a double of Porphyry's text, in which he claims to have "rendered every word, expressed or implied" (*Comm. Is.* I. 71A). His translation is then doubled by his commentary, and the first commentary by a second. The *Peri hermeneias* receives two commentaries as well, and the *Topics* receives two renderings, one based on Cicero's topics and one based on those of Cicero and Themistius taken together. It is a pattern that marks Boethius as belonging to a very late generation; his connection to his sources is so etiolated that he attempts to make up for the lack of immediacy by carefulness.[10] Like the shift of perspective and vocabulary among the major disciplines of natural philosophy, mathematics, and theology, the understanding of particular texts is also for Boethius a process comprised of movement through different perspectives, and, if not through wholly different vocabularies, at least through increasingly elaborated ones.

Commentary on the Isagoge

The Place of Logic

When introducing the discipline of rhetoric, Cicero concedes the evil and misleading uses to which the arts of language are put, but he still tells a positive tale of their discovery. The language arts make possible, Cicero claims, the peaceful and wise relationship of human beings in justice; it effects the persuasion of others to the conclusions of reason.[11] Boethius, by contrast, tells a tale of the problems created by language. The assumption that the structure of language corresponds to the structure of things is the source both of moral depravity and false natural philosophy in the Epicurean view that pleasure is the only good and the view that things are constructed of atoms, Boethius contends. Language is also the source of a kind of philosophical babble of confused and contradictory accounts of the nature of things (*Comm. Is.* I. 72C–73B). The "cure," according to Boethius, is to interpose the study of arguments before the study of things, to add a layer of words about words before coming to the application of words to things.

But how does Boethius think of the place of logic, this study of words and arguments, in relation to that of philosophy?[12] Is reasoning about how language and arguments work an end in itself? If so, logic is a part of philosophy. If not, language and arguments are instruments of philosophy, tools used to reach conclusions about things, either to be known or to be done. But even more is at stake. If we cannot get behind language to thought, or below convention to nature, then the study of language is an end in itself, and philosophy is identical with the study of language. If language refers directly and naturally to things, logic is the transparent instrument of philosophy.

The form of Boethius's well-known answer is ultimately more interesting than its content. As he will try to do with the main question of his treatise, the problem of universals, Boethius tries to have it both ways. Instead of choosing between logic as instrument or part, Boethius tries to craft different senses in which both are true. On the one hand, he concedes the independence of the study of discourse from that of things and, therefore, its status as a separate part of philosophy, but, on the other hand, he subordinates logic to the other disciplines, to the pursuit of truth or goodness (*Comm. Is.* I. 73C–75A). This move also makes of the language arts (as he already set them up at the outset) mediators between understanding and things. Moreover, it mirrors Boethius's own view of language: he attempts to carve out a space between the extremes of conventionalism and realism, based on the distinction *and* relation of convention and thing, thought and language.

The Problem of Universals

For Boethius, the problem of universals is completely germane to the theme around which he unites the other topics of Porphyry's introduction—the relationship and distinction between words and things. For Boethius rejects the Platonic view that genera and species correspond to forms, claiming instead that terms and things do not perfectly correspond (*Comm. Is.* 86A). The challenge, then, is to describe this noncorrespondence in a way that saves the truth of naming. Boethius does this, following Alexander, by arguing that we often consider things as other than what they are strictly speaking (*Comm. Is.* 84B).[13] We do so both by "composing" or uniting things not found together in reality and by dividing things that are united in reality. The products of composition are fictional constructions and thus false; though those of division and abstraction are not necessarily false (*Comm. Is.* 84C).[14] Universals are arrived at by abstraction.

Universals can be thought of in one way and can exist in things in another, Boethius explains, just as convex and concave lines are thought of and defined differently, yet are one and the same line considered from two different perspectives. Just as the same line is convex and concave "so also for genera and species, i.e., for singularity and universality, there is only one subject, but it is universal in one way when it is thought, and singular in another when it is perceived in those things in which it has its being"(*Comm. Is.* 85C–D). Words are not identical with the things they name, yet it is not false to call an individual by the universal name. For to consider the individual man and the universal man is to consider the same thing but from different perspectives.

On both universals and the place of logic, Boethius attempts to retain aspects of Platonic and Aristotelian views; he accommodates both views by making them different but true perspectives. So there is a sense in which it is true that in abstraction the mind beholds the universal "alone and pure as the form itself is in itself" (*Comm. Is.* 85A), as Plato thought, and another in which it is true that genera and species only subsist in sensibles, as Aristotle thought (*Comm. Is.* 86A). Thus Boethius accommodates Platonic and Aristotelian views by arguing that they are true from different perspectives.

Commentary on the Peri hermeneias

Relating the Elements of Language

Given the cryptic and classificatory nature of the *Peri hermeneias*, it is perhaps not surprising that Boethius's commentary attempts to fill out the text with a narrative connecting the various elements of language described.

The most noteworthy aspect of Boethius's commentary is his account of the relationship between written and spoken language and between understanding and things. In this commentary, only partially prompted by Aristotle's text, the binary relationship between words and things of the *Isagoge* becomes the four-part relationship between spoken and written language and between understanding and things (*Comm. PH* I. 1. 20. 15–25). Boethius gives us the plotline of the narrative relating these four. Letters cannot exist as letters unless some significant word exists out of these letters, and so also there are no words without understanding, nor any understanding without things (*Comm. PH* I. 1. 21. 27–33). There are, however, Boethius notes, "invented words [*voces invenies*]" which do not in any way signify anything, by which he seems to mean nonsense words like *blityri* (his example early in the commentary at I. 1. 5. 14–15) and the mere making of noise (*Comm. PH* I. 1. 32. 17–23). There are also understandings without any corresponding things, such as centaurs and chimeras (*Comm. PH* I. 1. 22. 1–5).

Thus, Boethius admits the possibility of the disintegration of the narrative of the dependence of letters on words, words on concepts, and concepts on things. His move to counteract the possibility of disintegration is to claim their ultimate union in the mind of God. "Whenever the thing is, so also is there an understanding, if not among men, then certainly for him, who by the divinity of his proper substance in his proper nature is not ignorant of any thing" (*Comm. PH* I. 1. 22. 8–11).[15] Thus God is the guarantor of the union of word and thing, of the truth of language. But he is so only in principle, not in directly giving intuition of the forms/ideas of things, as he does for Augustine, but only in guaranteeing that things have the intelligibility to be known and named by the human mind, which abstracts that intelligibility from them. This account of the union of word, thought, and thing in the divine mind is the linguistic integrity human language strives to imitate. While giving an account of the relationship *and* distinction between word, thought, and thing as they are in human language, Boethius notes both the possibility of their complete separation and their perfect unity. These extremes help locate the middle ground that Boethius is mapping and function as a cautionary note about the limitations of human language, its imperfect correspondence to things.

The order of the narrative connecting letters, words, thoughts, and things is reversed, Boethius claims, if we consider the position of one who learns, hears, and responds rather than the one who teaches, speaks, and questions. The former goes from names to understanding to things, while the latter proceeds from things to understanding to words. The different positions one may occupy in a dialogue, then, require different hermeneutics. That this order can and must sometimes be reversed is because of the discursive mode of knowing that is appropriate to humans.

Boethius also distinguishes between a "natural" pair (things and understandings) and a "nonnatural" pair (words and letters); the latter he describes as "constituted by position" (*Comm. PH* I. 1. 25. 1). Letters are the components of words only when the letters are placed in a certain order. It is how those elements are seen, what they are *taken to be*, which makes them function linguistically. Similarly, as we saw, one's "position" in communication (as speaker or hearer) gives different points of view on the linguistic process, different starting and end points. The recognition of different perspectives is a recurring strategy and intrinsic to Boethius's project of constructing bridges between different accounts and vocabularies as a way of resolving conflict. For the first step in communication is the recognition that others do not occupy the same position or perspective. People cannot read each other's minds; they must work backwards from what is said to what is meant to the reality one's understanding has grasped. This is the attitude from which Boethius composes his translations and commentaries.

Words, Thoughts, and Things
The crucial question posed by the *Peri hermeneias* for the Middle Ages is whether words signify "passions of the soul" or things. Boethius argues against the Platonists, whom he takes to have the view that words signify incorporeal forms, and against others who argue words signify sense objects or imaginations. Boethius makes sense and imagination intermediaries between things and understanding by weaving sense and imagination into the story of how sounds become understanding. Sensation, he explains, "gives birth" to imagination, and understanding "supervenes" on confused imaginings, resulting in the "perfect" or completed signification of nouns and verbs. This account, Boethius claims, solves "many old quarrels" by transforming rival claimants to be the referents of words (sensation, phantasms, understandings) into stages or mediators between words and things (*Comm. PH* I. 1. 29. 7–12; 21–27). Boethius thus takes a position—words directly signify passions of the soul, that is, understandings—but notes that all the elements can lay partial claim to be that which words signify. Thus rival accounts are true from different perspectives.

Boethius also distinguishes between three "sentences," the written, the spoken, and the understood in order to relate them in a similar way. Brian Stock applauds Boethius's distinction between spoken and written language but argues that it should have been more sharply drawn, leading to a clearer position on whether words (the units of spoken language) depend on letters (the units of written language) or vice versa.[17] But part of the reason for Boethius's apparent waffling on the issue comes from his understanding of the different directions from which the written word can be approached. As a writer, one goes from words to letters because one is moving from spoken to written language; as a reader, one moves from the letters on the page to the words of the spoken language. Thus whether words or letters are primary depends on where one begins. As Stock notes, Boethius's main concern is *connecting* spoken and written language, a move in the service of the larger goal of connecting understanding and things. Boethius first divides these four elements into two groups of two, those whose signification is "by position" (written and spoken language) and those whose signification is natural (understanding and things). Once Boethius has joined so many distinct elements in a single narrative he works very hard to keep the seams from splitting. Since his main focus is the distinction between the artificial and the natural, the two artificial elements and the two natural elements have to be firmly tied to each other.

A threat equal to the complete isolation of one element from another is their conflation. One such possibility Boethius argues against at great length is the view that words might be *naturally* significant. Naturally significant sounds (like weeping or barking) are *not* words in the same way that mere copper is *not* coin. In fact, Boethius argues, money is called money exactly for that by which it differs (*discrepet*) from other copper (*Comm. PH* I. 1. 32. 25–29). So too with words, then. That words are *in* sound means that that sound is *taken to be* significant. Thus what distinguishes mere sound from words is that words are sounds that can refer to letters (*Comm. PH* I. 1. 33. 2–15). Such a definition allows Boethius to argue for the connections between words and understanding. For to say sounds are linked to letters is to say that they can be understood by someone else, that they are, like coins, constructed in order to have the same value for different members of the community. It also means that they do not directly signify things but rather understandings of things.

Boethius continues to add layers to this picture, differentiating between the impression made on the soul by the thing and the "natural" impression by which "a shape [*figura*]" is "transferred [*transfertur*]" onto wax or marble or paper (*Comm. PH* I. 1. 34. 13–19). The impressions on the soul are as different from "natural" impressions as coin is from copper. Impressions on the soul, like sounds connected to letters, are *taken to be* significant and, hence, capable of being linked to understandings. The passions of the soul are created from these impressions. At this point, Boethius turns the line of his narrative into a circle, concluding, "for the same thing which is in the soul as a certain passion is indeed a similitude of the thing" (*Comm. PH* I. 1. 35. 20–21). Thus the word that signifies the passion of the soul is a similitude of the thing named.

The "happy ending" of this tale is the same as the happy ending of the *Isagoge* commentary's discussion of universals. Though both commentaries begin with the distinction between language, thought, and being, they end with their reconnection. But the connections hold only if the links remain distinct. Only by appealing to the distinctions and relations he has so carefully worked out can Boethius refute relativism (surely one of the "old quarrels" Boethius alluded to earlier as solved by this account of words). Relativism either argues for the absolute break between the order of language and being, so that language corresponds to no common reality, or asserts the simple identity of words with sensations, which are different for different people. Boethius's argument against relativism, under either construal, admits, on the one hand, the distinct "position" (i.e., conventional aspect) from which languages are spoken and from which "civil justice and goodness" derive. But on the other hand, Boethius insists that words and understanding and sensation and thought are distinct (*Comm. PH* I. 1. 41.

14–42. 6). Only because sensations and words can be different for different individuals and in different languages but thought and things common can there be an alternative to relativism, and an explanation for its apparent plausibility. That is, though individual sensations and languages can be different (making all things seem relative), through abstraction we reach the same thought referring to the same thing (*Comm. PH* II. 1. 41–42).[18]

This set of distinctions and relations is one Boethius returns to throughout the commentary, importantly in the course of the definition of *nomen*. The crucial characteristic of a name is that it signifies *ad placitum*. If names belonged to individuals naturally, they would never change and each thing would only have one name. Yet individual names change and the same things have multiple names; for example, "we say 'sword', 'brand' and 'blade' and these three aim at one substantial subject" (*Comm. PH* I. 2. 55. 31–56. 14).[19] Boethius also reiterates the conventional character of the noun, again marking the difference between animal sounds and words. We have names for the sounds animals make—barking, roaring, lowing—which are not identical with the actual sounds animals make, even though the animal sounds are significant and seem to be used by animals to converse with one another (*Comm. PH* I. 2. 60. 25–61. 1).[20]

When Boethius turns from the discussion of the noun to the verb, his concern shifts. For the noun, the most important thing is to distinguish it from naturally significant sound. For the verb, his concern is to distinguish it from the noun. Thus Boethius argues that verbs taken by themselves are names of things, though only in a certain sense. While a verb signifies what is said of or is in a subject (i.e., a universal or particular accident, according to the terminology of the *Categories*), it does not signify that subject as subsistent, as a noun does. So "tastes" does not signify the one who tastes, but rather the nonsubsistent tasting of that subject: "For just as a name [*nomen*] is a proper signification of some kind of thing as itself subsisting, so in the same way a verb is the signification of a thing not as subsistent through itself but through another subject and in a certain way as leaning on it as the foundation" (*Comm. PH* I. 3. 74. 5–9).[21] In this account of the relationship between nouns and verbs, Boethius bequeaths to the later Middle Ages a whole series of questions about nouns and verbs, about the relationship of grammatical categories to metaphysical ones, and about language in general. It is the nucleus, or perhaps something more, of the view, rearticulated and elaborated with ever more complexity, that words signify things in different ways, from different angles and aspects, not in a direct or one-to-one mapping.

The Larger Narrative: From Words to Things, from Logic to Metaphysics
Boethius opens the second book of his commentary with a reflection on the human tendencies toward work and idleness; we are motivated to

virtue, he notes, mostly by difficulty and demoralized by idleness. He stops, however, at this stage in his journey not out of laziness or before a threatening abundance, but out of ignorance. As he takes his break from the hard work of his commentary, he states his intention, God willing, to take up the much larger task of translating and commenting on all the works of Aristotle and Plato.[22]

Strange that Boethius makes a statement of his plan as a writer in the middle of the commentary. Or is it? The passage is dominated by verbs of motion and travel, their derivatives and opposites, *mitto, cedo, fero*. I can imagine Boethius wanting to preserve a sense of forward motion through this long project as one might stop to write out a plan for the whole book in the middle of the first chapter, as a break and as a reminder of where one is headed. Boethius's pilgrimage through Aristotle is so slow and careful even he (not to mention his reader) loses a sense of progress; he attempts to renew it with a reflection on the larger journey, stopping in the midst of the trees for a perspective on the forest. This famous passage seems to me like a kind of meta-comment on the text. As Boethius makes the transition from the account of words to sentences in Aristotle's text, he stops to reflect on his own project to go from translation and commentary on the individual texts of Aristotle (and Plato) to the construction of how they can be joined together in one interpretation. Boethius's "words" are his individual commentaries, and the "sentences" he hopes to construct are the joining and relating of Plato and Aristotle, just as sentences unite noun and verb.

Future Contingents

In a way Boethius's commentary on Aristotle's discussion of future contingents constitutes a kind of down payment on the way he might have tried to complete his project of harmonizing Aristotle and Plato. It also illustrates again how Boethius has moved methodologically and rhetorically away from Augustine. While Augustine's and Boethius's (in the *Consolation*) positions on providence are not that far from each other, they seem to have come to their views from different directions and to see the issue in different terms on the existential level.[23] The contrast mirrors larger differences in how the two thinkers construct both a language and a life that reaches toward God. Boethius both here and, as we shall see, in the *Consolation*, is worried about freedom's consistency with providence; he is moved to his greatest passion when considering the inefficacy of human action if it is determined by providence, while Augustine's overwhelming concern is to show the meaningfulness and unity of his life and actions by seeing in them the constant and sure hand of providence leading him to God. Though in the *Confessions* as elsewhere, Augustine contends that human beings have free choice consistent with God's complete and perfect providential activity, freedom in so far as it might be threatened by God's providence does not concern him in the *Confessions*. Rather he is concerned with freedom in so far as it is threatened by his own sinfulness. Augustine envelops his life in the life of God to make it make sense; Boethius works to preserve its autonomy in order to make its turn to God meaningful.

Boethius's desire to avoid determinism is so overriding that, prompted by Aristotle's account in the *Peri hermeneias*, he has been read as holding the same position as Aristotle. The terms in which Aristotle introduces the question of future contingents seem to leave little room for providence. First, Aristotle poses the question in a way that requires affirmation or denial: either events are truly contingent, or they are or can be correctly predicted or controlled, in which case they are necessary. Second, Aristotle argues strongly for the existence of real contingency, which seems to preclude providence. Given the nature of Aristotle's text, what is most striking about Boethius's commentary is that, even as it supports Aristotle's conclusions quite unconditionally, it accommodates much of the Augustinian picture, and opens up space for the more Neoplatonic account Boethius gives in the *Consolation*.

Boethius's prologue to the discussion proper sets up the Stoic position at one extreme and places his support clearly with Aristotle. On the Stoic view, Boethius claims, everything is determined, and what looks like a chance event is merely one whose cause is hidden from us. Moreover, the freedom that remains is in effect to choose the course for which one is fated (*Comm. PH* III. 9. 194. 23–196. 3). In the *Confessions* Augustine seems to hold a view not far from the Stoics as he struggles to see providence directing all the events in his life, including those that look like free choice or chance. I am not suggesting that Augustine's position is determinist, only that the perspectival shift which is a crucial part of his view is used by the Stoics as well, as is the view, reinterpreted in Christian terms, that freedom is a kind of submission to the foreordained plan. Both of these become elements in (though they are not the whole of) Boethius's discussion of providence in the *Consolation*.

Boethius begins his more direct support of Aristotle and rejection of the Stoic position somewhat paradoxically with an appeal to nature. The first and the most obvious problem with determinism, Boethius contends, is that it would mean that the order of nature is frustrated. For, he argues, it is part of the order of nature that human beings take counsel, an activity that would be pointless if all things happened by necessity (*Comm. PH* III. 9. 220. 8–15). Thus Boethius uses one form of necessity, the coherence of nature, to argue against another, determinism *tout court*. Boethius returns again and again to the counter-intuitive character of the determinist position. It makes nonsense of human deliberation, and thus of human nature, and the obvious differences between human beings (*Comm. PH* III. 9. 222–23). The claim that everything is necessary, like the claim that everything is chance, or that everything is subject to free choice is simply implausible (*Comm. PH* III. 9. 223. 12–20). As Chadwick notes, Boethius follows Alexander in the view that the nature of causes and effects is mixed.[24] Some are necessary, some possible, some subject to human manipulation, some matters of chance. Also following Alexander, Boethius argues that God's knowledge can only be perfect if he knows future contingents *as contingent* rather than necessary; to claim otherwise would be to make God's knowledge false (*Comm. PH* III. 9. 225–26).

What is rhetorically striking about Boethius's discussion is the way in which he ultimately places his view between the two extremes, the Epicureans, who hold everything is chance, and the Stoics, who hold everything is necessitated. Out of what began as a dilemma between affirming and negating determinism, a forced option between Aristotle and the Stoics, Boethius crafts a position as a mean between the two different extremes, like the possible itself (*Comm. PH* III. 9. 239. 24–240. 2).

Second, Boethius positions his view as the pluralist view, repeating on a number of occasions his view that "everything is mixed in the plurality of things in this composite world, and is not judged simply to be held together [*contineri*] by chance, necessity, or free judgement" (*Comm. PH* III. 9. 230. 23–26. Cf. III. 9. 232. 11–13; 240. 2–7).[25] Thus animals are subject to one nature, the stars to another, and rational beings to yet another. Plants and animals are governed by heavenly bodies, but human beings and heavenly bodies by their own will (*Comm. PH* III. 9. 231. 12–19). Moreover, humanity is itself a mixed nature in which the soul in itself has the faculty of free choice, but the body is ruled by a nature subject to imagination, desires, anger, and other passions. And everything, Boethius adds, is dependent on the divine will. Boethius concludes, "neither then is celestial necessity completely undermined, nor is chance by this disputation eliminated, but free choice is strengthened" (*Comm. PH* III. 9. 232. 3–10).

Boethius even manages to find some common ground between Aristotle and the Stoics, first, by finding a more extreme position, and, second, by making use of the Stoic appeal to perspective to explain apparent contingency. The more extreme view is that of Diodorus, who argues, according to Boethius, that if something is or will be, it is necessary to the point where the contrary cannot really be thought. Even Philo and the Stoics, Boethius notes, think that though things are necessitated, we can think the contrary quite coherently (*Comm. PH* III. 9. 234. 22–235. 20). This constitutes the transition back to Aristotle's conception of the possible as opposed to the necessary. The necessary is that of which the contrary cannot be thought. So snow cannot be conceived with the hot, nor fire with the cold, Boethius argues, echoing the *Phaedo*.[26] But Boethius adds yet another layer. If fire could admit cold and remain fire, the understanding of fire would be completely frustrated. And if we could not know the proper nature of anything, nature, accustomed to perfection, would be frustrated (*Comm. PH* III. 9. 236. 13–16). Boethius seems to be taking the *Phaedo's* argument one step further. Socrates argues from the axiom that nature does everything for the best to a kind of model that gives necessary and certain accounts of nature, for which the account of snow and fire are the examples. Boethius applies the same axiom reflexively, on knowers. If it cannot be known with necessity that snow cannot be hot, nothing can be known. That which seems to belong to human nature with the same necessity as cold does to snow is that human beings are rational and can, within certain limitations, know and choose.

Boethius uses a conception of providence as the rationality and coherence of nature to argue for the existence of genuine and distinct possibility and necessity. It is actually what he has been doing from the first lines of his commentary in this chapter. He begins with and returns to the argument that determinism makes everything peculiar to human nature a farce, a false appearance, making nature either a trickster or bumbler. In a way, Aristotle does something similar, for he argues against determinism by appealing to the experience of deliberation and the practices of justice as being incoherent if contingency is not real. But Boethius does so more overtly and in a way that ties in with his other strategies in the commentary.

Compared to both Augustine and the other ancient views he discusses, Boethius emerges as the proponent of compromise and pluralism, arguing for the partial and perspectival truth of a whole series of apparently mutually exclusive positions. He concedes more truth than does Augustine to both determinism and chance, and, notwithstanding the reality of both necessary and contingent outcomes caused by natural agents, he asserts the governance of all things by providence that knows and governs things in their complexity. For Boethius, the Stoic and Epicurean views are not completely false but partially true, true of sections of reality in much the same way physics, mathematics, and theology are true accounts of different ontological levels of reality. How these accounts of different levels of reality are all encompassed in a divine perspective without completely robbing them of their autonomy is in effect the question to which the *Consolation* turns. Here this conclusion is stated but somewhat unobtrusively and without full explanation.

Boethius does not reject providence or even the view that there is some sense in which chance is a result of a limited perspective rather than real randomness. Rather he rejects a providence that necessitates everything on moral grounds. Aristotle and Boethius make the moral grounds obvious: to ascend precipitously to the perspective that all things happen from an undifferentiated necessity makes human action nonsense. To take seriously the determinist conclusion that action is illusory amounts to an abdication of responsibility to intervene in the world on the side of good. Boethius's life is surely one that exemplifies a belief in the efficacy of intervention and the value of deliberation. It is no exaggeration to say that it was his commitment to these principles that caused his death as he tried to bring about reconciliation between king and senate, East and West. Boethius's life sheds light on the passion with which he writes against the view that denies the reality of human attempts to work for the good.

Moreover, a special temptation for the Christian and Neoplatonist is jumping too quickly and too simply to the ordering of all things by providence. Such a view amounts to a denial of one's own experience, the difficulty of one's choices, and the real pain of one's losses; more importantly, it drives one to deny the same elements in others' lives. Such truncated emotional responsiveness masked as a philosophical acceptance or Stoic fatalism is something we have all met with. Some might think Boethius tends to go in exactly this direction in the *Consolation*. I do think the progress of the *Consolation* is made through continual reinterpretation of Boethius's experience in ever higher and more all-encompassing terms, in some ways very close to Augustine's attempt to understand his life from the perspective of providence in the *Confessions*. Nonetheless, I want to argue, this does not amount to accepting the determinist view that Boethius rejects in the *Peri hermeneias* commentary. First, of course, even while arguing for universal providence in the *Consolation*, Boethius also argues for free will, which makes human action and deliberation real and efficacious. Moreover, the *Consolation*'s account of providence does not amount to a denial of the reality of the injustice he has suffered, the success he has achieved, nor the losses he has endured and has still before him. It does not amount, in other words, to a denial of the reality of secondary causality.

The Tractates: Creating the New Language of Theology

In the *Consolation*, just as Boethius and Lady Philosophy are preparing to delve into the problem of evil and the relationship between freedom and foreknowledge, Lady Philosophy challenges him to engage in a "clash of arguments," out of which conflict of reasons some "glimmer of truth [*scintilla veritatis*]" might emerge (*Consol*. III. pr.12. 302.70–72). Like the deep philosophical debates of the *Consolation*, the tractates are the clashing of arguments. First, they are clashes with the major philosophical and theological problems of his era, some peculiar to Christianity, some common to pagan and Christian belief systems. Three of the tractates (*De trinitate, Utrum pater, Contra Eutychen et Nestorium*) are obviously concerned with heresies related to the Incarnation and Trinity. Robert Crouse proposes the interesting thesis that *De hebdomadibus* and the *Consolation* too are connected to issues of the day, *De hebdomadibus* to Manicheanism, and the *Consolation* to Pelagianism.[27] If such a scheme is true, all of Boethius's writings are connected to matters of immediate and public concern. But the *Consolation* and *De hebdomadibus* hide their connection to public controversy. And while it is clear who Boethius's opponents in *De trinitate* are, Boethius takes a step back, using the more general and abstract language of Aristotle's *Categories*. Though the *Contra Eutychen et Nestorium* was provoked by a particular public event (the discussion of the Greek bishops' letter about the two Christological heresies), it is Boethius's own thoughts recollected in tranquillity. Moreover, it responds to the uproar by appealing to the complex meanings of the basic philosophical terms at the root of the debate. Boethius makes clear that the tract is also meant to have a larger and more long-lasting purpose: modeling Christian disputation, bringing to it the discipline and strategies of rationality, of philosophy. In fact, he makes it clear that modeling Christian disputation for the Romans who do not understand the need to reason about these things is a more important aim than coming up with the final or complete theology of the Incarnation.

There is, then, a second and deeper sense in which the tractates are a "clashing" of arguments. Boethius restructures these conflicts by going to their roots. In *De trinitate* and *De hebdomadibus*, the clash is between Aristotelian and Neoplatonic metaphysics; in *Contra Eutychen et Nestorium*, it is between the Greek and Roman approaches to theological issues. In the logical texts, Boethius develops his method of resolving conflict by making distinctions and creating different perspectives from which both opposing views can be true. In the commentary on Aristotle's discussion of future contingents, Boethius created a kind of space within the Aristotelian view for a Christian, Neoplatonic view. In the tractates, this becomes the more direct and difficult project of explicitly bringing both worldviews together.[28] Thus the project is integration, not refutation, and the instrument for the project is language. More specifically it is the distinction used to create hierarchies rather than contraries. Just as Boethius argues that different points of view on the nature of logic or universals or future contingents are partially true, that is, true from one perspective though superceded by a higher one, so he resolves theological disputes by reference to different meanings of basic terms, some of which are more proper than others. In this approach to resolving problems, the tractates are more scholastic than Augustinian and we see the roots and reasons for those scholastic methods in Boethius's strategy of integrating without completely submerging different perspectives in his own.

Contra Eutychen et Nestorium: Finding the Mean and Modeling Christian Disputation

The introduction and dedication to this work inaugurate the conflicts of authorship and audience, public and private personae, esoteric and Christian, which we will also see in *De trinitate* and *De hebdomadibus*. The prologue is Boethius's account of his experience of the meeting to hear the Greek bishops' letter questioning the coherence of the Latin church's position on the natures of Christ. He did not speak up during the meeting but found the Latin position that the Chalcedon formula of Christ as "in" and "of" two natures needed no further explanation, ignorant (*EN* Prol. 74. 31–33). Unlike the rest of the audience, he ruminates on the question instead of simply swallowing the papal resolution; the insight he reaches is not, at least not at first, clear understanding, but is about the nature of the problem (*EN* Prol. 74. 33–36). The lack of understanding among the Roman audience extends beyond the nature of Christ and even beyond the Greek bishops' objections to the Western formulation; it extends to their own words, which Boethius claims they do not understand and do not know that they do not understand (*EN* Prol. 76. 41–44). Their first and greatest sin is the covering up of ignorance; like the wounds Lady Philosophy will entreat the prisoner to uncover in the *Consolation*, ignorance must first be exposed in order to be healed (*EN* Prol. 76. 44–45). The first intellectual failure and the one the bulk of the ensuing text works to address is in not perceiving the gap between words and understanding.

But though Boethius addresses the failures of this audience, he does not address them directly. He writes to John the Deacon as his editor, ultimately intending his text for Symmachus, his adopted father/father-in-law (*EN* Prol. 76. 48–54). One motive for writing at such a distance from the original occasion and audience and for the esotericism of this text is Boethius's sense of the unworthiness of the public as audience. But Boethius is also motivated by his uncertainty of the value of his voice and by his fear of being attacked and misunderstood. The mob he heard discussing the letter from the Eastern church could just as easily turn on him, calling him a heretic for siding with the Greeks.[29] But there is something deeper at stake. The possibility of a solution depends on creating a certain distance from the very hot debate, transforming the discussion into a problem of language rather than power, philosophy rather than politics. Only under such circumstances does Boethius even have a chance of finding a place for the concerns of both Roman and eastern churches. Unlike Abelard and Alan of Lille, as we shall see, Boethius's desire is to integrate rather than refute opposing views, to diffuse conflict rather than raise the battle cry in a war of words. Hence, Boethius confronts the "self-contradictory" heresies of

Eutyches and Nestorius largely by carefully defining the terms (*natura* and *persona*) which are the sources of both the problem and the solution (*EN* Prol. 76. 59).

Boethius begins his own argument with multiplicity, the multiplicity of natures in Christ and the multiplicity of definitions of nature coming from different philosophical traditions and sources.[30] Boethius cites three applications of the term "nature": nature predicated of bodies alone, substances alone, and, lastly, of all things "that can in any way whatever be said to be" (*EN* I. 76. 1–3). The latter usage includes everything, even what cannot be understood except by "removal of forms" (i.e., God and matter) (*EN* I. 78. 13–15). When nature is predicated of substance, nature becomes "that which can act or be acted upon," a definition identical to that of substance (*EN* I. 78. 21–26). Restricted to corporeal substance, nature is the principle of motion (*EN* I. 80. 41–42). The last definition of nature, nature as "the specific difference that informs anything," is the definition that grounds the broadest usage of the term.[31] This is the one relevant to the Christological problem, the one according to which Nestorians and the orthodox agree that there are two natures in Christ (*EN* I. 80. 56–61). It is a point of agreement Boethius finds by first muddying the waters a bit, cataloging multiple usages of the term, and then searching for definitions that explain those uses until one is found on which the parties can agree.

In the definition of person, Boethius uses a different tactic to broaden and deepen the sense of its meaning: the etymology from the Greek. Though this is surely not the first time such an account is offered as evidence, it still implies a self-consciousness about his relationship to a philosophical tradition that he has taken over, as well as consciousness of the distance between ordinary and philosophical languages. Boethius's etymological remarks include a long account of the origins of *prosopon*, describing the masks and mentioning the characters of Greek tragedy (*EN* III. 86. 7–23). The effect of etymological explanation, especially when the original use is so far from the technical, philosophical one, is the same as using a metaphor; it provides a new perspective on the term and, hence, on the problem. Boethius's aim in his explanation of both nature and person is, I think, to loosen the hold of words on us so that they can reappear *as words* instead of things, giving him room to readjust their meaning and use.[32]

Boethius continues his strategy of making room for a solution in the discussion and definition of *essentia/ousia* and *subsistentia/ousiosis, substantia/hupostasis, persona/prosopon* (*EN* III. 88. 42–90. 78).[33] The Latin terms are defined and correlated with Greek equivalents in a way Boethius, citing Cicero, reminds us is imperfect. Boethius arranges these terms hierarchically, essence as applicable to being, subsistence as being that is not in a subject, substance as subsistent subject for accidents, and person as rational, individual substance (*EN* III. 90. 79–87). Even more than with "nature," Boethius creates a whirl of complex terms and then magically settles the dust by distinguishing and ordering their different meanings. Once this task is accomplished, the last step is to use these different layers to show that there is room to understand both unity and plurality in the Godhead (one God in one essence but three substances or persons) and in the second person of the Trinity (one person and two natures).

Boethius exhibits a certain flexibility in the use of technical vocabulary he has so carefully laid out. He concludes that we could, on his analysis, say that God is three substances and three persons, were not this use of language forbidden by the church (*EN* III. 90. 89–91.101). He leaves the exact language that should be used to the church and defends not the claim that God is three substances, but that God is substance because he is the principle underlying all things.[34] I take this suggestion not so much as a sign, as Stewart and Rand argue, of Boethius's readiness to submit to the authority of the church.[35] Rather, it is a concession that, like the rest of the linguistic reflection in the text, works to undermine obsessive and unthinking attachment to verbal formulas as if they were magic, as if they were fixed in or required by the nature of things. That kind of dogmatism is, after all, exactly what Boethius finds most intolerable about his fellow Romans: they simply repeat that Christ is in and of two natures as the orthodox formula that does not have to be further understood.

For Boethius the Christological problem is a problem of correspondence, in some ways like the correspondence of words to things. What Boethius argues against in both Nestorius and Eutyches is their model of one-to-one correspondence between natures and persons, not unlike the way he argues for the noncorrespondence, but connection, between words and things. These heresies, then, are like the two extreme positions on universals. Like nominalism, which denies any real connection between individual and universal, Nestorius denies any real connection between the divine and the human, leaving two Christs, one divine and one human. As in nominalism, only the usage of the same name connects the objects so named. One of Nestorianism's paradoxical consequences, however, is a kind of pantheism since everything has an equal right with Christ to be called God.

Boethius casts Eutychenism, by contrast, as a kind of realism, so uniting the nature of Christ that there is no real, particularized humanity in him. As in realism, the incorporeal, universal nature is what is real about the thing, overwhelming the particular and material in it. Its paradoxical consequence is to make the body of Christ human only in name and to break the connection between Christ and humanity. Just as surely as Nestorius, Eutyches undermines the Incarnation and the promise of salvation.

In the Chalcedon explanation, Boethius complains, what it means for Christ to "consist of two natures" is "an ambiguous formula of double signification" (*EN* VII. 118. 40–41). To solve the problem, Boethius substitutes another form of "duplicity," the duplicity of metaphor (i.e., see-ing one thing *as* another), for the "knot of ambiguity and equivocity" in the original formula (*EN* VI. 118. 46–47). One mode in which something is *of* something else is when one thing is completely confounded and changed physically into the other. This is the Eutychen view of how Christ is "of" two natures. The other mode of being "of" two natures is the "con-junction of the two so that both remain," for example, the conjunction of gold and jewels in a crown (*EN* VII. 118. 44–45; 116. 12–8). Boethius argues that Christ is of two natures in this sense. The two elements, human and divine, are related as elements in a metaphor—one is understood *as* the other, in terms of the other, but without losing its proper nature, and thus without becoming the other (*nec alteram in alteram transmutari*) (*EN* VII. 116. 27). "For if you understand [*intellegas*] man," Boethius explains, "the same is man and God, since man from nature, God by assumption. If, how-ever, you understand God, the same is God just as man, since God by nature, man by assumption. And in him nature is doubled and substance is doubled, since God-man and one person, since the same is man and God" (*EN* VII. 120. 66–74). Note the direct address of the reader in the second person verb, "*intellegas*," calling on the reader to participate in this seeing *as* in order to understand unity and duplicity in Christ.[36] Thus the mode of transfer is verbal and the solution is achieved by developing more than one perspective; the reality is not double but must be seen in two ways.

The treatise is through and through the redrawing of the lines of disjunction and conjunction; it engages in the "distinguishing and mixing" that, Boethius argues, has to be done by the understanding (*intelligentia*) to understand Christ (*EN* VII. 118. 59–61). Boethius's solution takes place in the expansion and multiplication of ways of seeing the second person of the Trinity rather than, as Eutyches and Nestorius advocate, in a reduction or oversimplification of Christ's reality.

Thus Boethius works to make the reader see between and beyond two extremes. It is, as Boethius says at the beginning and the end of the treatise, a search for the mean: "This is the middle way between two heresies just as the virtues too are a mean. For all virtue is fitly [*decore*] located in the mean of things" (*EN* VII. 120. 74–77). Though the model of thinking of a solution in terms of a mean seems to come from the original letter written by the anonymous Greek bishop appealing to Pope Symmachus to find a middle way between Nestorius and Eutyches, Boethius expands this view to orthodoxy in general, implying that theological reasoning itself is finding the mean.[37] While Boethius clearly does not mean that theology is practical science or that it should be moved by practical concerns, he does seem to imply that it is an act of balance and judgment more than an achievement of pure intellectual insight; its results are not certain but are subject to revision and consultation. Like the mean of virtue one can always be refining and tailoring, Boethius notes that he stands ready to take back his utterance in the face of better accounts (*meliori sententiae*), an attitude in marked contrast to the dogmatic response of his fellow Romans to the same problem. Finally, it is also a model of reasoning which mirrors the issue at hand in this case: Christ too is the "mean" or mediator between divine and human.

De hebdomadibus: The Logic and Rhetoric of Being

This work begins from the metaphysics of creatures rather than God, and with the problem and some of the language of Aristotle's *Metaphysics*. The task of the piece is to derive a Neoplatonic metaphysics from an Aristotelian one. Its question is this: given the reality of the world around us and its intelligibility more or less in the terms in which our language captures them (i.e., in Aristotelian language and principles), how can/must things be related to the One, first good (the Neoplatonic principle)? Boethius, then, unlike Augustine, does not reject the analysis of things into substance and accidents but places that view within another that understands them as real and knowable as participating in the One.

This comes, I think, to much the same thing Crouse claims about the work: that it is Boethius's response to Manicheanism.[38] The goodness of all things is established in a way that, on the one hand, saves the reality and independence of things so that they are not merely subsumed into the One, and, on the other hand, shows that those things derive their being and goodness from the One. Thus Boethius's account of the goodness of all things that can only derive from that which is goodness per se is constructed to withstand Aristotle's arguments against participation. A being must possess or be that which it is, lest we be left, as Aristotle thinks Plato is, holding the awkward view, on the one hand, that neither the good–itself is good, nor the real–itself real, or, on the other hand, that the particular thing which we call good or beautiful or human is not truly so since it is such only by participation.[39] The transmutation of the problem of Manichean dualism into this difficult and abstract philosophical problem could very well be how Boethius makes good on a promise he makes in the prologue. There he writes that he has decided to make his views inaccessible to the "impudent" and "wanton." He chooses, he says, the obscurity of brevity in order to hide the truth from the unworthy (*De Heb.* 38. 8–14).

The truth is ultimately that a thing can be good or be at all only if it is related to that which is Being and Good in a perfect unity, that is, to God.

The desire for union with the perfect good both defines things and divides them from the One they desire. In themselves and until they achieve union with this being, all things except God lack internal integrity. The language appropriate to their condition, then, is not the language of logic, of identity, but that of rhetoric, of desire. Hence, stated in yet other terms, the text is about the relationship of logic to rhetoric. Its project is to make consistent the identity between subject and predicate (the metaphysical subject and its predicates of being and goodness) the logician posits, and the internal fragmentation of particular, composite beings and their distance from their desired object the rhetorician strives to describe and then traverse.[40] True to the propensities we have seen in Boethius's logic, his solution is not to choose between these two languages and the ontological situations they describe but to bring them together by ordering them hierarchically.

The Structure of the Text

The argument of the text as a whole is a *reductio ad absurdum*. As a matter of mental separation, Boethius leaves aside the Neoplatonic metaphysical principle, the One from which all things derive, in order to show that such an assumption leads to absurdity (*De Heb.* 44. 86–48. 128). We can put this argument in terms of the relationship between logic and rhetoric. Boethius will show that the identity of a thing with itself that logic seeks is impossible without the difference and division within the thing and its distance from and desire for the One and the good described by the language of rhetoric. Thus, without the One as origin and end, the world of language and experience described by Aristotle could not exist.

Boethius sets up his *reductio* by pinning the reader on the horns of a dilemma to which he or she is bound only in so far as he or she accepts an Aristotelian metaphysics in which predicates belong to things either substantially or accidentally (*De Heb.* 42. 56–44. 85). If things have their natures or qualities by participation or accidentally, either they or the form in which they participate cannot be said truly to have that nature or quality. Conversely, if things are substantially good, they are wholly good, good in their being, and thus identical to the first good. On my reading, then, these middle two portions of the tractate, the dilemma and the *reductio*, are "Aristotelian" in this sense: they argue from entities composed of substance and accident, and consider things and take them to be intelligible on their own terms and without relationship to a source on which they are dependent for their being and goodness.

By contrast, the first and last parts, the axioms and the solution are Neoplatonic. The form and style of the axioms clearly imitate the structure and obscurity of Proclus and they operate on the oppositions of diversity and unity, simplicity and complexity, and participation and purity (*De Heb.* 40. 18–42. 55).[41] These contrasts map out two layers of composition in finite being, first, of *esse* and *id quod est* and, second, of substance and accident, laying the groundwork for the argument proper in which goodness is attached to *esse*. That the concluding solution is Neoplatonic is perhaps beyond dispute, given its assertion of the dependence of all things on the first good for their being and their being good (*De Heb.* 46. 119–50. 162).

The Logic of the Text

The argument of the text is to distinguish between three different kinds of predicates, being (and being good), accidental predicates (e.g., being white), and substantial predicates (e.g., being human). The well-known problem of the text is to develop a consistent interpretation of Boethius's distinctions between *esse* (or sometimes *ipsum esse*) and *id quod est*, and between *esse aliquid* and *esse aliquid in eo quod est*.[42] The whole argument revolves around the difference between these two pairs. To be (*esse*) and to be something (*esse aliquid*) (e.g., white) must be different so that Boethius can then argue that being good attaches to being (*esse*) rather than merely belonging to something as an accident (*esse aliquid*).

The difference between the pair *esse aliquid* and *esse aliquid in eo quod est* is the clearest. The expression, "<u>esse aliquid in eo quod est</u>," Boethius says signifies substance; "to be something" signifies an accident (*De Heb.* 40. 38–40).[43] The presence of "signifies" reminds us that part of what is to be worked out is the relationship between saying and being. Boethius is in effect noting that even though the sentence structure ("A is B") is the same whether the predicate is a substance or accident, the predicate can relate to the subject in different ways. This difference is not reflected in ordinary language, but it *can* be reflected in language—though only in a language whose complexity is inversely related to the simplicity of that which it attempts to capture. Thus, the longer and clumsier *esse aliquid in eo quod est* signifies what the thing is more primarily: substance, and the simpler *esse aliquid* signifies that which the thing is only in composition with its substance: accident. Boethius's aim is to show that goodness is a predicate more like (but not just like) substantial predicates than accidental predicates. It is, then, an argument for yet another way in which the structures of being and saying are not symmetrical.

The more difficult and controversial issue is how to understand the distinction between *esse* and *id quod est*. While most scholars agree that *id quod est* refers to the concrete particular being, the debate is over the meaning of *esse* and *ipsum esse*. For some it is essence, for others, existence. L.-M. de Rijk argues that *esse* must mean essence or the *forma essendi* (e.g., humanity) while *id quod est* is the concrete individual.[44] The standard argument against *esse* as existence is that the distinction between essence and existence derives from Avicenna and that Aquinas anachronistically reads this distinction into Boethius.[45] However, besides Ralph McInerny, who takes Aquinas to have correctly interpreted Boethius, there are Neoplatonic interpretations of Boethius that argue nonetheless for taking *esse* to mean existence.[46] Pierre Hadot argues that the distinction between *esse* and *id quod est* mirrors the distinction between existence (*huparchis*) and substance (*ousia*), a distinction made by Neoplatonists such as Marius Victorinus and Candidus.[47] Thus, Hadot argues, *esse* means pure being without determination, while *id quod est* is the limitation of *esse* in a concrete thing which exists according to a certain form.[48]

I think Hadot's interpretation fits the evidence in the text; Boethius does seem to have in mind two different distinctions (between *esse* and *id quod est*, and between *esse aliquid* and *esse aliquid in eo quod est*) and three different kinds of participation (in *esse*, in the *forma essendi*, and in accidents). Moreover, Hadot's account of the distinction between *esse* and *id quod est* is implied in the very grammar of *id quod est*. The distinction is, then, between the *id quod*, the "that which" or the "what," and its *esse*. For without a subject (in the grammatical sense) the finite verb *est* remains the infinitive form, *esse*. Thus, when Boethius claims that the *ipsum esse* "is not yet," he means that it has not yet received determination, a grammatical subject that turns *esse* into *est*. So only with a *forma essendi*, a determination for its being, do we get the composed *id quod est* (*De Heb.* 40. 28–30).

The contrast throughout the axioms is between the complexity of the kinds of substances described by Aristotle's categories and the simplicity of the being that is the ground of Neoplatonic metaphysics. Axiom six seems to imply that the most important break is between *esse* and the other kinds of "whats" something may be, substantial and accidental, not between substantial and accidental being, as it is for Aristotle.[49] Thus we have two modes of participation, the participation in *esse* in order to be, and the participation in something else to be something.

Axioms seven and eight assert the unity of simple being to contrast with the layers of diversity of composed being. These two axioms, then, are the counterparts to the account of composite being already given, describing simple being. Axioms two and five on composite being begin with "*diversum est*," noting the distinction between *esse* and *id quod est* and between substance (*esse aliquid in eo quod est*) and accident (*esse aliquid*). By contrast, axiom seven asserts that *esse* and *id quod est* of a simple being are one, and axiom eight asserts that the *esse* and *id quod est* of the composite being are diverse (*De Heb.* 42. 45–48).[50]

The last axiom (IX) notes that diversity always causes tension or "discord," and similarity causes desire (*De Heb.* 42. 49–52). This last axiom is less technical than the others, easily skimmed after the density of the preceding ones. But it is important. For it asserts that a thing "naturally reveals" itself through what it desires. Thus, it grounds the possibility of the ultimate union of lover with the beloved even as it describes that which separates that which desires from its object of desire. The ontological relationship between a thing and its desired end gives the dynamism to composite being and to Boethius's argument. Unless it is agreed that things are like what they desire, Boethius cannot get to the claim that things are good because they desire the good.

What Boethius leaves unstated in the last axiom is that desire, like plurality, is also a negative sign, a sign of what something does not have yet and is not yet. This is stated explicitly in the *reductio* part of the argument: "If things were nothing other than good" (nothing other than what they desired), "they would not seem to be things [*res*] but the principles of things, or rather not *they* would seem to be, but *it* would be the principle. . ." (*De Heb.* 46. 111. 114–15). To forestall the conclusion asserting not the likeness but the identity of composite being and goodness, Boethius must argue for a distinction between the goodness of composite things and the goodness of the principle of things (*De Heb.* 46. 122–48. 126).

Boethius expresses this difference between composite beings and the first good in two different ways. First, unlike the first good, composite beings are not good in every way; and, second, unlike the first good, they are something other than good (*De Heb.* 48. 130, 134–35). These claims, though verbal inversions of each other, come to the same thing. Composite beings can be described in terms of what they *have* (qualities besides good-ness) that the first good lacks (it is only good); they can also be described in terms of what they *lack* (a wholly good being) that the first good has. To understand that both say the same thing requires a shift in perspective. For the first speaks from the perspective outlined by ordinary experience and ordinary language in which each determination of the things by substance or accident is added to the list of predicates affirmed of it and is seen as a positive growth of its being and possibilities. The second speaks from the point of view of the One, in which each new determination is a narrow-ing, a fragmentation of its being and power. Particular goods are substan-tially good but not identical with the first good because they are not simple. And because they are not simple, they depend for their existence on the first good.[51] And in order to understand the nature and extent of that complexity, the reader needs the ontology laid out in the axioms.

Method and Audience: the Pedagogy of the Text
The relationship between the axiomatic and argumentative portions of the text raises a more general question about the axiomatic method and

esoteric character of the treatise. Boethius himself makes the method a part of the argument rather than something assumed by it. He does so first in the preface in which he asks his reader not to "take objection to obscurities consequent on brevity"; these are, he continues, "the sure treasure house of secret doctrine and have the advantage that they speak only with those who are worthy" (*De Heb.* 39. 11–14, Tester's translation).

Boethius also draws attention to his method in the first axiom. Here Boethius lays out his well-known definition of a "common conception" as "an enunciation which anyone approves as soon as he hears" (*De Heb.* 40. 18–19). True to his position in the *Peri hermeneias* commentary, Boethius makes the connection between propositions and understandings, rather than words and things. His claim is that "common conceptions" have a kind of integrity, an immediate correspondence to thought and a direct mapping onto things. Not to everyone, however, Boethius notes, preparing the reader for the difficulty in the axioms to follow. The paradox is that the axioms, which should assert only the immediately intelligible, are in fact intelligible only (and just barely) to the learned. He gives no explanations of the axioms, noting that the "prudent interpreter" will be able to supply them (*De Heb.* 42. 53–55). Further, he shrugs off the difficult task of connecting the axioms with the argument as if it should be just as obvious as the understanding of the axioms. It is, of course, just as obvious, which is to say not obvious at all.

The other method Boethius uses is that of mental separation, a technique we recognize from his commentary on Porphyry. Things which cannot be separated in actuality, Boethius explains, can be separated in thought, just as in mathematics we consider the triangle without the matter of which it is composed (*De Heb.* 44. 87–98). This strategy is in effect the opposite of the axiomatic one, for it requires the reader to break the connection between word, thought, and things. This kind of separation ought to be difficult because it requires thinking of things other than as they are, but the part of the text that uses this strategy is much more accessible than the axioms.

The reversal of the reader's expectations, the self-evident axioms as less accessible than the more complex abstraction of the *reductio*, serves Boethius's thesis. For the argument of the tract is to show how the surface of the world of our experience, of plural beings composed of substance and accidents, has as a condition for its possibility the linking of those beings with the One, the first good and absolutely simple being. This is the deep structure of being mapped by the axioms. It is also the most intelligible level of reality, not to us but in itself, while what is most intelligible to us is what is further from the ontological roots of being, a world constructed of individual, independent beings composed of matter and form. Thus the reader finds the text accessible in an order opposite to ontological order and to the way Boethius presents it. The path Boethius creates for his reader is one along which he will discover his own lack of understanding when faced with the axioms. That understanding finds a foothold in the assumptions and arguments of the *reductio* section, and emerges to an understanding of the metaphysics described by the axioms. Boethius's text is esoteric, but its esoteric meaning can be penetrated by anyone willing to follow its pedagogy.

The last part of the argument draws the moral and spiritual consequences from the metaphysical condition of all things (dependence of all things on the first good), and the epistemological condition of the reader (not understanding the nature and extent of that dependence). It comes in Boethius's reply to the objection that if the first good is just in its being, then all things, because they are derived from the first good, must be *just* in the same way that they are good (*De Heb.* 50. 162–67). Boethius responds by saying that the first good is just, but since being and acting are not the same for us as they are for the first good, we are good but not just in our being (*De Heb.* 50. 165–71). The interesting part of Boethius's response is his very pointed shift in pronouns to discuss beings other than the first good. Throughout the treatise, compound beings have been discussed in the third person neuter, either singular or plural. As he concludes, however, Boethius shifts to the first person plural: "For *us* to be [*esse*] and to act are not the same," "Nor is it therefore the same for *us* to be good as just, but it is the same for *all of us* to be that in which *we* are [*in eo quod sumus*]" (*De Heb.* 50. 168–71, my emphases). Thus, Boethius turns the reader's attention from an abstract and distant metaphysical problem to his own fragmentation, his own imperfect possession of justice, and dramatically shifts the story from an abstract consideration of goodness and being to one which is a description of both the reader and the writer. The closing words of the tractate summarize what is also the bittersweet conclusion of the *Consolation* on providence and human life: "Therefore, some things are just; other things are otherwise; but all things are good" (*De Heb.* 50. 174). This is exactly the perspective toward which Lady Philosophy leads her pupil, that providence governs all things for the good, even while human beings endowed with free will are in their free actions (and sufferings) often unjust.

Like the *Consolation*, *De hebdomadibus* is the story of the origin and end of all being, including Boethius's. This is exactly what is captured by Boethius's richly enigmatic dedication of the text: "From the same to the same." Of course, on one level, Boethius is referring to himself as the "same" author of another tractate, and to one of his adopted fathers, Symmachus, his father-in-law, or John the Deacon, his "spiritual father," as the "same" one who received another of Boethius's texts. But given the subject of this carefully constructed and esoteric text, it must also refer to the content of the text, which itself imitates the Neoplatonic pattern of emanation and return; thus all creation emanates from and returns to the same One. And since the story is Boethius's as well as that of all composite being, both readings can go together. Boethius as writer attempts to return to one or both of his two "fathers," giving back what he has learned. At the same time, his progress mirrors that of all being, made perfect when and to the degree to which it returns and is reenfolded into its source, its true father.

De trinitate: Supporting the Foundation of Faith

Audience and Method

Like *De hebdomadibus, De trinitate* is an encounter between Aristotelian and Neoplatonic categories. In this text, Aristotle's categories—substance, quality, quantity, relation—are rewritten to form a "Neoplatonic logic" and pressed into service to describe God as triune. Boethius describes his choice of the language of the categories to discuss the Trinity as driven by esoteric motives. The combination of brevity and new words protects the study of divine things from those who are too dull and too clever (the dull are too lazy and the clever, too envious). On these he "looks down [*deieci*]," while he hopes Symmachus's eyes will "turn toward [*convertitis*]," his work; the rest are unworthy even to read the words of his text (*De Trin.* Prol. 4. 12–22). Like the opening to *Contra Eutychen et Nestorium*, this opening narrates Boethius's struggle to direct his attention toward the right audience and away from the wrong one, to distract the unsympathetic and incapable and attract the worthy, in this case only Symmachus. And as in *De hebdomadibus*, he attempts to accomplish this by partially cloaking rather than fully revealing his own thoughts in his words.

Almost as a concession, Boethius adds another account of his language as originating from the limitations of reason itself. Reason's seeing or contemplation (*intuitus*) can only mount so high (*conscendere*) toward the divine; like medicine, all the arts have some sort of limit or goal (*finis*) that the *via rationis* approaches though does not always achieve (*De Trin.* Prol. 4. 23–28). The healing of the gap between our understanding and the divine, between word and thing, is the goal Boethius's medicine will fall short of. And so Boethius ends his prologue not by criticizing others but asking for pardon for his own failure (*De Trin.* Prol. 4. 29–30).

What, then, is the leading motive for Boethius's language? Is it chosen for its ability to "veil" the matter from the unworthy? Or is an indirect language necessary because there is no language that is truly proper and directly revelatory of the subject matter? Esotericism is motivated by a sense of one's superiority over the many from whom important truths must be hidden. The sense that there is no appropriate language, by contrast, brings with it a sense of one's own unworthiness and inability to reach truths that are beyond all human understanding and language. When Boethius compares himself to those who are unaware of their own ignorance (as he did in the prologue to the *Contra Eutychen et Nestorium*), he sees himself as knowing and looks down on those mortals below. When, by contrast, he focuses on the reality of God, he looks upward at a goal a great distance from him, a location he shares with other human beings.

Whichever is the main motive, both esoteric and failed languages are asymmetrically related to the reality they attempt to signify, and this is the theme to which the work returns over and over again. Thus, for example, section one emphasizes the single, universal, orthodox formulation of the Christian faith in contrast to the plurality of claimants on that faith. Further, in order to reach unity, both of the three-in-one God and of doctrine for the one, universal church, Boethius begins with plurality, the plurality of speculative sciences (physics, mathematics, theology) and their respective discourses.

Many Names for the One God

As Boethius starts his discourse he notes two different truisms about knowledge: first, that we can only consider things insofar as they can be understood, and, second, that we should attempt to form our beliefs about things as they actually are (*De Trin.* II. 8. 1–4). What Boethius does not make explicit is that these two pieces of advice are in the present case at odds with one another. He will not be able to consider the Trinity as it actually is because it cannot be fully understood by us. The "solution" in a sense to this problem is to consider things in different ways, according to different disciplines, according to different terminologies. Thus, Boethius implies, mirroring the nature of things more closely requires not one but *different* approaches, different ways of seeing and, hence, different modes of expression.

Even though Boethius quickly moves through and beyond the lower "perspectives" of physics and mathematics to divine science, the same kind of strategy is used throughout the treatise. Thus, Boethius continues to construct different perspectives or terms for the same thing, a single perspective or term for a diverse group of things, and "higher" perspectives superseding lower ones. First, Boethius points out that from the perspective of "divine science," which deals with forms separate from matter, only such pure forms truly are and are only "this" and not "this" and "that" (they have no accidents); they are, then, their own "*id quod est*," and therefore truly deserve their names. Forms in matter, by contrast, even though they have their principle of being and their name from their forms, are nonetheless incorrectly called forms, but are merely "images" or "simulations" of form (*De Trin.* II. 12. 53–4). Boethius is not just, as Stewart and Rand point out, signaling his Platonism, his belief in pure and separate forms.[52] He is also noting that the most proper language, that which most clearly corresponds to the order of things, is not ordinary language, in which material objects are named from their forms. Composites of matter and form, unlike pure forms, are not only or wholly those forms. In order to grasp this, one must shift from an ordinary perspective and language to a less enmattered one, the kind of shift that is required several times more as the work progresses. By this path to form, then, Boethius arrives at unity, at the absence of difference and plurality in God. And so, he concludes, one can truly say "God is God."

However, Boethius must move from the unity of the divine nature to the plurality of the divine names. The divine names are of three sorts: synonymous names signifying the single divine nature, names with different meanings signifying the one God, and nonsynonymous names of the different persons of the Trinity, which are the "same [*idem*]" but not "identical [*ipse*]" (*De Trin.* III. 16. 47).[53] Synonyms, the first type of name, create only verbal but not real plurality. Thus we can say "God," "God," "God," like "sun," "sun," "sun," and even "sword," "brand," "blade," without multiplying the number of things discussed (*De Trin.* III. 14. 33–40).

Even predication of terms with truly different meanings need not multiply realities. For just as we may "speak of the same thing many times," so we can speak of a single thing in many ways (*De Trin.* III. 14. 28). Names signifying substance, quantity, quality, and the like, are predicated of God in this way. In order for such terms to be predicable of God, Aristotle's categories are reinterpreted twice. First, Boethius rearranges the categories themselves. Substance, quantity, and quality "show the thing in a sense [*quasi rem monstrant*]"; the others—relation, time, place, habit, position, activity, and passivity—show "the circumstances of the thing in a way [*quasi circumstantias rei*]" (*De Trin.* IV. 24. 100–101). The significant division for Aristotle is between substance and accident, not between substance, quantity, and quality, on the one hand, and the rest of the accidents, on the other.

The second change is that quantity and quality are said of God differently than material beings; since he is not a subject, these cannot be said of him as subject; instead "God is named by a predication according to the substance of the thing [*secundum substantiam rei*]" (*De Trin.* IV. 24. 107–108). That is, as later formulations have it, quantity and quality are not accidents but substantial predicates of God; he is good and great not accidentally but substantially.

This whole account of how the categories work is explicitly made within the realm of how we talk about things rather than directly about the way things are. Boethius emphasizes this within a few lines, repeating verbs of saying and showing. Things are "said," "called," and "named" in different ways; different predicates "show" or "point to" different aspects of the thing (*De Trin.* IV. 24. 99–108). The concentration on what we say about things rather than things themselves are characteristics of the chapter as a whole. *Quasi* is repeated as modifier of predication, as a signal of the gap between being and saying.[54] Though in the course of the chapter these verbal hints occur in the context of distinguishing between natural and divine predication, they also have the effect of adjusting the focus onto language itself, to bring the reader to see language, to see that *in terms of which* we ordinarily see everything else. Boethius's strategy seems to be the following: one must see first that language is not just simply a mirror of "the way things are" in order to see how terms apply differently to God than creatures. Once we have shifted our focus to the medium, we can think of different kinds of pictures, and then perhaps of a different kind of picture of a different kind of thing.

And so in the space created by this difference between what we say and how things are, Boethius posits two different kinds of predication appropriate to different kinds of things, according to their simple or complex character (*De Trin.* IV. 18. 26–29). Since God is simple, that is, nothing other than that which he is, things are predicated of God in a conjoined or united way. But human beings, on the other hand, are not "wholly [*integre*] themselves" and thus are *not* substance (*De Trin.* IV. 18. 32–36). So, Boethius explains, to be God is the same as being a just God, but to be human is one thing, and to be a just human being, something else (*De Trin.* IV. 18. 39–41).[55] In the earlier chapter, the model is something like "a human being is this and that and so forth," and here it is, "a human being is not wholly him/herself"; with this shift, complexity becomes fragmentation, the failure to achieve integrity. Complexity *is* fragmentation for Boethius; the important thing is to come to see it *as* that.

God as Triune

Having discussed the ways in which terms falling under the categories are predicated "according to the thing" (substance, quantity, quality), Boethius turns to the ways in which terms falling under the category of relation pertain to God. Relation is, of course, the category under which God as three persons falls. Boethius's account of relation emphasizes, first, the ontological fragility of relations. A relation is completely dependent for its slender hold on reality on its counterpart, which is completely external to it (the master's status as master depends on the slave). Second, he notes that the thing remains unchanged by the predication of relations of it. So while, on the one hand, "master" completely disappears without the slave, on the other hand, that which is called "master" is in itself neither added to, subtracted from, or changed by this relation (*De Trin.* V. 26. 17–19, 30–33). Relation consists only in a kind of "being in comparison" either with something else or with itself. Thus relations consist in a seeing something *as* something, *as* related to something else or itself.

Because Boethius has emphasized the way in which relations do not effect the being of things in relation, he can describe the relationship of persons in the Trinity in a way that leaves the unity of God undisturbed (*De Trin.* V. 26. 33–28. 40). The relations of the Trinity are not even the relations of two things compared to each other, as master and slave, but are the relations of a thing to itself, like the relations by which we say that equals are equal, likes are like, and identicals are identical. Hence the Trinity is the relation "of that which is the same to that which is the same" (*De Trin.* VI. 30. 21–22).

Changing One's Relationship to the Trinity

The last two sections of the treatise emphasize, on the one hand, the stability of the divine nature and, on the other hand, the plurality of the relational predicates and the plurality of Boethius's approaches to it. Boethius uses an example to illustrate the nature of relation that is emblematic of his text as a whole. A man who does not move when approached first by a man from the left and then from the right by another is said to be to the right and then to the left of the man approaching. Without moving or changing, that man finds himself in relationship with those who approach him (*De Trin.* V. 26. 22–29).

Analogously, Boethius ends the treatise with the contrast between the stability of the truth he approaches and his own multiple and uncertain approaches. He notes the stable and "unchanging judgement [*normam iudicii*]" of John, to whom he writes (he hopes) with "*recte decursa*" (*De Trin.* VI. 30. 27–30). His argument, he tells us, is really superfluous, functioning as a support for what already stands firm, addressed to someone whose judgments are already the standards for truth (*De Trin.* VI. 30. 30–33). Like someone approaching the same man from different directions, Boethius's own treatise approaches the Trinity from different directions. Like the man approached, the Trinity does not change, but Boethius's relation to it does as he attempts to understand it more fully and in different ways.

Boethius follows this with a rhetorically obligatory humble closing much like the closing of the *Contra Eutychen*. He again attributes success to others and failure to himself, but in this work, he uses terms of the motion of approach as opposed to stability. If his work has reached its goal (*perfectus*), he writes, joy "will return whence the effect came," going full circle, returning to approach that from which it originated (*De Trin.* VI. 30. 33–34). But "if human nature cannot make this ascent," if the work fails to reach its goal, cannot close the circle by returning to its source, Boethius writes, "however much weakness removes [*subtrahit*], prayers will supplement [*supplebunt*]" (*De Trin.* VI. 30. 30–36).

So considered, the text ends, I think, with a less ambiguous answer than we began with to the question of whether Boethius's language fails to perfectly mirror his subject for esoteric or for more systemic reasons. For Boethius ends on the note of supplication, of prayer, in the position of humility not just in relation to his addressee, John, but in relation to the subject. This humble position is that of humanity. Thus, Boethius is not ultimately and finally assuming a superior position of the esoteric writer over against those unworthy of reading his book. Rather he is noting the failure of his language to map onto the thing he seeks to explain. Since he cannot complete the circle of return to his source, his language remains the language of rhetoric, repeating the distance between himself as speaker and his subject.

But these gaps—between speaker, subject, and audience; word, thought, and thing—are the concern in the three tractates we have considered and, as we saw, in the logical commentaries. In the tractates, Boethius's task has been mediation of conflicting terminologies and perspectives. Boethius has worked at stretching language from this world to the next in order that the mind might follow.[56] Though expressed in different form, this is the same as the task of the *Consolation*, to which we turn next.

The *Consolation* and the Transformation of Perspective

While virtually all readers of the *Consolation* would agree that the project of the *Consolation* is the transformation of Boethius's perspective on his own suffering, many of the *Consolation*'s best interpreters have taken there to be insuperable tensions and oppositions within the work.[57] While I agree with these scholars that there are different voices in the work, I think that Boethius is largely in control of these voices, weaving them into a single spiritual vision.[58] To the degree that Boethius gives voice to worldly and unphilosophical perspectives, they are expressed so that they may be converted. As de Vogel points out, Boethius the prisoner is neither Christian nor philosopher; "he is just depressed and shows himself in all his human weakness." Thus Boethius begins with his real feelings and responses, working through them under the guidance of philosophy. To the degree that these feelings and voices are not completely converted, Boethius is expressing the inherent limits of human understanding and will.

Thus, the position of Boethius the author is not simply identical with that of Lady Philosophy.[59] Rather he seems even as he writes to be in the process of attempting to synthesize the voice of his own suffering and misfortune with the voice of his own philosophical knowledge that these merely external losses should be disregarded.[60] This is the progress the text traces as Boethius works to develop in his persona, the prisoner whom Lady Philosophy addresses, ever broader and more encompassing perspectives within which he can in some way come to understand his own fate and, more importantly, the workings of and presence of God in the world. In this way Boethius struggles, in large part against himself, to catch a glimpse of a single and unifying perspective. Each step toward this new perspective brings with it a new language, with the radical redefinition of the terms in which Boethius at the beginning misunderstands his fate—fortune, freedom, happiness, justice, virtue, chance, and, ultimately, good and evil.

As in the *Republic*, one of the first views to be rejected is that of the poets. But even more explicitly than the *Republic*, the *Consolation* uses poetry after having rejected it. I contend that at least in the case of Boethius it is far too easy to close the gap between what he says (the poets must go) and what he does (write poetry) simply by arguing that he banishes those poets who lie and continues with a reformed or redeemed poetry in the service of philosophy and truth. Even though she criticizes them, we shall see that Lady Philosophy takes over the language, methods, and perspective of the prisoner and the poetic muses at different points throughout work. But more importantly, I will show that the voices of the poets continue to speak and are never completely sublimated into the higher perspective for which Boethius has supposedly been freed by Philosophy.

My contention is that the *Consolation*, then, repeats the strategy I have argued is found throughout the Boethian corpus. The project of the work is development and hierarchical arrangement of different perspectives on Boethius's suffering. Moreover, Boethius lets us see these different points of view and allows their echoes to remain even when they have been superceded.

Baring the Wound

In the *Consolation*, Boethius casts himself as a student rather than a teacher, a patient rather than a doctor, and the one to be consoled rather than the consoler.[61] The tables have turned from the esoteric *De hebdomadibus* and other tractates in which he casts himself and his audience as those who know, protecting the precious truth from the unworthy and unwilling. At the opening of the poem, it is Boethius who is unworthy and unwilling.

Philosophy appears on the scene banishing the muses with the explanation that they "accustom" rather than liberate from disease (*Consol.* I. pr. 1. 134. 34). Though she continues to distinguish her task (curing the prisoner) from theirs (offering a forum for complaint) (*Consol.* I. pr. 2. 138. 1–2), she quotes Homer in asking the prisoner to "speak out" and "not hide his heart" (*Consol.* I. pr. 4. 144. 4). "If you are looking for [*exspectas*] the work of curing, it is necessary that you uncover the wound" (*Consol.* I. pr. 4. 144. 5–6). So in form, by quoting, and in content, by asking to hear Boethius's complaints, Philosophy takes up a position vis-à-vis the prisoner close to that of the muses who have just been banished.

The prisoner accepts the offer to bare his wound in a long speech followed by a poem. Boethius's version of the charges against him saves his strongest outrage for the distortion and perversion of his principled causes—the preservation of the senate and the study of philosophy—into crimes.[62] Out of this anger comes the poem contrasting the beauty and order of the natural world with the disorder and instability of human life. For him the order of human life is completely turned upside down and inside out, virtue has become vice, merit becomes the justification for punishment, learning has been turned into ignorant superstition (*Consol.* I. m. 5. 160. 28–48).

As the next prose passage begins, however, the prisoner refers to this speech as "ranting [*delatravi*]," contrasting it to the impassivity of Philosophy, who is unmoved by his complaints (*Consol.* I. pr. 5. 160. 1–2). Thus Boethius shifts his perspective, stands apart from and looks back at his expression of anger and pain as an animal-like roar. He perhaps means to caricature his outburst as not yet language in the true sense, as a "natural" rather than truly linguistic expression of unhappiness, as he did the animal sounds in the *Peri hermeneias*. Philosophy takes the same somewhat harsh perspective the prisoner does, arguing that he is responsible for his own unhappiness, that he has "driven himself [*ipse pepulisti*]," rather than been "driven [*pulsus*]" (*Consol.* I. pr. 5. 162. 6–8). Quoting Homer again she refers to his *patria* as that in which "one is lord, one is king," a land from which he can never be involuntarily exiled (*Consol.* I. pr. 5. 162. 12–19). Though the prisoner sees Lady Philosophy so, she is not unsympathetic, she says, but she is "moved by his face," not by his imprisonment (*Consol.* I. pr. 5. 162. 21).

It is not just Boethius the prisoner who shifts his (worldly and self-pitying) perspective to move toward the greater wisdom of philosophy. Lady Philosophy also does a fair amount of adjustment to Boethius's position. She literally comes down to his level (*Consol.* I. pr. 3. 140. 10–12). She stands with him against his enemies. She also concedes the importance of his feelings. She requests the telling of his story (the "showing of his wounds")

(*Consol*. I. pr. 4. 144.4–6), she wipes his eyes and is moved by what is going on within him (*Consol*. I. pr. 2. 138. 12–18). Philosophy views the prisoner as suffering from spiritual illness and sees herself as therapy for his illness.[63] Like any good therapist she does not simply correct him but starts with him where he is, attempting to bring him to bring about changes in his own condition. Significantly, Philosophy quotes Homer to express some of her most important truths: the unity of God, the need to speak one's heart (*Consol*. I. pr. 4. 144. 3; pr. 5. 162. 12). She shifts her view of his complaints following the prisoner's shift, but she corrects his overly harsh view of her perspective, claiming that she is indeed moved by him, just not by his external predicament.

Philosophy thus grants the truth of his complaints but draws a conclusion different from that of the prisoner's. Nature is ordered, and if human life seems disordered it is because humanity has itself precipitously deserted that order (*Consol*. I. m. 6. 166. esp. 20–23). The cause of his illness is that he knows the *source* but not the *end* of all things; he knows that he is a rational, mortal animal but nothing else (*Consol*. I. pr. 6. 168. 19). His partial grasp of the truth leads him to the false conclusion that "evil men are fortunate and powerful," a conclusion begotten of the vicious circle of forgetfulness, false opinion, and further confusion (*Consol*. I. pr. 6. 170. 45–46, 55–63). The language of vision, of looking in different directions, up and down, toward end and beginning, fills the entire book in a complex way. The shifts of vision are not just the prisoner's but also Philosophy's. As we shall see, the shifts of perspective and language throughout the *Consolation* are not always or simply upward and toward unity.[64]

Redefining/Reenvisioning Fortune and Happiness

Philosophy begins from Boethius's original complaint: Fortune's desertion. Philosophy, first in her own voice and then taking up the voice of Fortune, attempts to "remind" the prisoner of the "real worth [*meritum*]" of Fortune (*Consol*. II. pr. 1. 174. 10). And so the third female character vying for Boethius's affections enters the drama. The muses were the first, dismissed by Philosophy as "harlots" or paid lovers (*meretriculas*). Fortune's *meritum*, like that of the harlot muses, is also deceptive; seen through Philosophy's eyes she appears like nothing so much as an abusive lover, catching Boethius in a kind of addiction to her charms, charms that are ever disappearing or threatening to disappear. "Is fortune so dear to you while she is with you," Philosophy asks, "even though she cannot be trusted to stay with you, and will bring you sorrow when she leaves you?" (*Consol*. II. pr. 1. 176. 40–44, trans. Tester). Dramatizing herself as Fortune, Philosophy presents her, quoting Homer, as the cool and playful dispenser of evils and blessings who satirizes the "cry of tragedy" as a kind of immature lack of comprehension of the rules of the game (*Consol*. II. pr. 2. 182. 38–43).

This shift in perspective does not yet console Boethius. He complains that his sense of the evils he has suffered is "*altior*," meaning both "higher" when seen from below and "deeper" when seen from above. Philosophy's response is to try to bring him to a still higher/deeper view of his condition. His present place of exile is home to the inhabitants around him, she notes. Human beings, looking outside rather than inside for happiness, have "so turned around the nature of things that a rational animal, in merit divine [*divinum merito*], can seem splendid only in possession of inanimate equipment." In such a way, one's value, "not undeservedly [*haud immerito*]" falls below the things one possesses, Philosophy adds (*Consol*. II. pr. 5. 204. 72–75; 82–84). Boethius began by lamenting that the world was turned upside down by his misfortune, and by the world's evaluation of his virtue as vice; Philosophy argues instead that it is Boethius who has inverted the real hierarchy of value (*meritum*), valuing his goods and his position more than himself.

Philosophy attacks his clouded vision, his distorted perspective, and false estimations expressed in his language. "You delight," she complains, "in falsely naming things, which are themselves otherwise, by names that are easily refuted as false by the effects of the things themselves. And so that cannot justly be called riches nor that power nor this honor" (*Consol*. II. pr. 6. 212. 62–65). She notes the limitations of any human being's power over another, over the body, or fortune. Moreover, she argues, offices and powers have "no natural and proper good" since they can be possessed by evil men. As Socrates does in the *Gorgias*, Lady Philosophy argues that for power to be real power, it must be only for the possessor's good. Echoing the *Phaedo*, she argues for the purity of the realities as opposed to the mixed beings the prisoner calls "riches," "power," or "honor." So Philosophy concludes, bravery is in the brave, swiftness in the swift, music in the musician, rhetoric in the rhetorician: "the nature of each thing performs what is proper to it and is unmixed with contrary effects and further rejects what is adverse" (*Consol*. II. pr. 6. 212. 52–56). This is the order of reality, but Boethius cannot see it and, hence, cannot mirror it in his language use.

True language should follow the reality of things in which dishonorable results cannot come from what is truly honorable, nor want from what is truly riches, nor lack of control from true power. Boethius gives the negative version of this argument:

> Indeed abundance cannot quench insatiate avarice [from *aveo*, want], nor power [*potestas*] make one master [*cumpotem*] of oneself whose vicious desires constrain him by indissoluble chains; and the conjoining of the inferior with

honorary office [*dignitas*] not only does not make them honorable [*dignos*], but rather proclaims [*prodit*, which can mean "appoint to office"] and shows their dishonorable character [*indignos*]. (*Consol.* II. pr. 6. 212. 56–61)[65]

Honorary office *should* derive from honor, earthly power from self-mastery, material abundance from lack of want or satiation, and *would* if these things truly possessed the nature their names suggest. But since honorary office coexists with dishonor, riches with want, power with lack of self-control, these offices, riches, and powers must be wrongly named. And so, Philosophy concludes, fortune per se is not good, coexisting with evil men and evil results (*Consol.* II. pr. 6. 212. 66–214. 69). The poem that follows describes the life of Nero, an appropriate example of the way in which high office, riches, and power can lead to disastrous results (*Consol.* II. m. 6. 214).

In light of these discoveries, Philosophy asks Boethius to shift his perspective on the universe and his position in it. She has him look down from a distance back on the earth, look across his borders and around the world. From such a vantage point, he will be able to see the insignificance of the parochial offices and privileges he regrets and the impotence that passes for human power in the scheme of the infinite universe. Philosophy ends with two paradoxical conclusions: the philosopher is the one who would never proclaim himself such (because he so thoroughly rejects the glory and fame of the world), and adverse fortune is more beneficial than good (since it allows one to see the true nature of fortune and makes it possible to distinguish true friends from false ones) (*Consol.* II. pr. 7. 220. 66–77; pr. 8. 224. 5–8). The language that sees and names things truly is paradoxical and is the inverse of the way things are ordinarily seen and named.[66]

Book III is supposed to mark the change from seeing happiness in terms of what it is not to seeing it in terms of what it is. But before the prisoner can see happiness on its own terms, he must take another look at the earthly vision of happiness. "That subject which is better known to you I will endeavor first to describe in words and delineate," Lady Philosophy explains, "so that from this perspective [*perspecta*], when you turn your eyes to the contrary, you can recognize the form [*species*] of true beatitude" (*Consol.* III. pr. 1. 230. 17–26). The perspective she directs him toward is the one he still occupies, which sees riches, power, and honor as being constitutive of happiness. The shift she wants to bring about is for him to see these same things in a different way. She wants him to see that those who pursue riches, power, and honor are seeking the good, but are looking for it in all the wrong places. Philosophy asks, "Do they seem to err who strive to want for nothing? Is not the best what is most honorable? Is not happiness a condition of plenty? Power [*vis*] the most eminent? The most illustrious the most excellent? Is not happiness without sorrow, anxiety, suffering, and pain?" (*Consol.* III. pr. 2. 234. 54–236. 71). In this way Philosophy asks Boethius to attend to the good within the things that she spent the last book showing are not true goods. Mistaken though it is, the soul that seeks honor, plenty, and power "nonetheless seeks again its good, but, like a drunk, does not know by what path to return [*revertatur*] home" (*Consol.* III. pr. 2. 234. 51–54).

Of course, Philosophy does not hesitate to go on to add that these things judged good by worldly standards do not deliver the goods, the true goods, which they promise. But the focus even in these considerations shifts to the positive and real goods desired even when they are sought in the wrong place, whetting the pupil's appetite for the real instead of the ersatz version of these goods. She then bids him to look thoroughly and attentively ("*perspicaciter intueris*") at the false form of happiness to see the true. He sees clearly, he says, that "neither can sufficiency be achieved by wealth, nor power by kingship, respect by honored positions, nor renown by glory, nor joy by pleasures" (*Consol.* III. pr. 9. 262. 3–6). But he can barely see why; he says, he seems to see as though "*in rimula*," through small cracks or fissures (*Consol.* III. pr. 9. 262. 8–9). The prisoner's vision is, then, still fragmented, unable to see the unity of sufficiency, power, renown, respect, and delight.

The task, then, is the reintegration of the prisoner's vision. The first step is toward understanding the true unity of the goods that are ordinarily named and pursued separately. So she argues that the good is one, that real sufficiency implies the possession of power, that it will be worthy both of reverence and fame, and will give the greatest joy to its possessor. Philosophy concludes, "Indeed it is necessary by these [arguments] that the names of sufficiency, power, renown, respect, and delight are diverse, but in no way do they differ in substance" (*Consol.* III. pr. 9. 266. 41–44). In light of this new and unified perspective on the good, she describes human pursuit of good fortune once again as the mistaken pursuit of a fragment of the good that cannot bring happiness. "That which is one and simple by nature, human perversity splits up and while he strives to obtain a part of something which has no parts, he attains neither a portion of it, of which there are none, nor the thing itself, to which he does not in the least aspire" (*Consol.* III. pr. 9. 266. 45–49).[67] Philosophy then commands Boethius, "Now turn around the mind's insight in the other direction," to see true happiness (*Consol.* III. pr. 9. 268. 76–77). Her pupil replies, "[T]his is seen clearly [*perspicua*] by the blind" (*Consol.* III. pr. 9. 268. 78).

The famous poem, "*O qui perpetua*," follows this glimpse of true happiness, part of a series about the order of nature. It differs from the preceding ones in its description of the source of all things, in its emphasis on the return of all things to the one, and its use of the second person to address God directly.[68] God is described as one who perpetually governs things in time, who, remaining stable, moves all things, who is "beauty most beautiful," perfect and commanding perfection (*Consol.* III. m. 9. 270.1–272.9). After intoning the familiar theme, the order of nature binding together diverse and opposing forces, the poem describes the natural order itself as returning to its source. "You, God, beget the lower souls," the poem asserts, "you convert [*conversas*] them to you and make them with returning [*reverti*] fire come back [*reduci*]" (*Consol.* III. m. 9. 272. 21). This single verse contains a threefold emphasis on the return to God. The poem ends with a prayer asking to ascend and "rediscover" the light and to approach the source of good, to satisfy the desire to approach and to see God (*Consol.* III. m. 9. 272. 22–25).

The story of the relation of things in nature told at the outset of the *Consolation* has not been changed, but it has been extended, receiving a beginning and an end. The earlier poem directly addressed to God on the order of nature was in the voice of the prisoner; in it he lamented that human beings seem to fall outside this all-encompassing power (*Consol.* I. m. 5. 158–60). Meter nine gives a more exact picture of the source the prisoner always claimed to recognize, but that source comes into focus as source because it is now seen as end. So the poem ends with a summary of this progression expressed as a list of the names of God: "Principle, bearer, leader, path, and end, the same" (*Consol.* III. m. 9. 274. 28).[69]

From the unity of all goods in the one Good, Philosophy argues for the connection between goodness and unity in all things, deriving their goodness from their unity. Things strive to preserve their unity and resist dissolution; since unity is goodness, all things desire the good. The true order of nature, then, is the unity of all things in their direction toward the One. However, Boethius's grasp of this principle (applauded by Lady Philosophy as "the very center [*mediae*] of truth)" (*Consol.* III. pr. 11. 294. 118) is expressed as a disjunction: "Either," Boethius proclaims, "everything is not related to one thing and will flow around [*fluitabunt*] as if in a whirl [*vertice*] without direction, or if there is something toward which the universe of things hastens, that will be the highest good of all" (*Consol.* III. pr. 11. 294. 113–16). It may be the "center of truth" but the prisoner's hold on it is somewhat tentative.

Redefining/Re-envisioning Freedom and Constraint

The end of all things in the One is a truth dimly remembered by all nature, according to Lady Philosophy. Hence, all things long to escape the bonds of their prison and return to their true nature, which is to incline toward the good. True freedom consists in re-finding one's nature and giving in to its "bonds." Boethius makes this clearest in meter two of Book III. The poem opens with the order of nature, stressing the "indissoluble bonds" of nature's laws "restraining each thing" (*Consol.* III. m. 2. 236. 1–6). But the poem's examples of nature's "bonds" are of things that break free from human attempts to restrain and control. Exposure to blood reawakens the tiger's nature; it attacks its master in retaliation for being chained and beaten. A well-fed caged bird, seeing the trees under which she belongs, suicidally scatters her food and sings to the woods; a sapling bent to the ground, once let go, turns back to the sky (*Consol.* III. m. 2. 238. 7–30). It is a violent picture both of nature and the contrary, asserting both the "bonds" of what is according to nature and what is contrary to it. One suspects a warning to earthly tyrants, whose "tigers" will turn on them and whose "caged birds" will reject the golden handcuffs by which they are held. The poem expresses the prisoner's justified anger at his persecutors, but it is an anger that has been transformed. What angers him now is not having been deprived of honors and riches but having lost the connection to his nature, his very self.

Within the space of a few lines, the poem shifts its view of what counts as freedom and constraint; to be constrained by nature's laws means being "free" from earthly/human chains. Like the tiger and the caged bird of the poem, Boethius, against his will and nature, is jailed by a tyrant. And like the tiger and the bird, Philosophy wants Boethius to see and act with his true freedom, freedom from human standards and, thus, to find his nature. Though, according to the poem, he still has only "minimal perspective [*minime perspicaci*]" into these matters, he "sees from a distance [*prospicitis*]" the true good toward which his natural inclination leads him (*Consol.* III. pr. 3. 240. 1–5).

This new understanding of freedom and constraint creates apparent paradoxes. As the argument progresses, Boethius describes himself as more and more "compelled" by the argument, more stable and less uncertain in his opinions. Over and over again, he confesses himself to be constrained by Philosophy's conclusions.[70] Echoing her student, Lady Philosophy describes his progress to this point as the "fixing" of his mind (*Consol.* III. pr. 11. 294. 118). In these responses, Boethius presents himself in the traditional role of the student in the philosophical dialogue whose main task seems to be to affirm the conclusions of the teacher. But he does so in a way that shows that those responses enact the conclusions about freedom and imprisonment they have reached. As he is "forced" to consent to arguments that show that he is only now free and no longer imprisoned, he is experiencing the real freedom of reason exercising itself without the constraints of passion.

The poems throughout Book III carry forward the process of defining, redefining, and refining the notions of freedom and constraint. The first poem ends with an exhortation to draw one's neck from the yoke of vice (*Consol.* III. m. 1. 230. 11–12). The second poem, examined in some detail above, contrasts the "indissoluble bonds" of nature with the breaking free from the bonds created by human passion. The next poems then recount the bondage of the avaricious, the tyrant, the hedonist, the ignorant (meters 3, 4, 5, 7). After the redefinition of sufficiency, power, and fame in prose nine, the famous meter nine intones the stable and binding order of nature, followed by a call to free all captives in meter ten.

Returning to Earth

Book III does not end in certainty of its achievement but closes ambiguously and ironically; with increasing self-consciousness the parties recognize the possibility of failure on their quest. Philosophy herself brings out the barely repressed desire to fall back, to return to the earlier senses of all the terms they have redefined by bringing up "the stories [*fabulis*] of the giants provoking heaven" (*Consol.* III. pr. 12. 302. 69–70). These giants understood freedom as freedom from divine control and bondage as subjection to the gods, exactly the opposite of the perspective just reached by the prisoner. Philosophy declares, on the one hand, that "[the giants] were put in their proper place by a benign strength," yet she proposes to her student that they engage in their own challenge of heaven, that they "clash their arguments [*rationes*] against one another." To which Boethius replies (we must suppose with a smile, given the recent discussions of freedom and constraint), "as you choose" (*Consol.* III. pr. 12. 302. 70–74).

The "clash" Philosophy provokes results from a continuation of her line of thought. Since God can do everything but cannot do evil, evil must be nothing (*Consol.* III. pr. 12. 302. 74–304. 82). This redefinition of evil as nothing provokes Boethius, the victim of considerable evil, to object and to voice the suspicion that their whole discussion has been a trick, a game she is playing with him. "Are you playing a game [*ludisne*] with me, weaving [*texens*] an inextricable labyrinth with your arguments [*rationibus*], since at one time you go in where you are going to come out again, and at another come out where you went in, or are you folding together [*complicas*] as it were a wonderful circle of simplicity of God?" (*Consol.* III. pr. 12. 304. 82–86, trans. Tester).

Ludere has a number of meanings besides the general one captured by "play"; it can also mean to deceive, mock, imitate, or banter. All are uses of signs that seem to but do not represent things as they are. Not just the Boethius who "plays the role" of Philosophy's student in the text, but also Boethius, the author of the *Consolation* and the *Peri hermeneias* commentary, would have to admit the possibility of deception as intrinsic to the nature of language. For language signifies only by convention; that which is so artificially related to things can be made to *seem* but not *be* correctly related to things. The question is about the nature of the connections Philosophy has drawn: are they artificial, merely woven, a kind of confusing and circular web of question begging strategies, or an "enfolding [*complectans*]" of all things into *the* circle of emanation and return to God? Like his earlier response to Philosophy's arguments (either everything is ordered to the One or everything is in chaos), this doubt is also expressed as disjunction. Either everything Philosophy argues makes perfect sense, or it is all a jumble of deception.

Like the reference to the giants, Boethius's reference to Orpheus in the closing meter of Book III is ambiguous.[71] On the one hand, Orpheus is a negative example. In the myth, he looks back on his way out of darkness and loses everything; like Orpheus, the prisoner has just expressed the desire to turn back, suspecting Philosophy of deception. Moreover, Orpheus was brought to the underworld in the first place by a previous looking back, by his grief for his wife, a grief not unlike Boethius's grief for his losses at the opening of the poem. And, like Boethius's, his grief was expressed in poetry. So Orpheus is doubly or even triply wrong, wrong for being overcome with grief for the loss of an earthly love, wrong for composing poetry of unabated grief instead of taking the path of philosophy, and wrong for turning back once on his way toward the light. As Book IV opens and Boethius approaches the problem of evil again, the prisoner refers back to the poem about Orpheus. Boethius admires Philosophy's "soft" and "sweet" song about Orpheus; like Orpheus, he is, he says, still immersed to some degree in his own grief (*Consol.* IV. pr. 1. 312. 1–4). Orpheus's turning back mirrors and repeats Boethius's temptation to return to grief, a sign of his recalcitrant vision that to some degree still sees things from below. As Winthrop Wetherbee remarks, the story of Orpheus is "admonitory exemplum" but it also "gives eloquent expression to the very impulse it is intended to curb, the attachment to earthly things which is at the heart of the metaphor of imprisonment."[72]

But even this is not quite complex enough to capture all the undertones of the closing of Book III. Orpheus's turning back brings to mind two other conversions or reversions. First, the poem, which appears directly before the one about Orpheus, refers to another kind of turning around, reminiscence in the Platonic sense. Those who seek the truth, the poem claims, must "turn back into oneself the inmost light of vision," and "bend their movements into a circle in order not to fall down wrong paths" (*Consol.* III. m. 11. 296. 1–5). Second, the final lines of the poem about Orpheus recommend turning back: "On you this fable reflects [*respicit*, literally "looks back"]/ Who seek to lead your mind to the upper day . . . ." (*Consol.* III. m. 12. 310. 52–54).

The poem exhorts the reader to turn back, to reflect on the tale of Orpheus, a tale whose moral is not to turn back, as part of the larger movement of returning to God. Thus reflecting back on Orpheus (even given the danger that Boethius will not look *at* Orpheus's turning back but will imitate it, falling back into an earthly perspective) is somehow necessary to make the grander motion of return to the true origin.

Redefining Evil

Philosophy's response to Boethius's hesitation is to try to "give her pupil's mind wings," to carry him on an "ascent" which is also a "return home" (*Consol.* IV. pr. 1. 314. 35–38). The first poem of Book IV promises an ascent "transcending the whirling [*verticem*] of fire" (a reference to misdirected passion as well as to natural philosophy). The vantage point to which she promises to bring him is so high, it looks back on clouds and stars and sees "the tyrants whom wretched people fear as fierce" as "exiles" (*Consol.* IV. m. 1. 316. 6, 15–18, 29–30). The speed continues to accelerate as Boethius "runs ahead" in an "indication of an already erect and resistant nature" (*Consol.* IV. pr. 2. 322. 71–73).

Boethius's grief takes new form; it is caused by the co-existence of evil and an all-good ruler of the universe. Philosophy's response is to deny that this is the state of the universe; "those who are evil I do not deny that they are evil; but that they are, purely and simply, I do deny" (*Consol.* IV. pr. 2. 326. 108–10). Philosophy continues, "he who can only do good things can do all things, and they cannot do all things who can do evil" (*Consol.* IV. pr. 2. 328. 128–31). The ability to do evil is not power but impotence. The poem (*Consol.* IV. m. 2) that follows reenvisions "powerful" kings, stripping away and seeing beneath the surface of their apparent power in order to see their chains, their impotence.

"From this perspective," Philosophy continues, "the good never lack their reward, and the criminal never lack their punishment" (*Consol.* IV. pr. 3. 330. 2–4). From this perspective, in other words, a new kind of vision of verbal and moral integrity results. Power and being have been redefined, revealing the powerlessness and even non-being of evil-doers. The resulting vision brings with it a new, more truthful and more consistent language, in which "goodness [*probitas*] is itself the reward for the good [*probes*] men, just as for wicked [*improbis*] men, worthlessness [*nequitia*] is itself the punishment" (*Consol.* IV. pr. 3. 332. 36–38).

However, Boethius the prisoner is still troubled by the remaining loose ends of the new reversed vocabulary. He notes that though the evil have lost their nature and lack real power, they still seem to have enough power to destroy the good. Philosophy replies using the terms with the new meanings she has argued for. The evil suffer from a threefold misfortune: they desire, are able, and actually carry out evil (*Consol*. IV. pr. 4. 338. 5–340. 15). Boethius replies that he wishes "that they would quickly lose this misfortune by the possibility of accomplishing [*patrandi*, also "to father"] crime deserting them" (*Consol*. IV. pr. 4. 340. 17–18). At the beginning of the poem misfortune is what he suffered at the hands of his persecutors; now, Philosophy argues, it refers to what his persecutors have done to themselves. In Boethius's ironic reply, it has *both* meanings.

Philosophy is not discouraged by his irony but continues her attempt to convert his perspective and his vocabulary more thoroughly. She tries to point out the relatively short duration of the "power" the evil have to do evil to others in the larger scheme of things; she argues, as the *Gorgias* does, that the evil are even more wretched when they remain unpunished.[73] She is only partially successful. For again Boethius, like Orpheus, looks backward to his older view of things, unable to envision this new world. From human standards of judgment, the prisoner complains, her arguments would not only not be believed, they would not even be heard (*Consol*. IV. pr. 4. 346. 93–94).

In response, Philosophy draws on Aristotle's analogy between all-too-human judgments and the blindness of owls accustomed to the dark being blinded by the light of day. But she goes further and asks her pupil to engage in a kind of mental alternation of perspective, looking on lower things and then to higher things (*Consol*. IV. pr. 4. 346. 101–108). The result will be, she claims, a shifting impression of where he himself stands (*Consol*. IV. pr. 4. 346. 104–108). Her claim seems to be ultimately that his self-understanding is relative to his point of view; to turn to higher things in effect is to place oneself among them and vice versa. Further, Philosophy argues, if the vicious "were allowed to catch sight [*aspicere*] in some fragmentary way [*aliqua rimula*] of the virtue they had left behind," they would ask to be punished and therefore freed from their vice (*Consol*. IV. pr. 4. 350. 141–46). Seeing through cracks (*rimula*) is the same way Boethius described his own understanding in Book III. Even such a fragmentary and partial glimpse, she claims, would suffice to shift the understanding of power, sufficiency, and honor to that developed in Book III. Lady Philosophy ends with a plea not to bother hating the wicked, who are diseased in spirit and thus deserve pity more than hate (*Consol*. IV. pr. 4. 350. 147–54).

But Boethius persists in the view that there is some truth in the popular notion of fortune. He cites as proof the preference, even of the wise man, to be "powerful in his wealth, revered for his honors, efficacious in his power, and to flourish in his own city" (*Consol*. IV. pr. 5. 352. 6–7). He still objects that the order of the world is up-side-down since "the punishments due to the wicked oppress the good, while the wicked seize the rewards due to virtue" (*Consol*. IV. pr. 5. 352. 13–15, trans. Tester). And once again Philosophy's reply turns on the way things in the world are viewed. "It is no wonder" that "something is believed to be confused and fortuitous when the reason of its order is unknown" (*Consol*. IV. pr. 5. 354. 22–24).

Redefining Fortune from a God's-Eye View

Prose six of Book IV is the longest sustained prose passage in the work. It develops the most important thesis of the work, that the world is not governed by random fate but by providence, which orders all things for the good. One of the most surprising reversals of the work follows from this claim: that all fortune is good fortune. To see things from this perspective is to see them from a God's-eye view. Fate and fortune, Philosophy explains, are lower, more distant, diffused circles, rotating around the center of Providence.[74] Those things further from the center are more diverse, complex, and apparently random than those things closer. Nonetheless, things governed by fate and fortune are not more but rather less free. The more things move toward the simplicity of the one, Philosophy explains, the more free they are, and the more they strive to diffuse themselves, the "more tightly enmeshed" and less free they are (*Consol*. IV. pr. 6. 360. 69–76).

Boethius's inability to contemplate this order, to see the hierarchy from the top down, explains why, seen from below, fate looks random rather than ordered and arranged for the benefit of the evil rather than for the good. For the confusion emerges especially when human beings suppose themselves capable of "seeing into [*intuieri*] the inmost mixture of souls" (*Consol*. IV. pr. 6. 364. 110–11). The fates devised for different individuals seem unjustified, just as the doctor's treatment of healthy and sick might seem irrational to those who do not know the causes of health and illness, especially when the ignorant see that even different healthy people and different sick people receive different treatments (*Consol*. IV. pr. 6. 364. 112–21).

Lady Philosophy even goes so far as to suggest that things are really the opposite of the way they seem to us, that those human beings seen as the most just might be exactly the opposite. Even if human and divine judgments agree on who is just (a rare occurrence, she implies), we do not know, as God does, what the person needs. Perhaps he is weak and needs not to have his justice tested by hardship; perhaps he is so perfectly just that providence rejects any adversity for him. And so on. In the pages that follow Philosophy gives any number of explanations for "good" and "bad" fortune (in the ordinary sense), supporting her view that there is at least one way to view the diversity, cruelty, and absurdity of some human fortunes such that all can truly be judged good (*Consol*. IV. pr. 6. 366. 33–368. 79). She ends with the greatest paradoxes of all: that the evil can make the evil good, that for the divine, evil is good, and that slipping from the divine order is part of the divine order of providence (*Consol*. IV. pr. 6. 370. 184–95).[75]

Philosophy stops herself at this point with the line from Homer: "[I]t is grievous that I should talk of all this as if I were a god" (*Consol*. IV. pr. 6. 370. 196).[76] She began this section with an account of the insufficiency of any discourse on these topics, about which doubts grow like the heads of the hydra "unless compelled by the liveliest fire of the mind" (*Consol*. IV. pr. 6. 356. 6–10). The warnings, I think, apply to the impossibility of really seeing both extremes of the picture she has been trying to paint. There is, on the one hand, the simplicity of divine providence and, on the other, the detailed and complex account of how particular fates might be appropriate to different individuals. Thus though Boethius may have had the "beginning" and the "end" of the story since the famous meter nine of Book III, it is a story whose extremes Boethius cannot grasp in detail and in all. Philosophy withdraws to a somewhat less complete perspective, saying "*tantum perspexisse sufficiat*" ("let it suffice to have seen only this"), outlining the source of all things in God, the direction of all things toward him in a way that eliminates evil by the "chain of fate" (*Consol*. IV. pr. 6. 370. 199–204). She ends deep in the subjunctive: "[I]f you were to see [*spectas*] the disposition of providence, you would not consider there to be evil anywhere" (*Consol*. IV. pr. 6. 370. 205–206).

Boethius's continued objections show that human beings do not, by and large, find it natural and more freeing to see bad fortune as good. Believing that everything is guided for the good by providence, Boethius notes, is not just a difficult but an "impossible opinion [*inopinabiles*]" to hold. "The common language [*sermo communis*] of human beings," often "calls [*usurpat*]" some fortune evil (*Consol*. IV. pr. 7. 376. 11–14). Philosophy's student admits that her proof that all fortune is good must be true, but he adds, "none would dare to confess it" (*Consol*. IV. pr. 7. 378. 37–38).

Reverting to Ordinary Language: Classical Models of Virtue

Philosophy's response to this objection is to return to a description of fortune in ordinary, human language. "Do you want us to have recourse for a little while to common [*vulgi*] language, lest we seem to have withdrawn too far from human practice [*humanitatis usu*]?" she asks (*Consol*. IV. pr. 7. 376. 14–17). Given her earlier description of true freedom as finding and returning to one's true nature in enfolding oneself in the One, virtue should be the path toward reintegration into the natural order, finding the true nature toward which one naturally inclines. Instead she notes that virtue is so called from *vires*, strength, because it is a kind of struggle against adversity, against being turned around or away from the first good (*Consol.* IV. pr. 7. 378. 44–45). The battle must be joined against every kind of fortune, she continues, lest we be oppressed by bad fortune or corrupted by good (*Consol.* IV. pr. 7. 378. 47–50). In this whole speech, Philosophy returns to the ordinary meanings of good and bad fortune, those she earlier rejected; she thus reassumes a lower position, one which the prisoner still occupies. From this perspective, she admits the reality of adversity, of things being turned away rather than toward God, the reality of a bad fortune that can burden or even crush, and the reality of struggle and conflict.

We must read the final meter of Book IV in the light of this definition of virtue, this retreat to a more human perspective on human life. This poem is concerned with examples of human struggle and conflict from Greek poetry. "War" is its first word and it recounts the tales of Agamemnon, Odysseus, and Hercules. They seem to be put forward as positive models of those who have struggled against evil and won; Hercules is explicitly called a "great example" of "the struggle against earth for the stars" (*Consol.* IV. m. 7. 382. 32–35). But like Orpheus, they are ambiguous examples. The fortunes of all three are extraordinarily harsh, unfairly and even whimsically imposed by uncaring gods, and their struggles against their adversities were also struggles against nature and natural feeling. The violence committed by each in order to survive, to fight against their fate, is appalling. And it is this violence that is the main subject of the poem.

All these figures had been read allegorically by Stoic, Neoplatonic, Cynic, and Christian thinkers before they were used by Boethius.[77] Positive interpretations range from considering Odysseus as a figure for intelligence, for Stoic virtue and strength, or for Platonic wisdom; others view Odysseus negatively as the errant soul, tempted by and, at times, succumbing to vice or, worse, as ruthless promoter of his own interests. Seneca writes of Odysseus and Hercules: "We Stoics have declared that these were wise men, because they were unconquered by struggles, were despisers of pleasure, and victors over all terrors."[78] Agamemnon is the most unexpected; unlike Odysseus and Hercules, he was not often the subject of allegorical readings, and as O'Daly points out, his story is the stuff of tragedy not epic.[79] His struggle, as Boethius relates it, amounted to the sacrifice of his daughter in order to win a war, "buying winds with blood" (*Consol.* IV. m. 7. 380. 5).[80] He is hardly seen, especially in Roman versions of his tragedy, a positive model of virtue; Agamemnon's bargain is thoroughly condemned by Cicero and Lucretius, as well as by Seneca, whose play Boethius clearly alludes to here.[81]

The impossibility of the position Agamemnon was placed in illustrates the cruel and arbitrary character of fortune, and, worse, the impossibility of avoiding committing and suffering terrible wrong at the hands of fortune. However, Agamemnon does not seem to struggle against being seduced by fortune; rather, he both suffers the ill-fortune of being forced to sacrifice Iphigenia, and suffers the good fortune of victory which corrupts him and sends him home to die at his wife's hands. As Wetherbee notes, "the sacrifice of Iphigenia is the harshest possible image, indeed a grim parody, of the renunciation of mortal affections, reminding us of the danger that in making such sacrifices one may only reap the wind."[82]

Odysseus appears next, for the second time in the poem. Earlier, in meter three, we heard the story of Odysseus's encounter with Circe. Just as Odysseus resisted the seductive Circe, whose potions turn her guests into various animals, so Boethius needed to resist the poetic muses who tried to seduce him.[83] Boethius does not present the "wily Odysseus" who out-smarts evil on his own; rather he presents Odysseus receiving salvation through the pity of Mercury (the god who brings messages), just as Boethius is saved from the muses by the good graces of Philosophy (*Consol.* IV. m. 3. 336. 17–20). This setting of Odysseus implies that one does not so much resist seduction by the charms of earthly power and riches as one is delivered from them.

In meter seven, Odysseus's epic struggles are summed up in the episode with the Cyclops.[84] This episode seems to make Odysseus a mixed example; he suffers the loss of his comrades and stands alone before the powerful, monstrous tyrant; hence, we pity him. He succeeds in taking his revenge, as Agamemnon succeeds by winning the Trojan war, and we admire his courage and resourcefulness. But his act against the Cyclops is in retaliation, the angry battle cry of the wounded. It is a reaction like that of Boethius at the outset against his persecutors, the very reaction Philosophy has been attempting to change since Book I. Like Agamemnon, Odysseus, having been wounded by Fortune's wiles, struggles to get on her good side.

Over half the poem is dedicated to Hercules. It is a litany of Hercules's labors told in quick succession with an emphasis on their overwhelming difficulty, their painfulness, and their weight against which human strength must muster every ounce. It concludes "[G]o then, you brave, where the lofty path of this great example leads," and asks, "[W]hy do you turn your backs in indolence? Earth overcome grants the stars" (*Consol.* IV. m. 7. 382. 31–35). The exhortation is an echo of a line in Seneca's *Hercules Furens*, in which Juno taunts Hercules to hubris, in what Lerer describes as "an exhortation to do something disastrous."[85] The Hercules in Seneca's play is the victim of Juno's infinite desire for revenge. He is also the mad Hercules, who having accomplished all the tasks set for him, goes mad on his return, threatening violence to the gods if they do not accept him and committing violence again after having expiated an earlier violent episode by his labors. Seneca's play ends with Hercules sentencing himself to exile in the underworld.

The question is whether Boethius means to invoke Seneca's Hercules, with his flaws and horrific fate, or rather the successful hero whose labors Boethius summarizes in this poem, holding up the heavens in his last labor.[86] Boethius does not mention the events of Hercules's tragedy, yet the verbal echoes of Seneca's *Hercules Furens* and placement of Hercules with another tragic figure, Agamemnon, sound dissonant to Hercules as the pure hero and unalloyed positive model for the prisoner. Within the *Consolation*, Hercules most readily calls to mind the giants who arrogantly and ignorantly rebelled against the gods, sealing their own bondage in their attempt to gain freedom from divine control. Those very same giants also provide the example for the "clashing together of arguments" Lady Philosophy and the prisoner dare to engage in (*Consol*. III. pr. 12. 302. 69–74).

Both Lerer and O'Daly conclude, by different paths, that Odysseus, Hercules, and Agamemnon fit without remainder into the picture of human life portrayed by Lady Philosophy. Either these figures fit into this text easily and without change in their classical context (O'Daly), or they are recast and their stories rewritten by Boethius in order to be assimilated into the argument of the text (Lerer). For Wetherbee, as for me, there is a double message conveyed by the poetic retelling of the stories of the classical figures. Wetherbee argues that there is an unresolved tension between Lady Philosophy, for whom "the heroic images she presents are models of decisive, liberating action, repudiations of fortune and the ties of fears of earthly life," and the prisoner (like the reader), for whom they are "images of the difficulty of such renunciation and transcendence."[87]

There is also a tension between the account of fortune, honor, freedom, riches, and power given by Lady Philosophy at the culmination of her argument in Book IV, prose six, on the one hand, and the values expressed in the stories of these figures, on the other. Lady Philosophy argued in prose six that there is no such thing as evil fortune; hence, there is no such thing as being a victim of fortune, and, thus, no way to make Agamemnon as victim or victor or hero. Moreover, the moral lesson Philosophy teaches is that moral failure is not failing to win good fortune but seeking good fortune in the ordinary sense at all; hence, for Philosophy there is no way to make Odysseus's victories over fortune heroic. Thus the figures of Agamemnon and Odysseus do not represent the heights reached in Lady Philosophy's discourse but are still bound by fortune in their attempts to struggle against it.

Hercules, even given the dark side to his fate alluded to by Boethius, comes closer to embodying a heroic model Lady Philosophy could accept.

Hercules was most often read allegorically as a positive model of virtue, as exemplifying the struggle to free oneself from the bonds of earth.[88] But the stories of Agamemnon, Odysseus, and Hercules, even read as exemplifying virtue, paint a portrait of the virtue of "common language," not virtue as described by Lady Philosophy. In these stories and in popular opinion, virtue is at best a struggle against oneself, others, fate, and the gods. This, incidentally, is the false picture of virtue Plato accuses the poets of painting—making virtue look hard and vice easy (*Republic* 392). Like Plato's, Lady Philosophy's picture of virtue (before she retreated to this more earth-bound picture) was of virtue as the natural inclination to the good that all desire.

Because Boethius cannot maintain the heady vision Philosophy brings him to, she reverts to a more accessible way of seeing the same goal. Vice as going against nature, as choosing bondage over freedom, as impotence and nonbeing, is the truer picture, but it is not, to use Boethius's distinction from *De hebdomadibus*, that which is more accessible to us. Boethius experiences virtue as a struggle and the vicious as strong. So Philosophy uses the examples of those who share above all their experience of struggle to exhort Boethius to engage in the struggle when he cannot see virtue as his (and the world's) natural inclination.

Redefining Chance: the New Perspective and its Limits

Book V opens with a Boethius sobered and still struggling. The struggle to understand Philosophy's conclusions now focuses on chance. Chance, she explains, fits within the all-encompassing power of providence, but, of course, from such a perspective, it disappears. Boethius repeats Aristotle's example of the man digging in the field who happens to be on a treasure hunt from the *Peri hermeneias*. Lady Philosophy first gives the Aristotelian account of chance as the "unexpected [*inopinatum*]" outcome of concurring causes. But she adds the Neoplatonic twist that the concurrence of those causes to produce particular effects has its source in providence from which those causes "proceed in an inevitable connection" (*Consol.* V. pr. 1. 388. 53–58). She comes closer than the *Peri hermeneias* commentary, at least at this point, to expressing the Stoic view that chance is an illusion based on ignorance of divine intentions. Freedom is not a contradiction to this view but fits within it. For freedom is, she explains, a matter of the direction of vision: "[H]uman souls are necessarily more free when they conserve themselves in contemplation [*speculatione*]." When, on the other hand, they "lower their eyes" from the "light of the highest truth," consenting to destructive affections, they become "in a way captive of their own freedom" (*Consol.* V. pr. 2. 392. 16–29).

However, Philosophy's pupil is "confounded by a more difficult ambiguity" in all this, the problem of the consistency of freedom and foreknowledge (*Consol*. V. pr. 3. 394. 1–6). Prose three, completely devoted to Boethius's objections to universal providence, repeats many of the arguments against the necessitation of all events Boethius gave in his *Peri hermeneias* commentary. To these he adds the argument that the necessitation of all events dissolves the only possibility of "intercourse [*commercium*]" between the human and the divine—prayer.[89] If things are necessitated, both prayer and hope become senseless. Instead of the harmonious union of all things held together by love and directed by providence that Lady Philosophy has established, the prisoner argues, if all is determined by providence, "it will necessarily follow that human kind will be torn apart and disjoined from its source," unable to connect and adhere to God (*Consol*. V. pr. 3. 402. 111–12).

Meter three considers whether the conflict between "two truths" (freedom and foreknowledge) might be in the nature of things, or might be wholly a result of the inability to see and understand the real coherence and unity of things (*Consol*. V. m. 3. 1–10).[90] But Boethius refuses to take refuge in either obscurantism or gnosticism; rather he supports the rationality of seeking that which he does not yet understand. Like the *Meno*, the poem argues that we could not seek if we did not already know or dimly recall something of the single truth we grasp in parts (*Consol*. V. m. 3. 402.11–404. 27). The dialectic the poem depicts is not one that posits straightforward progress of the understanding. Instead, the picture is of a more cyclical process, by which one achieves a sense of the heights only to lose sight of the parts, returning to those forgotten parts in an attempt to add them to the whole (*Consol*. V. m. 3. 404. 28–31).

The response attempting to harmonize freedom and foreknowledge is true to this picture of the dialectic of human reasoning. On the one hand, Boethius points to the manifest limitations of the human power of knowing, the incompleteness of its perspectives. On the other hand, Boethius attempts to expand on and make plausible a divine perspective from which freedom and foreknowledge are no longer in conflict but cohere in the simplicity of the divine nature. These two strategies come very close to being the same in so far as exposing the limitations of the human perspective amounts to the possibility of imagining another higher, simpler, and more complete perspective.

Lady Philosophy lays out the problem this way. She assumes that Boethius can see that merely knowing that something is going to happen does not cause it to happen. Nonetheless, Boethius is unconvinced that no necessity results from divine foreknowledge, because the future is known as future and is known by a perfect knower, God (*Consol*. V. pr. 4. 408. 53–66).[91] Moreover, if things are genuinely contingent, there can be no foreknowledge of them (*Consol*. V. pr. 4. 408. 65–68). The cause of this error, Philosophy explains, is that we think whatever is known is rooted in the nature and power of the thing known instead of in the knower (*Consol.* V. pr. 4. 408. 72–410. 74). Things are known, she argues, not according to themselves but according to the power of the knower (*Consol.* V. pr. 4. 410. 75–77).

Paralleling the development of different perspectives each one surpassing the other, Boethius describes the different modes of knowing—sense, imagination, reason, and intelligence—as ordered hierarchically, each "higher" perspective encompassing those below (*Consol.* V. pr. 4. 410. 84–92). Sight grasps the roundness of the sphere all at once, while touch grasps its shape in parts and sequentially (*Consol.* V. pr. 4. 410. 75–82). Like sight, intelligence "looks down from above," grasping the whole at once, while reason is like touch, in some sense blinded and using clumsy tools to try to put together the whole out of the parts it cannot grasp all at once. And reason is what humans are stuck with, not the unitary and synthesizing vision of intelligence (*Consol.* V. pr. 5. 416. 17–18).

This account of knowledge does not sound quite as shocking as it should until we remember that Lady Philosophy has attributed Boethius's lack of understanding of divine foreknowledge to a kind of naive realism, the view that, "knowing things other than as they are" is contrary to "the integrity of knowledge [*scientiae*]" (*Consol.* V. pr. 4. 408. 70–71). She rejects this view to argue that knowledge is somehow knowing things as *other* than they are. This is the last, most important, and most shocking of the reversals of perspective of the *Consolation*. First, it explains the coherence of freedom and foreknowledge in the divine mind, and second, it justifies Boethius's method of shifting perspectives in the text as a whole. So divine intelligence can know future things with certainty not because those things themselves occur necessarily but because that is intelligence's mode of knowing, knowing with certainty even the uncertain (*Consol.* V. pr. 5. 419. 39–420. 56).[92] Further, the *Consolation* itself follows its own account of knowledge in presenting things according to different modes of knowing. Like the path of knowledge from the senses, through imagination, reason, and intelligence, the *Consolation* moves through different ways of understanding good, evil, virtue, and fortune.

But it cannot reach the culmination of this process, knowing by intelligence. Instead of intelligence, which knows even the imperfect perfectly, Boethius can go no higher than reason, which knows even the perfect only imperfectly. Hence, the text closes by exhorting the reader to turn away from vice, cultivate virtue, lift the soul to righteous hopes, and offer humble prayers to heaven (*Consol.* V. pr. 6. 434. 172–76). These are all gestures of the one standing below striving to reach upward. The completion of the text is, then, completely consistent with Boethius's casting of himself throughout the work in the role of a puzzled, frustrated student and an angry, grief-stricken prisoner. He begins and remains a supplicant in the work, occupying a position that looks upward from below rather than downward from above at the truth. Thus, at the close of the *Consolation*, Boethius rejects his esoteric tendencies even more completely than he does at the beginning. He understands himself as the one without full understanding, identifies with ignorance, and even feels anger and resentment. His humanity is not fully transformed, is not yet divinized (as Lady Philosophy promised the fruit of true happiness to be) in this text; only the direction of his vision is turned.

Even the ability to look upward only lasts for a moment. For the penultimate poem notes that the dialectic of human understanding always must descend to the parts it has lost and forgotten from the heights it has achieved (*Consol.* V. m. 3. 402. 22–404. 31). In linguistic terms, this means that Boethius must move to and from the meanings of those terms appropriate to those different places along the path from or back to God. The text as a whole has this same movement. Philosophy must repeat her arguments and revert to previous levels she has already transcended to bring along her pupil; he is like Orpheus and she turns back with him. Moreover, she must goad her pupil on to be like the warriors of struggle, Agamemnon, Odysseus, and Hercules, engaging in endless battle against two false positions, the view that he knows all and the view that he knows nothing. True to the genre and title, Boethius is only consoled for his loss; he does not have what was lost restored to him.

The Consolation of Fragmentary Vision

To ask why Boethius leaves the seams in the text he has woven exposed is to some degree the same as asking why Boethius wrote *Consolation* without availing himself of the consolations available in Christian scripture and/or by appeal to the Incarnation. This is not to ask whether Boethius writes the *Consolation* as a Christian or not. As both Chadwick and Pelikan point out, the *Consolation* covers much of the same ground and is missing the same explicit references to Christianity and revelation as the early Augustinian dialogues.[93] However, what seems to be absent from the *Consolation* and cannot be missed in Augustine is the distinction between the Neoplatonism which is consistent with Christianity and Christianity itself. Accepting that Boethius is a Christian in the *Consolation* "pressing reason to the very boundaries of faith," Pelikan wonders why "this orthodox theologian in the hour of utmost need, found solace more in philosophical contemplation based on natural reason than in the Christian revelation to which his theological works point."[94]

Like these commentators I think that the muffled character of the *Consolation*'s Christianity, even once the Christianity of its author is taken as given, needs to be explained. Why does Boethius choose the rhetoric for this work that he does, from the language and stories of pagan philosophy and culture? Why does his last work and the most complete vision of the human condition and the order of creation work its way up through the worldly, Stoic, and Neoplatonic accounts of the good life, but stop short of the experience of grace, of the Word made flesh?[95]

Two recent interpretations have argued that Boethius is showing the failure or at least the limits of philosophy. For Joel Relihan, the *Consolation* is meant to ridicule philosophy's ability to console; for Marenbon, Philosophy's arguments are deeply flawed and her power limited in ways she recognizes. In an important sense, I agree with Marenbon's conclusion about the limits of philosophy—though not how he gets to this conclusion. For Marenbon, Philosophy's most important arguments simply fail.[96] I have argued instead that Philosophy—as matter of pedagogy, not inconsistency—shifts her ground, moving her pupil ahead and, at times, coming back down to meet him when he cannot quite move higher with her.

I think that pedagogy becomes clearer if we look at the work not as isolated arguments and in terms of its place in the corpus of a writer who sought to translate, explain, and reconcile Plato and Aristotle, as well as bring together East and West, king and senate. That trajectory moving from logic up through the liberal arts to theology to a glimpse of the divine is a long one that Boethius took the time to build up in many stages in his writing and in his public life. Boethius's method of gathering, weaving, and ordering all the different sources at his disposal in his writings are, we might say, the formal and linguistic counterparts of the life Boethius lived, as Roman and Greek, citizen and theologian, politician and philosopher, careful scholar and speculative thinker, logician and rhetorician, servant of the king and member of the senate. One can imagine him dealing with the complexity created by so many concerns by carefully differentiating them, and ever so delicately ordering and relating them as mutually consistent but different functions. In the *Consolation* this project faces its most radical test in Boethius's existential condition as prisoner under the death sentence. Here the life of multiple and carefully balanced modes of vision and action falls apart, as his accusers essentially charge him with being unable to live all those roles at once. So the *Consolation* displays the crisis that threatened the world constructed by those careful distinctions, the suspicion that they perhaps could not peacefully coexist. Boethius's response to that crisis was to create a more complete and definite hierarchy of those layers and the path through them in a dialectical upward path.

However, at the same time, Boethius is very clear that reason, philosophy's instrument, falls short of completing the task. Where reason falls short, poetry steps in. Thus, the poetry in the work cannot be seen as mere ornament or entertainment.[97] It is integral to it, first, as a first step along the path Philosophy and her pupil tread; second, it is a sign of failure, a way of signaling an apotheosis desired but not quite achieved. Poetry and poetic perspectives also remain in a third and more positive way, as an attempt to imitate more fully the completeness of the divine perspective, which, unlike that of the prisoner or Philosophy, need not sacrifice particularity for universality, the means for the end, nor the part for the whole. Poetic language is not surpassed; it remains a sign of where Boethius has been, a sign of the goal at which he has not yet arrived, and a sign imitating that at which he is aiming.

Hence, Boethius's choice of language and style has to do with the fact that the *Consolation* as a whole ends not with this glorious vision of the unity, beauty, goodness, and order of the created world, a world in which all are pulled back toward God as "end," "source," "maker," "lord," "path," and "goal" portrayed in meter nine of Book III. Rather it ends with Boethius struggling to keep his very fragmented vision of the divine before his eyes, struggling to keep his will committed to virtue. He ends, in other words, with an incomplete and fragmented vision, one in which different perspectives remain, awaiting but not achieving the transcendent vision of the divine.

Late in Book III, Philosophy quotes Parmenides's description of the divine as "like the body of a sphere well-rounded on all sides"; it does not, she explains, receive anything external to it (*Consol.* III. pr. 12. 306. 103–105). Human reasoning and language in the *Consolation* are something less than the closed, perfectly rounded sphere. Boethius's struggle is for integration of all his different roles and allegiances, a task, I have tried to show, that characterizes his work from the logical commentaries to the *Consolation*. But unlike the self-sufficient divinity, Boethius needs all kinds of external material, from Aristotle to Greek literature, to imitate the completeness of the divine material he cannot enclose within his text without remainder, without the loose ends protruding and disrupting the perfect line of the sphere. The form of this work, its syncretism and its less than divine perspective are connected: both are ways of expressing and attempting to ameliorate the limitations of human reason.

CHAPTER 2

ABELARD: A TWELFTH-CENTURY
HERMENEUTICS OF SUSPICION

Keeping Open the Wound of Exile

Abelard's career is as characterized by struggle and opposition as Boethius's is by mediation and integration. Abelard presents himself as constantly engaged in a battle to overtake his masters and enemies, in a fight against the envy and incompetence of others. He struggles with himself as well, attempting to justify his work in a context of intense criticism and attack. The earlier view of Abelard as rationalist rebel, fighter for the autonomy of reason over faith and authority, has been recognized as an anachronistic projection, but no other picture giving unity and coherence to Abelard's work has taken its place. Most have looked at his life, as controversial in modern scholarship as it was in its time, and seen disorder.[1]

The truth of these comments notwithstanding, I want to argue that there is a coherent set of motives that characterizes much of Abelard's work. These motives are reflected in his views on language and furthered by the emphasis on language in his theological and philosophical work. In positive terms, my claim is that Abelard's tendency to turn all narratives into narratives of conflict is a manifestation of the desire for authenticity in his own work and an uncanny ability to sniff out the absence of it in others. What I mean by authenticity is the union and coherence between inside and outside, surface and depth, use and meaning.[2] It expresses itself in Abelard's work not just in trenchant criticism of the failures of others but also in a style of straightforwardness, simplicity, and critique, and in the rejection of esotericism or mysticism. Abelard's views on language are central to a reading of him according to this problematic in two ways. First, the gap between word and meaning is for him a version of the gap between surface and depth; second, language becomes the medium for dealing with that gap. Luscombe points to the same link in noting that Abelard's principle of analysis is always "penetration beyond an actual text to its underlying purpose," an analysis that "requires the use of hermeneutics."[3] Thus, "authenticity" as I am using it is an ethical goal pursued by knowing oneself, one's depth, and seeking to appear as one truly is, but it is at the same time a hermeneutic principle whose project is to look carefully, indeed skeptically, at all surfaces to see how they might belie their depths.[4]

The hermeneutic uniting Abelard's work can also be expressed in negative terms as a "hermeneutics of suspicion," to borrow Paul Ricoeur's phrase, leveled not only at words and texts but also at actions, practices, and narrative constructions. Thus Abelard's constant task is to look behind surfaces toward elusive and often impenetrable depth. Ultimately the negative characterization takes precedence over the positive because his work, I contend, is less about matching surface and depth than about seeing the ways in which surface and depth cannot be made to match.

This is, I think, the most consistent theme of the *Historia calamitatum*.[5] Abelard's version of his story is unified by this quest for coherence and integrity and by his failures to achieve it, failures caused both by his own hypocrisy and that of others.[6] The battles Abelard describes in the *Historia* are aimed at displacing the complacent masters of logic and theology, exposing the incoherence of reigning logical and theological opinions, and reforming corrupt religious communities.[7] Abelard's criticisms of Anselm of Laon make him (whether truly or not) a spokesman for the traditional method of reading and interpreting Scripture based on accepted authorities.[8] The contrast Abelard sets up between his own and Anselm's theological method is between surface (use) and depth (meaning), between mere facility with language and understanding (*HC* 68. 168–74).

The *Historia* returns repeatedly to the contrast between surface and depth. At the Council of Soissons condemning Abelard's work on the Trinity, Abelard is both humiliated and frustrated at being forced to recite but forbidden to explain the Athanasian Creed—after having been criticized for espousing a view on which Athanasius was the authority (*HC* 87–89). He also speaks of being asked for the authority (Augustine) for the claim that God did not beget Himself, but being cut off from explanation and interpretation of both his own and Augustine's remarks (*HC* 84–85). Abelard's criticism of his accusers is the same he leveled at Anselm of Laon, the same as Boethius made of his fellow Romans: they are concerned only with surface correctness rather than with inner meaning or understanding. They think of theology as following the received tradition blindly, Abelard contends, rather than questioning and reordering it. Rejecting the performance of an outward act uninformed by the control, expertise, or understanding that would make it one's own, Abelard seeks to give his words the interiority his accusers' words lack; he will not follow their tracks but will make his own, relying on his own *"ingenium"* (*HC* 69. 204–205).

There is in this story a different kind of restlessness than that in, for example, Augustine's *Confessions*. Augustine asserts the restlessness of the human heart until it rests in God, but Abelard's is a restlessness motivated by disappointment and persecution. It is a kind of flight from the false rather than a journey toward the true. For Abelard, the ability of the external sign to signify an internal reality is, in a world in which everything has been turned upside down, negative. Most poignantly, this is clearest in the way in which the deep meaning of events (that known and planned by providence) is the opposite of that reflected in their surface appearance as fortunate or its opposite: persecution by corrupt human judges signifies acceptance by Christ. Hence, paraphrasing Jesus' statement about not being "of this world," Abelard writes, "if you belonged to the world, the world would love you as its own" (*HC* 108. 1574–75, 1571–72). To Heloise quoting Proverbs he writes, "Whom the Lord loves he reproves," and he adds from Hebrews, "[He] lays the rod on every son whom he acknowledges" (Ep. 4. 91; Proverbs 3: 12; Hebrews 12: 16).

Abelard envisions the point at which this inverted world order will be overturned only in a distant and attenuated sense. While Augustine's assertion throughout the *Confessions* is that God is directing his life toward a good end, Abelard (though the founder of a oratory called the "Comforter") allows words of comfort, the assurance of a happy ending, to appear only in the last lines of his *Historia*. And then they come only in a form which looks toward this end in the most general way. God in his goodness lets nothing occur outside of his plan, Abelard notes, glossing this claim with two scriptural quotations: Paul's "All things work together for good for those who love God" (Rom 8: 28) and the proverb, "Whatever befalls the righteous man it shall not sadden him" (*HC* 108. 1597–98, 1599–1600; Proverbs 12: 21). Boethius struggles toward (even though he does not achieve it) a vision of all fortune as good fortune; Abelard concludes only with both irony and melancholy, "Every unhappy life is happy in its ending" (*Ep.* 4. 143).

Abelard's struggles seem to be against a world in which all relationships and natures are the reverse of what they should be, a world of constantly disappointed expectations, consistently failed projects. His teachers should have been his students, those examining his heresy were the ones without real understanding of their faith. In the rest of this chapter I trace how this sense of dissatisfaction with the disordered and inverted hierarchies of meaning, practice, and authority presents itself in Abelard's logical, theological, and poetic writings.[9]

Abelard's relentless criticisms of various forms of realism describe them as specious modes of uniting (external) word and (internal) meaning, of confusing (superficial) usage with (deeper) significance. His compilation of conflicting authorities in the *Sic et non*, and the long list of possible objections against the doctrine of the Trinity in the *Theologia "summa boni,"* are likewise the exposure of gaps between different explanations of faith in the tradition which must be directly and honestly confronted. In parallel manner, his *Ethics* reveals the absolute separability of true morality from external act and conscious desire, leaving the conclusion that *the* ethical problem is discerning the true motives and intentions beneath one's actions.

The painstaking and finely tuned analyses in Abelard's logic, theology, and ethics are *mutatis mutandis* carried over into Abelard's poetry, letters, and hymns where they serve the search for an authentic spiritual life. In the letters and hymns, Abelard takes up his role as religious reformer. His letters to Heloise put less emphasis on outward rules and practices than on the creation of the conditions for an authentic spiritual life. Abelard also argues that questioning and rethinking one's basic beliefs and traditions are crucial to religious life. The spiritual goal of infusing the outward form of words and practices with meaning and life is explicitly the motivation *behind* Abelard's rewriting of both the words and music for the hymns of the liturgy and the Benedictine rule for Heloise's community.

Abelard's *planctus* do not build toward union and fulfillment in God as Boethius's *Consolation* does. Boethius at least projects a divine perspective on the narrative of human life, culminating in a happy ending union with God. The figures in Abelard's laments do not envision divine union or if they do, it is seen as sacrifice rather than consummation. Here as in Abelard's other "solutions" attempting to unite word and thing, human and divine understandings, Abelard does not so much find a means of achieving union so much as he works toward revealing the gaps that cannot be overcome.

Logic: Dissolving Old Narratives and Making New Fictions

If Boethius's goal in his logical commentaries is to distinguish in order to unite, Abelard's goal seems simply to distinguish. Boethius's construction of a narrative from Aristotle's cryptic remarks in the *Peri hermeneias* is one Abelard follows carefully and also criticizes, finding Boethius's connections more a confusion than a synthesis of the elements in Aristotle's text. He argues that Boethius constructs a unity that is inauthentic, which asserts a happy ending, a union between language, understanding, and the world that is not quite achievable. His own corpus of commentaries breaks down this narrative to consider its parts much more carefully.

Abelard's perception of gaps in Boethius's narrative and his desire to take it apart is signaled in many ways. It comes across at a general and formal level in his account of the relationship between the *Categories* and *Peri hermeneias* in his later glosses on Porphyry (known as the *Logica nostrorum petitioni sociorum*). In these later glosses, he argues that Aristotle's two works are not two pieces of a single narrative, an account of words leading to one of sentences, as Boethius claims (and as was a tradition Abelard himself follows in his earlier glosses), but the separate consideration of words insofar as they signify things (the *Categories*) and words insofar as they signify *intellectus* (the *Peri hermeneias*) (LNPS 508. 32–37). Beginning with this division, then, I would like to consider Abelard's account of the distinction between words and things in the earlier *Glosses on Porphyry* and the later gloss on Porphyry, and between words and understanding in the *Commentary on the Peri hermeneias*.[10] I will attempt to examine the kind of a narrative Abelard constructs, insofar as he constructs any, of the processes of abstraction and sentence construction.

Glosses on Porphyry

Abelard presents his battle to overtake William of Champeaux in logic as a battle of coherence against incoherence, honesty and thoroughness against double-talk and superficiality. Abelard's *Glosses on Porphyry* reads like a series of assaults against the walls of realism's fortress, walls that crumble like façades before Abelard's critiques. The irony is that *realism*, which stands in a sense for the view of the substantiality of language, is for Abelard a superficial and simplistic theory of the fit between language and reality.

When Abelard comes to the famous questions on universals posed by Porphyry he makes additions that exaggerate the gap between words and things already noted by Boethius. First, Abelard adds "the question of the common cause of imposition of universal nouns, namely, what is that cause in virtue of which different things agree?" He also adds "the question of the understanding of universal nouns, in which no particular thing seems to be conceived, nor does the universal word seem to be concerned with some particular thing . . . ." (*Gl Por* 8. 12–16). These two additions assume Abelard's position on universals, that is, that universals are not things to which words correspond and that there is an asymmetry between words and things. Only given the different and discrete character of individual things and the lack of any shared nature must one ask what is found common to them grounding their common nomination, or, conversely, how the common and abstract understanding of the universal noun applies to those particulars.

Abelard also adds another question to the list: would the universal continue to function meaningfully, signifying understanding, even if the things named by the universal are destroyed? (*Gl Por* 8. 16–22). This question envisions the absolute independence of words and understandings from things. The autonomy of the understanding, its ability to function in the absolute absence of the object, constitutes its most distinctive feature for Abelard. But it is also what makes words and things difficult to match up with each other and leaves Abelard's account with very little of the flavor of the Aristotelian model of understanding as a kind of unity with the object.

The list of authorities who argue that universality is a property of things as well as words includes the best: Aristotle, Porphyry, and Boethius (*Gl Por* 9. 21–22). Nonetheless, Abelard's attack begins abruptly and unequivocally: "while authorities seem to agree very much upon it, physics opposes it in every way" (*Gl Por* 11. 10–11). In a way we could well expect from the author of the *Historia*, Abelard places authority on one side and himself along with truth on the other, even when, as in this case, it means giving a somewhat distorted picture of Aristotle and Boethius.

Abelard then proceeds, as Stock puts it, to "play logical havoc" with the realist position.[11] Abelard's first arguments are against a very extreme form of realism that, he argues, leads to monism and asserts the simultaneous presence of contradictories in the same object. Abelard's *reductio ad absurdum* essentially collapses the Porphyrian tree as one would an umbrella. When that common trunk connecting all the branches is taken to be a thing, all the branches become identical to the trunk and, hence, each other. Thus since animal, the genus, includes the rational as well as the irrational animal, the same thing, animal, is both rational and irrational, and Socrates and the ass become identical. The identity of individuals with their species, of species with their genera as well as the root identity of all members of the highest genera—substances, qualities, and quantities— follows from this very simple version of realism.

According to Abelard, the more complex versions of realism all ultimately assert that there is some*thing* in virtue of which individuals are called by the same name; hence, they are obfuscations of the same realistic view. The view that the universal is a "collection" of individuals still ends in monism, because it makes individuals identical with the collection, which receives contradictory predicates (*Gl Por* 14. 40–15. 11). Similarly, the view that individuals are not essentially the same but merely "agree" with each other also comes to naught. It fails to explain why we should predicate "man" and not "Socrates" of other men since Socrates surely agrees with all other men to exactly the same degree as "man" does. Nor does another moderate view, that Socrates "does not differ from Plato in man," solve the problem since neither do the two differ in stone. The latter versions of realism fail to give enough distinguishing content to the universal, fail to account for the unity between individual and universal, just as the former versions identify them too firmly. In none of these accounts, in other words, has the right fit between individuals and universals been achieved.

The "fit" Abelard tailors is of the "one size fits all" variety, claiming that the universal is "common to all and proper to none" (*Gl Por* 21. 34). The fit is, strictly speaking, not between universals and things, but between the common (but not proper) conception "pertaining" to individuals and those individuals. The "common cause" of the denomination of different individuals by the same word, on the one hand, and the formation of a "common conception," on the other, are processes Abelard wants to keep separate. The "common cause" by which different individuals are called by the same name is their "*status*"—that they are human beings. *Status* is most definitely not a thing and not a concept, not even of the "common to all and proper to none" variety. Abelard writes, "So this *vox* 'human being' names singulars from a common cause, namely that they are human beings [the *status*], because of which it is said to be a universal, and constitutes a certain common but not proper understanding [*intellectus*], namely pertaining to singulars of which it conceives the common likeness" (*Gl Por* 19. 9–13). But *universals* do not constitute this common understanding; they only nominate, and the conception, the fruit of this understanding, is not the cause of imposition of the name.

Abelard is emphasizing that there are three different orders that may not be confused. There is a universal, a common conception, and a common cause (the *status*), but these are not identical to one another. Universals name things; they name because of the cause, the *status* of the thing in question, and they signify conceptions. Unlike Boethius, however, Abelard does not close this circle, uniting the *status* of the thing with the conception in the mind.

The problem is how the understanding works to form these concepts and to connect them with things. First, Abelard distinguishes between the understanding (*intellectus*) and a form of the thing conceived by the understanding: "understanding [*intellectus*] is a certain action of the soul, by which it is called understanding [*intelligens*], but the form to which it is directed is an imaginary and fictive thing which it makes for itself when and how it wishes, like those imaginary cities which are seen in dreams . . . ." (*Gl Por* 20. 28–33). The product of understanding, the form or image it conceives, is, Abelard explains, like the image in a mirror, which "is" only in a sense. The mirror image is the subject of sight, the thing seen, but it is, in another sense, nothing. So the form is the subject of the understanding but is of itself nothing, and it is surely nothing of which we could predicate the qualities that we predicate of the thing (*Gl Por* 21. 6–17).[12]

Abelard notes that some have identified this image-concept with the understanding itself while others, like Priscian, have identified it with the divine ideas. Abelard, however, argues that they are distinct. Unlike God, Abelard explains, to whom all things "are known through themselves" and who "knows them before they are," human beings do not reach beyond "the exterior sensuality of accidents" to simple and pure understanding (*Gl Por* 22. 27–23. 11).

Abelard's position on divine ideas is mixed. On the one hand, Abelard does not claim that concepts can or should try to move closer to divine ideas, nor indeed does he assert any common ground of causality or likeness between human conceptions and those of the deity.[13] On the other hand, however, Abelard does not jettison divine ideas; he retains them in order to contrast them with human concepts. Human concepts are shallow and fictional constructions which, unlike God's ideas, do not penetrate to the reality of things. Divine ideas remain the standard for knowledge, but for Abelard they are a standard we simply fall short of, not something that human conceptions approach, even in principle.

In Abelard's account of abstraction, the view that we find seeds of in Boethius emerges in full force—that abstraction is a kind of "fiction" or making. What distinguishes true from false abstraction is, again as only hinted at in Boethius, the way it is considered by the one who makes it. Hence, Abelard explains, abstraction is not false even though one considers only one quality rather than all aspects of a thing. "The 'only,' " Abelard explains, "refers to the attention alone, not to the mode of subsisting. . . . For the thing does not have only it, but it is *considered* as having only it" (*Gl Por* 25. 26–29. My emphasis). Thoughts of the future in providence and the past in memory are analogous to abstraction for Abelard. They are not false as long as they are not mistakenly thought to be of the present; in the same way, abstraction is not false unless it is mistakenly taken to be more than what it is, a certain incomplete way of conceiving something (*Gl Por* 26. 35–27. 7).

The role that all these distinctions (between thing, universal, image-concept, and understanding) play is to distinguish and separate universals, things, and understandings, thereby outlawing any transfer of properties from one realm to the other. Thus, on the one hand, universals name the corporeal, concrete individuals and, on the other, name them incorporeally, that is, indeterminately and confusedly. Universals subsist in sensibles in the sense that they signify an intrinsic substance of a thing sensible by its exterior forms, yet that substance is distinct from these sensible forms (*Gl Por* 27. 39–29. 38). Abelard's account of the process of coming to know and name is one of very carefully drawn distinctions, the elements of which have only very tentative, indirect links drawn between them.

When it comes to the most important link, between understanding and things, Abelard again distinguishes rather than unites. He argues that we have only opinion, not knowledge, of abstract forms like rationality and paternity since those forms are not accessible by sense. Of sensible forms, Abelard claims, there is understanding, but not because understanding, which is the result of abstraction, gets to and grasps the real nature but only because "the inventor [of the universal for that form] intended that they [universals] be imposed according to some natures or properties of things, although even he was not able to think out completely the nature or the property of the thing" (*Gl Por* 23. 20–24). Thus it is the intention of the inventor to capture the form, not his actual grasp intuition of it that grounds that knowledge as knowledge.[14]

Boethius began his account with the narrative of the "fall" of confusing words with things, born of the expectation of one-to-one-correspondence, and he ended by constructing a narrative of how, despite the difference and imperfect mapping from one realm to the other, words and things are nonetheless connected. Abelard, on the other hand, ends his account with the difference between the orders of words and things, and a warning to those who would "transfer" characteristics from one realm to another, a category in which Boethius, according to Abelard, belongs.

For Abelard, as Boethius, the point of making careful distinctions is to save the truth of the language we use. But even though that goal and some recognition of the asymmetry between words and things is common to Boethius and Abelard, Abelard's need to keep the realms of words, thoughts, and things separate overrides his interest in uniting them.

Logica nostrorum petitioni sociorum

The *Logica nostrorum petitioni sociorum*, a later gloss on Porphyry, shows certain signs of maturity in the discussion of universals, and of some distance from the arguments with and about the supposed realism of William of Champeaux. Instead of beginning with the caricature of realism found in the *Glosses*, Abelard sets up the whole text in the form of a *quaestio*, lining up authorities around the three views of what universals are: things, understandings, or words. Unlike in the earlier *Glosses* he lists Aristotle as among those holding the view that universals are words. Further, he attributes to Boethius the view that species/universals "are more *sermones* than things" (*LNPS* 515. 6–9). The arguments against realism have the same structure as those in the first *Glosses* but come to the point more quickly and more directly: realism leads to monism.

Abelard's own view turns on the distinction between *sermo* and *vox*. *Vox* is the thing, the sound, and *sermo* is by its institution a word that is used of many. Thus, a word is universal or particular because it was instituted as such. *Vox*, the sound, on the other hand, is a natural creation and is simply particular as all existing objects are (*LNPS* 522. 28–31). Thus Abelard "distinguish[es] the physical component of language from its capacity to signify" arguing that singularity and universality belong to *sermones* not *voces* or things.[15] Abelard explains the connection between the two aspects, natural and conventional in this way: "The nativity of *a vox* and a *sermo* are different, though wholly identical in essence" (*LNPS* 522. 22–23). "But voces are things in no way universal, though it happens that all *sermones* are *voces*" (*LNPS* 522. 30–31). Characteristically, Abelard states his own view in the most provocative language possible. Abelard does give an analogy explaining his own view, likening the relationship between *vox* and *sermo* to that between a stone and the image in a stone statue. Abelard says "this stone" and "this image" are entirely the same, but the stone is the work of God, the image is that of a human artist. The "status of stone" is conferred by God, and the "status of image" conferred by human agreement.

Abelard concludes that in an important sense it simply is the case that abstract understanding conceives things other than as they are. "Hence, the understandings of this sound [*vox*] 'body' has another mode in being conceived than body in existence, since understanding conceives this substance only with corporeity, so that namely it attends to some form, but body does not exist with only this form" (*LNPS* 530. 11–15). Still understandings are not mere fictions because understanding attends only to one aspect of a thing; it does not pretend that the thing has only that one aspect, while fictions do falsify the object by pretending to be a complete presentation of it.

The analogy Abelard draws is the following: when I say I want a golden castle, I want something, but there is not something that I want, rather I have "some want [*aliquam voluntatem*]" (*LNPS* 532. 1–3). Similarly, Socrates and Plato agree in something, that is, in so far as they are human beings, but this does not mean "they participate in some *thing* [*ex aliqua re qua inter se participant*] but rather that they have some agreement [*aliquam convenientiam habere*]" (*LNPS* 531. 35–39). The "something" in each case is understood not as an independent, external existent, but as a determination or modifier of the agreement or of the want.[16] So Abelard can conclude, thoroughly enjoying the paradoxical sound of it, "Thus when I understand a chimera, though there is no thing which I understand, nevertheless I understand something" (*LNPS* 533. 7–9). Such arguments bring abstractions and fictions much closer to each other and further from things than they are for Boethius. But Abelard's motive is not to undermine the legitimacy of abstraction any more than his collection of contradictions among theological authorities is meant to undermine faith; rather his aim is to distinguish abstraction and the product of abstraction from the individual things that receive a common name.

Particular names do not escape all the problems which befall universals, even though the asymmetry between words and things (discrete things receiving common names) does not afflict them (*LNPS* 524. 32–35). Particular names are unsuitable for describing, for example, "something present or absent in all men," because they (particulars) are inconstant, "having substance in one way and in another not," and they are infinite and, hence, unknowable (*LNPS* 532. 10–15; 50).[17] Hence, they fail to capture common and knowable features of things just as universal names fail to capture individuality. The implication is that the function of words is not just to refer to individuals or to stand in one-to-one correspondence with things, for Abelard; if that were all that words were supposed to do, proper names would be perfect names. As Jacobi notes, for Abelard, unlike for Frege, semantics is not reducible to the "paradigm of naming."[18]

The indefiniteness that is characteristic of universal words is also characteristic of whole sentences. Even what should be the model of a clear predication, a simple sentence like "Socrates runs," Abelard argues, "do[es] not show how or how much he runs" (*LNPS* 532. 23–25). Hence all language and all ways of conceiving things are incomplete; we do not and cannot attend to every aspect of things even in the most particular and most determined thoughts and propositions. Abelard implies that language, being, and thought fail to mirror each other in a number of ways, ways we usually do not notice. While this does not hinder the successful functioning of ordinary language in ordinary life, it does need to be recognized as a condition within which we live, speak, and understand.

Glosses on the Peri hermeneias

In this commentary, Abelard again considers the question that occupied him in the *Glosses*: whether words signify understandings (i.e., passions of the soul *GPH* 312. 15–16) or things (*GPH* 312. 29–33). The question is triggered by Aristotle's mention that words are symbols for "passions of the soul." Abelard begins by distinguishing between sensation, imagination, and understanding. Imagination and understanding are substitutes for the sensation of the absent object and are that through which understanding takes place. Just as in the *Glosses*, he gives these images a considerably lower status than Platonic ideas; they are not the *things* that universal words name; they are not things at all. Like the imaginations of the city of Rome or a fictive tower, like fantastic castles and dreams, these images have no substantial reality (*GPH* 314. 25–27; 315. 18–21). Moreover, these images are not identical with understanding itself, because the intellect cannot transform itself into the likeness of things to understand them (cannot become length or breadth, be in motion or stable), and, hence, cannot become identical with what it thinks (*GPH* 314. 32–35). Because products of the imagination and understanding are for Abelard fictions rather than Platonic ideas, they cannot be what are primarily named or designated by words. Abelard calls them "*intersigna*"; they are used to know things but are not the things known or named (*GPH* 315. 27–30).

Clearly de Rijk is right that Abelard "intended to look for the object of human understanding within the acts of understanding themselves" rather than externally, in something like Platonic forms. But Abelard does not do this, in order to dispose of divine ideas as soon as it is safe to do so, prefiguring Ockham's razor.[19] Abelard does reject the idea that human understanding seeks to grasp the divine ideas, but he does not thereby simplify the problem of knowledge because they remain as a standard so distant as to be unrelated to our conceptions. Moreover, the slot filled by the Platonic form remains occupied by the conception, but it does not become, as it was for Boethius, that which unifies thought with thing. Abelard illustrates his view using the statue of Achilles: the fiction in the understanding is not the reference for the reality any more than the statue of Achilles is the reference for Achilles; to the degree that it is confused with Achilles or taken as the subject of thought or language about Achilles the statue is falsely understood (*GPH* 315. 37–316. 12). But we still make and still need the image.

Having distinguished between sensation, to which the object is immediately present, and imagination and understanding, which are distanced from the object, Abelard turns to the difference between the latter two. Abelard argues that understanding discerns the thing really and not just *in* or *as* an image or fiction (*GPH* 317. 15–18), but he describes understanding as an elaboration of the image: "By imagination, therefore, we grasp only the image of the thing; hence, perhaps imagination is so called from the image it grasps. By understanding this same image, as was said, we paint [*depingimus*] that which by imagination we grasp and hold, so that imagination only holds the image, somewhat confused, as if stupefied and admiring and not attending or defining anything it is as the understanding does" (*GPH* 318. 1–9). Abelard then likens imagination to holding a block of wood while understanding colors and carves it; imagination outlines the figure while the intellect paints it in (*GPH* 318. 9–19).

Thus understanding is like the activity of an artisan; it is a making rather than a receiving, more "fictional" (i.e., made) than even the "fictions" of the imagination.[20] Such a depiction of understanding accords well with Abelard's tendency to see accessing the true and authentic, in this case the understanding of natures, as a deeper, less immediate, and more arduous task, and as a self-conscious activity rather than a simple taking over of external forms. Here the preference for depth over surface, for what is self-made over what is received, gets its epistemological correlative: under-standing is not an immediate or passive presence of something to the mind; it is something developed and achieved by the knower.

The distance between understanding and imagination is parallel to the difference between understanding and language. Abelard spends much less time than Boethius focusing on the artificial character of words and letters; however, he too is concerned to note, as Boethius did, that it is institution that makes a linguistic sign a sign. He does so with a characteristically fine and paradoxical sounding distinction: many things actually signify that are not significative. What counts is that something be *instituted* to signify, not that it does actually or potentially signify (*GPH* 336). Further, words, which are instituted to signify, can signify in ways other than the ways they were instituted and in these cases they are not significative in the strict sense. So a word can signify itself (e.g., "human being" is a noun) by a kind of transfer rather than institution, just as a meadow can be said by transfer to laugh (*GPH* 336). So while Abelard insists on there being a *proper* mean-ing, he insists equally strongly that propriety is the product of institution, a mere conventional procedure.

Abelard is also less concerned than Boethius about any shift or loss of meaning in the translation between different languages. Abelard considers with some sympathy the view that since it is the interior understanding which counts and since this is the same between different languages, both words and understandings are the same in different languages (*GPH* 323. 17–18). Why words too? If what makes understanding possible between persons and across languages is the similarity of the mode of conception, then words in different languages are essentially or physically different as things but have the same mode of signification, for example, *homo* and *anthropos* (*GPH* 323. 18–27). The best way to understand this view is as a sort of extension of his view of the word as consisting of *vox* and *sermo*, the sound and the institution. The word as *sermo* is, in a sense, the same between different languages since it is instituted to signify the same under-standing; only the *voces*, the sounds, are different. Though Abelard in the end does not quite go so far as to claim that words (in the sense of *sermones*) are common to different peoples, he does contend that understandings and things are common; only "the form or office of signifying for both sounds and letters is changed" (*GPH* 323. 37–39, 324.15–19).[21]

It seems naive of Abelard to assume that the different sounds and letters in different languages are *merely* cloaks covering a common understanding of reality. And in a way it is, but it is consistent with his approach to other issues. Abelard analyzes problems by distinguishing between apparent surface and real depth. Thus he reads the difference between different languages as a merely exterior difference and understanding as the common reality beneath. In the same way, the verbal formulas of theology are super-ficial coverings of no value or importance when compared with deep and real understanding. Further, Abelard has a fairly radical view of the diffi-culties attending translation within the same language. As we shall see, Abelard argues that propositions that seem to say the same thing often really do not and those which seem to say something different from one another in outward form are often really saying the same thing. Hence, for Abelard to claim that all languages share the same understandings does not neces-sarily imply a simple doctrine of one-to-one-correspondence across lan-guages since correspondence even within a given language is a complex matter that requires looking beneath the surface.

Abelard also notes that a true proposition can generate a false under-standing and a false proposition, a true understanding (*GPH* 328. 1–2). It depends, Abelard explains, on what the understanding attends to when the claim is proposed. If the proposition is about the past and the understand-ing attends to the present and an image or conception based on that presence (where Socrates is sitting, for example), then the truth value of the understanding and the sentence can be different (*GPH* 328). Two people may, Abelard continues, form different images of insensible things (he seems to have in mind here abstract concepts like paternity) and still understand the "*vim naturae*" (the inner power or reality of the thing) in the same way (*GPH* 329. 3–6).

Moreover, Abelard explains that one can consider the same thing in different ways—as oak, wood, matter, and so on. Here the Porphyrian tree Abelard wanted to fold up like an umbrella and put away is rehabilitated; no longer taken literally, it is turned into a tree of different ways of consid-ering things rather than different modes of being. This "discretion of atten-tion" (*GPH* 329. 21), the ability to attend to different aspects of the same thing, is characteristic of rationality (*GPH* 329. 25–26).

Abelard's account of the verb is often taken to be the most creative element of his commentary and it continues the theme that the surface of language often belies the inner reality. In his account of the verb, he goes further in rejecting an understanding of language based on grammatical cat-egories. Abelard first attacks Priscian's view that verbs signify action and passion. Abelard can barely conceal his contempt for the shallowness of such a view, simply noting in exasperation a few of the many exceptions to it. He describes the contortions those holding Priscian's view must perform to make this view work, because they are forced to maintain that verbs such as "sit," "lie," "live," "have" signify action or passion but have to admit that they also can signify a situation or a having, that is, signification proper to nouns not verbs. Moreover, any number of common verbs do not by any stretch of the imagination signify actions, for example, verbs like "continget" or impersonal verbs such as *"taedet"* or *"piget,"* or importantly *"esse"* (*GPH* 348). Abelard will have none of such *ad hoc* attempts to add qualifications and complications to a content-based account of such verbs to make them fit Priscian's view.

Although he does not object as strenuously to Aristotle's location of specific difference for verbs in their (con)signification of time, his analysis and examples are such as to qualify and effectively diminish the importance of this as a distinguishing feature of verbs as well. Abelard argues that time signification is really something that characterizes the sentence, not just the verb. Moreover, time signification is not something a verb carries in a fixed way but is affected by other verbs in the proposition (*GPH* 350. 1–5; 10–12). Given these reflections on the verb, Klaus Jacobi concludes that the direction of Abelard's thought is toward "giving up the difference between nouns and verbs altogether and continuing to observe only the functional difference between subject position and predicate position."[22]

Courting Difference and Complication

Jacobi characterizes Abelard's logic as having an "essentially negative character," by which he means that Abelard's investigations, arguments, and distinctions are all "warnings against reductional accounts."[23] Abelard resists attempts to come up with a simple, content-based account of the differences between different parts of speech or an analysis of propositions as if they were composed of independent components. Abelard argues that like words, propositions have two meanings, one relating to things, another to understandings, but, also as in the case of words, the relationship of propositions to things is not based in some *thing* onto which the proposition maps. Just as universals are predicated of many not by virtue of some *thing* in which those individuals share but because of their *status*, so too propositions connect to the world through their *dicta*, what Abelard calls the "quasi-thing" they have reference to (*GPH* 367. 9–13).[24] Further, Abelard rejects an atomic view of meaning for propositions just as he does for words; the content of a proposition is not the sum of the content of its components. Abelard argues that what makes a proposition a complete word string is its assertive character, its claim that something is the case. Thus propositions *propose* something (e.g., Socrates is sitting) while verbal phrases (e.g., that Socrates is sitting) do not (*GPH* 327. 27–40). Abelard would prefer to have a complex but accurate account rather than a unified theory of all propositions.[25]

One of Abelard's main targets in his commentaries is the grammatical analysis of sentences. He sees his role distinctly as that of a dialectician, not of a grammarian, downplaying even the grammatical evidence Aristotle quite frequently calls to his aid. He disparages the grammarian's interest in outward form and opposes it to his own in real content and deep structure. Unlike grammarians, Abelard pulls away the curtain of irrelevant differences of form, which obscure the commonalities of real meaning and understanding, to reveal the noncorrespondence of thought and language. Hence, Abelard is fond of pointing out that propositions and phrases can have the same meaning but different forms, and have similar words or forms but different meanings and truth values. In his restless critique of his contemporaries and of the tradition, Abelard considers views so radical that they would have completely overturned the Aristotelian conception of logic and language, yet Abelard does not quite take these last steps. This is surely because, as Jacobi argues, it would have been impossible for Abelard "to free himself from this tradition to such an extent as to be able to recognize the far-reaching consequences of his line of thought."[26] But I think it is also because Abelard's aim is not to reform language, by, for example, abolishing grammatical distinctions so that surface and depth might match. Though Abelard, like Ockham, is certainly critical of realistic and reifying tendencies, Abelard's effort is not to get rid of supposedly useless extra objects, but to reveal the confusion between different aspects and layers of language and knowing. Moreover, Abelard clearly enjoys the complexity and paradox he uncovers and creates; he is not looking for a technical language that might escape the incongruities of ordinary language he exposes.

The result is a certain tension between Abelard's rejection of the realist theory of how language maps onto thought and things and the realities he refuses to part with even given language's inability to capture them. Martin Tweedale is a bit frustrated by Abelard claiming that there are only two types of things: individual substances and individual (accidental) forms, even as he "helps himself generously to a host of non-things as well: *status, dicta,* natures, properties, states, and events, among others."[27] Abelard, Tweedale concludes, is in both his logic and theology "deeply committed to this way of having [his] ontological cake while throwing it out at the same time."[28] Jolivet describes this as a kind of combination of "nonrealism" and Platonism, or as a Platonism "freed from the realism of genera and species."[29] The rejection of realism is in the determination not to find for either words or propositions a *thing* or essence to which they correspond; Platonism, on the other hand, is expressed in the independence of truth from both things and human knowledge.[30] We see the former in Abelard's analysis of universals and propositions; we see the latter in his insistence in the commonality of meaning across languages and in grammatically different expressions.

Abelard's analysis of language posits a kind of Platonic reality even while he makes it clear that our words and propositions do not capture it; thus he carefully disengages the functioning of words and sentences from things to which or on which they might be supposed to map. For Abelard, even when we achieve knowledge by abstraction, what we have is not knowledge of the "real" thing. That is a kind of Platonic reality in the mind of God and in the thing at a level we cannot quite reach. While Boethius recognizes the distinction between the order of things and words, he joins them in principle, positing a point at which the trajectories of word, thought, and thing come together. For Abelard, words, divine and human understanding, sense perceptions, images, and things themselves are simply of different and nontransitive orders. His theology and poetry, like his logical work, we will see, is in parallel ways preoccupied with absence, separation, and difference.

Theology: Sounding the Battle Cry

Abelard's penchant in his logical work for exposing the gap between surface and depth in the arguments of others and constructing fine distinctions we shall see displayed in his theological writings as well. And just as Abelard's criticisms of realism do not lead to a solution that would dispense with all asymmetries between language, thought, and being, so Abelard's theological reflections do not criticize the solutions and explanations of others only to replace them with those that pretend to illuminate the divine perfectly.

There is in Abelard's theologies a combination of bravado and skepticism that I would like to suggest is explained by a view of theology as an engagement in theology as a battle.[31] The battle cry gathers and emboldens the troops for the fight, but it does not envision the possibility of transcending the struggle or emerging from it unscathed. Like battle cries, Abelard's theological texts are a combination of tremendous confidence in their arguments to defeat opponents and grim reminders of their failure to comprehend the great truths they seek to explore. Thus, I do not just mean that Abelard's theologies are battle cries because his rhetoric is polemical (something common to any number of theologians of the period), rather I want to argue that the very way he constructs theological texts and theological answers is as one under siege. I take it this is not simply because Abelard felt himself to be beset by enemies (though he surely did and he surely was) but rather because he extrapolates this into a more systematic position on the nature and possibilities of theology. Thus, his project is to fight off enemies rather than achieve peace, to stave off contradiction rather than attain transcendent insight and understanding.

The *Sic et non* exposes the gaps and inconsistencies in the tradition and among authorities and leaves their resolution to the student/believer.

Its goal is essentially Socratic, revealing the ignorance of those who pretend to possess knowledge, in this case the theologians rather than dialecticians. In the first version of systematic theology, the *Theologia "summi boni,"* Abelard takes his enemies to be dialecticians who have misused the art of dialectic and misread or ignored the works of the philosophers in their pursuit of theological victory. The last version of his systematic theology, *Theologia "scholarium,"* is a defense of dialectic against those criticizing its use in theology.[32] In neither case does Abelard cast himself as occupying the sane middle ground between extremes; in both he sees himself as an extreme defender against both opposite extremes. As Abelard's conception of the enemy shifts, the nature of the battle also shifts to some degree, from defense against outsiders to criticism and questioning of the authoritative tradition, with a goal of ongoing reform and self-evaluation. But what remains constant is firstly, the sense of an enemy who is always understood as accepting surface rather than seeking depth and, secondly, the conviction that questioning is a path toward a truer grasp of and more authentic commitment to the Christian faith.

The Rhetoric of Battle

Abelard introduces and justifies the dialectical portion of his first systematic theology on the Trinity as follows: "the time of miracles has passed, evil has grown, fallacy has unleashed its army against the truth; for those of us who cannot fight back by acts, it remains to fight back by words" (*TSum* II. 114. 15–19). The terms of this opening salvo remind us of Abelard's presentation of his calling as dialectician in the *Historia* (*HC* 63. 25–28). As Abelard prepares for the battle against the formidable army of objections to the doctrine of the Trinity, he reminds his readers that this is a fight using the very same weapons as the enemies who attack the faith, "to fools according to their folly." Abelard's aim is to crush their assaults and disperse their forces, defeating them as David did Goliath (*TSum* II. 122. 220).

In the *Theologia "scholarium,"* Abelard works to justify his project of reasoning about God and the Trinity in terms of the need to fight an ongoing battle. One might think, he notes, that the problem has already been solved by making accessible what was hidden, in which case Abelard's work is superfluous. Further, he adds, no more heresies or doubts against which arguments and defenses must be made might arise. Or the ineffability of the Trinity might be so intractable that it cannot be made accessible (*TSch* II. 425). Abelard offers no response to this last objection, in effect conceding to it. To the other two, Abelard essentially replies, "Would that it were so!" He adds a raft of scriptural quotations predicting conflict, division, and unbelief in almost apocalyptic fashion and counseling clear and careful speech in defense of the faith (*TSch* II. 425).[33] Thus Abelard sets up his project of explanation and defense of the faith against doubts from within and attacks from without as an unending battle.

Abelard's *Sic et non* uses authorities not to solve but to raise questions as it reorganizes the tradition around questions like "that God is threefold and contra" and "that God is not a substance and contra" (*SN* 709 qq. 6, 9). Abelard seeks and arranges the authorities to highlight their differences, forcing the student into a battle of ideas by tearing asunder the curtain of continuity and agreement in the tradition.[34] Although the principles of interpretation Abelard lays out in the prologue connect to a tradition going back to Augustine and through practices used even by Anselm of Laon, the way Abelard weaves the quotations he selects from Augustine and others underlines his preoccupation with the fallenness of language and human understanding, even the supposedly redeemed language of Scripture and the Fathers.[35] The reader is left with a strong impression of the overwhelming odds against arriving at any correct interpretation. Abelard gives a litany of the ways in which texts and our interpretations can fail to represent reality and their author's intentions. A text may be miscopied or misattributed to an authority, may cite opinions not held by the author, may only lay out problems rather than solutions, or may take a human rather than divine perspective in its use of language (*SN* 90. 54–56, 91. 78–85, 93. 114–17, 93. 134–37, 94. 149–51, 95. 168–69, 95. 177–80). In contrast, although Augustine recognizes as many difficulties of interpretation as Abelard, he chooses to place them in the context of the multiplicity of possible readings consistent with the faith, reveling in the plenitude rather than, as Abelard does, in the poverty of meaning.[36]

This project of exposing contradiction in the tradition seems to emerge from a spirit contrary to Boethius's model of theological argumentation in the *Contra Eutychen* as finding the mean. However, it is too simplistic to say that Boethius dissolves and Abelard provokes dissention. Boethius's strongest criticism in the *Contra Eutychen* is for those who find no need for an explanation of doctrine. Moreover, a crucial step in Boethius's version of theological reflection involves laying out of the multiplicity of meanings of key terms. The effect of differing authorities in Abelard is like the effect of different definitions in Boethius. It dispels the notion that there is a clear and unmediated connection between words and thought in order to focus on the need for reflection and on the truth one is trying to grasp.

The difference, of course, is that Boethius puts the emphasis on ordering meanings and reconciling differences while Abelard dwells on the conflict. Discussions of and differences with the Fathers and teachers of the church is an exercise Abelard calls "salubrious"; Abelard writes, "in reading works of this type [writings of the fathers and later authorities] what is necessary is freedom of judgment, not belief"(*SN* 100. 178–80). The problems Abelard creates by revealing the dissonance in the tradition are to be solved by the student/believer who must develop his own understanding of these questions and is forced into constructing and taking responsibility for his own interpretations. Deepened faith emerges from an attitude of questioning and self-reliance on the part of the student. Hence, Abelard concludes that his aim for his collection of dissonant authorities is to "provoke students to engage in the most important inquiry into truth and make more acute their skill at inquiry." "For," he continues, "the first key to wisdom is assiduous and frequent questioning. . . . For by doubting, we come to inquire and by inquiry to the perception of truth" (*SN* 102. 230–39).

In the service of giving student the tools to engage in the theological task, Abelard defends the use of pagan philosophy and poetic fiction over a mass of objections.[37] Abelard argues in defense of poetry not that it is true but that the reading of no secular art should be forbidden unless it means foregoing some more important good. "There is," he adds, "nothing false in teaching, nor corrupt in words. . . ." (*TSch* II. 421. 433–34). Abelard's use of "similitudes" of the poets or philosophers or of his own not only follows divine example but is necessary to teach enemies and bring understanding (*TSch* II. 424. 523–28). This conclusion is bolstered by three passages from *De doctrina christiana*'s fourth book on the role of eloquence in Christian teaching. These passages praise the use of clarity over eloquence, improper speech, which produces understanding, over propriety, which does not, and the "wooden key," which opens what has been closed, over a "golden key," which opens nothing (*TSch* II. 424. 530–42).[38]

Those who mistake knowledge of evil for doing it and who prefer false propriety to real understanding should heed the prophet Isaiah's warning, "Woe to you who call evil good and good evil" (*TSch* II. 423. 499–514; Is. 5: 20). What is significant, of course, is that Abelard is arguing for a kind of reversal, calling what is normally taken to be evil (knowledge of evil) good. Abelard's arguments in favor of poetry are constructed as polemical arguments expressed by a lone voice against zealous, powerful, and numerous enemies, taking a contrarian point of view against appearance and authority. The appearance of truth and the lining up of unimpeachable authorities on behalf of a position does not guarantee its truth; moreover, the dangerous content and unorthodox authorship of pagan philosophy and poetry does not necessarily guarantee its falsity and uselessness.

When the systematic theologies actually try to answer the questions they raise, the rhetoric of battle predominates. In all the versions of his theology Abelard takes the view that the best defense is a good offense, beginning not with the objections to the doctrine of Trinity but with excessively optimistic claims about the knowledge Jews and pagan philosophers had of the Trinity. To this end, he turns to Genesis, then to the prophets and wisdom literature. The series of citations and interpretations from this literature, Abelard argues, shows the clarity with which the three persons of the Trinity are announced in the Old Testament. The following example is typical: Abelard quotes Psalms 32: 6: "By the word of the Lord were the heavens made, and all their host by the Spirit of his mouth," and takes the "Word" to refer to the Son, and "Spirit" to the Holy Spirit (*TSum* I. 94. 227–30). What we might take to be a fancifully anachronistic reading of Hebrew Scripture, Abelard presents as its self-evident, literal meaning, something Augustine does not do even though he offers similar interpretations.

The same claim of a kind of self-evidence of his own position and of the unthinkable character of the opposite continues in Abelard's examination of the testimony from pagan philosophers. The testimony most heavily stressed is found in Plato, the equation of *Nous* with the Son, and, in the equation of the Holy Spirit with the World-Soul.[39] The World-soul placed at the center of the world and spreading itself throughout is an allegory for "divine grace offered in common to all" (*TSum* I. 6. 104. 507). Such readings of Hebrew Scripture and pagan philosophers are surely not unique to Abelard but the bravado with which they are put forward as incontrovertible surely is.

Interpreting this evidence allows Abelard once again to cast himself as the combative unveiler of the core hidden beneath the surface; in this case, he takes the covering of the truth by fictions to be both a divine and philosophical strategy. He quotes Hebrew Scripture and Cicero in defense of the clothing of truth in the protective covering of fiction. He adds his own formulation of the benefits of indirection based on the contrast between surface and depth: "That which appears at first to be fabulous or fictitious and very far from useful when one rests on the surface of the text, becomes more worthy of interest in proving to be afterwards rich in mysteries and full of most instructive teachings" (*TSum* I. 99. 368–72). Abelard adds to this a standard Neoplatonic argument for the benefit of fictitious coverings, arguing that the reader becomes more attached to truth extricated at such great price; the more difficult the text, the greater the benefit to the reader (*TSum* I. 100. 373–76).

Abelard concludes that if we do not read Plato on *Nous* and the World-Soul allegorically, we must concede that he is "the greatest of fools" (*TSum* I. 101. 431). For, he continues, "what is more ridiculous than to think that the entire world is a single, rational animal if we do not take it as said allegorically?" (*TSum* I. 101. 431–34). There are more embarrassing difficulties confronting a literal reading of the *Timaeus*: How does the world sense (as it must if an animal)? Does it "feel" the digging of earth more or less than the gathering of leaves or the chopping of trees? (*TSum* I. 101.435–103. 468).

Because the literal, surface meaning of Plato's text is completely unconvincing, the truth must be purposefully hidden beneath the surface.

Structuring the Battle

The structure of the reasoning part of Abelard's systematic theologies is exclusively defensive. In the *Theologia "summi boni"* an opening statement of his thesis on the Trinity is followed by a series of objections from two sides, one set on the unity of the triune God and a second on the plurality of the one God. These are followed by a highly rhetorical attack on the attackers and then responses to particular objections.

This form is significantly different from Boethius's *Contra Eutychen et Nestorium* and later discussions in disputed questions on Christology and the Trinity. First, Abelard's gloss of the orthodox view precedes the objections as something more than a credal statement and less than a theological explanation. It stands while those grounding themselves on the unity of the divine essence attack the diversity of persons, and those grounding themselves on the diversity of persons assault the unity of the divine essence. Thus Abelard positions the Trinity to fight off objections; it does not, as Boethius has it in the *Contra Eutychen*, emerge as a mean in opposition to the two extremes. Further, Abelard gathers all the objections to the Trinity together; they gain a force that makes a successful defense difficult to imagine. And, lastly, Abelard constructs no answer of his own, just a series of responses to the scattershot objections.[40]

Later discussions, like those of Peter Lombard or Thomas Aquinas, break down the problem into a series of smaller questions; each one is more focused and less overwhelming, and with each partial solution, the position being constructed gains stability. Boethius works to establish the unity of the divine nature and its distinction from creatures before turning to the plurality of persons. But Abelard places the Trinity under attack from all sides, taking every opportunity to make his defensive task more difficult. Faith is battered by understanding (in the form of the arguments of the dialecticians); it is not supported by it. Arguments are deployed by the enemy to attack the faith and by Abelard to defend it; they are not the "seeking," which joins faith and understanding.

Saving the Words in the Absence of Experience

Abelard's responses to objections to the Trinity use two main strategies. First, Abelard develops verbal formulas that save the content of faith from contradiction; second, he justifies the complicated and paradoxical formulas of faith by finding their equivalents in ordinary language.

The objections to the Trinity Abelard presents focus on problems of disjunction and noncorrespondence on many levels—between words and things, persons and things, names of substance and names of persons, singular and universal names, multiplicity of predicates and singularity of being. Why can we not say triune Father as well as triune God, Abelard asks (*TSum* II. 130. 442–43). Why, if we can say "there are three persons," can we not say "they are" or "they are beings?" (*TSum* II. 131. 468–69). On the other side, objecting to divine unity, Abelard notes that we identify the sitting man and the white man when both whiteness and sitting are predicated of the same substance; so too, then, should not we identify Father and Son, conclude that the Father is incarnate and even that God engenders himself since the Father engenders the Son? (*TSum* II. 133. 519–31).

Though Abelard does in fact go on to offer an account of the divine nature in terms of the three persons of the Trinity, he also notes that his ability to understand the Trinity is extremely limited. While the three persons of the Trinity can be explained in terms of the three characteristics of power, wisdom, and goodness, other attributes, like eternity, seem to have an equally central claim on the divine nature, and, conversely, contradictory qualities, like generosity and vengeance, are contained in one person/aspect (in this case, that of goodness) (*TSum* II. 154. 1079–155. 1100). Abelard notes he cannot explain *why* the divine nature has these three persons but only *how* God is to be understood in these terms. Moreover, Abelard concludes, "it could probably have been described in many other ways" (*TSum* II. 155. 1101–1105). The orthodox account of the Trinity, that the three persons are associated with three properties, is simply supported by authority, which also, Abelard notes, grounds many a philosophical claim (*TSum* II. 156. 1111–13). Like Boethius in the *Contra Eutychen*, Abelard does not attach necessity to any particular account (including the orthodox one). The reason we have the one we do is because it is more suited to human understanding, not because it mirrors the divine nature better than some others might. Abelard does not and cannot unite what believers say (the credal statement on the Trinity), what they understand (the persons in terms of the properties of power, wisdom, and goodness), and what is (the Triune God per se).

Abelard meets the particular objections he has enumerated by a combination of analogies between the Trinity and ordinary things and ordinary language. So, Abelard explains, like the Trinity, the soul is really one in its essence but multiple in its properties; in the same way human being is one in its definition and multiple in its capacities for laughter and navigation, and one Socrates is three grammatical persons (*TSum* III. 157.1–158. 57). When he turns to the problem of why it does not follow from the predication of three persons of God that God is three, he argues that even in ordinary language we cannot, for example, go from "something appears broken" to "something is broken," or "he is a great thief" to "he is great," nor, then, can one go from "the Word is made flesh" to "the Word is made" (*TSum* III. 159. 66–71).

Though each person is God and substance, there are not many gods or substances, Abelard argues; just as there are multiple understandings of the term "human being," multiple instances of names, passions of the soul, and vocal sounds. Each is an essence but together they are not many essences (*TSum* III. 166. 278–89). Moreover, we say that a man is three artisans (e.g., carpenter, glazier, and blacksmith) because he has three skills, not because he is three men (*TSum* III. 167. 322–24). Abelard finds example after example of what we say and know to be true that sound easily as paradoxical as formulations of Trinitarian relations. So he writes, "though the same vocal sound is sometimes a noun and sometimes a verb, or at the same time a word and a sentence, we admit nonetheless that the noun is not the verb . . . and the word is not the sentence" (*TSum* III. 171. 386–411). Abelard argues that just as we cannot infer from the propositions "this man is this body" and "this body is the matter of this man" that "this man is the matter of this man," we cannot conclude from "the Father is God" and "God is the Son" that "the Father is the Son" (*TSum* III. 175. 516–176. 541).

The same strategies return for the discussion of the procession of the Word from the Father and of the Holy Spirit from Father and Son. Abelard again uses examples from ordinary language of the ways in which words shift meanings in particular sentences in a way that prevents equivalencies and substitutions from sentence to sentence. Abelard explains the Nicene Creed's account of the Son's generation from the Father as "God from God, light from light" by appeal to the parallel ways in which ordinary terms change meaning based on their context; thus different instances of the same term need not have the same meaning. So when we say, "dead man," "man" shifts in meaning; when we say "Achilles was greater than all the Greeks," "all" is understood not to include Achilles. In the same way, then, in "God from God" we must understand the first "God" for the Father and the second for the Son (*TSum* III. 184. 785–95). This property extends to verbs as well. So, for example, "sitting" in "he was sitting" no longer signifies the present; the same is true for pronouns in different contexts (*TSum* III. 184. 807–185. 821). Abelard's strategy for dealing with theological language is not, as Alan of Lille does, to argue for the exceptional character of language that has God as its subject, but rather to argue that linguistic ambiguity is universal and ordinary rather than peculiar to theological language.

Abelard draws the line between what can and cannot be said of God in a way that has less to do with substantive standards grounded on the real

structure of divine and creaturely natures than with what will benefit the
faithful. So, for example, Abelard distinguishes the persons in terms of their
activities in the created world, distinctions carried over into liturgical and
prayer life. The Father, he argues, is connected with creation from nothing, with commanding and disposing things in the world; to reflect this,
there are special prayers of the solemn mass addressed only to the Father.
To the Son is assigned that which concerns wisdom and judgment, activities especially reflected in Psalm nine. To the Holy Spirit belongs that
which concerns divine grace, especially recognized in the sacraments, such
as baptism, penance, confirmation (*TSum* III. 177. 574–179. 612). Plato's
account of the World-Soul as divisible and indivisible, the same and other,
is an allegory for Trinitarian relations in which the Holy Spirit is both one
in essence with the Father and the Son and yet personally distinct from
Father and Son. Abelard glosses Plato not in the traditionally more significant metaphysical direction but in a way that connects the Trinity to the
world: sameness and otherness signify "the multiplicity of his [God's]
works, multiple works which he accomplishes while remaining absolutely
simple in himself" (*TSum* I. 105. 527–28). As Buytaert writes, "the Trinity
in the *Theologia "summi boni"* is described exclusively as 'economical,' i.e., in
connection with creation and salvation; it does not attempt to penetrate the
life of God."[41]

Boethius's account of the Trinity is part of his project of the conversion
of an Aristotelian perspective to a Neoplatonic one, showing that the first,
more worldly Aristotelian account is incomplete without the second, oth-
erworldly Neoplatonic one. But Abelard's project from the first version of
his theology right through the last is to see the Trinity in the world.
Abelard explains the reason for this in essentially pastoral terms, "This
analysis of the Trinity . . . is also very useful for inculcating in human
beings attachment to the divine cult" (*TSum* I. 87. 37–40). Power and
wisdom, Abelard explains, move one to fear, and goodness, to love (*TSum* I.
88. 43–46). Moreover, the theologian must also be concerned about how
much the community of believers can tolerate. One cannot say that the
Father is the principle of the Son because it would appear to remove eternity from the Son, and hence would cause scandal. So Abelard concludes,
"it is not appropriate to say everything which is true, given that the respect
for decency deters not just the obscenity of facts but also of words, and in
place of proper terms one often uses transpositions which have the same
sense" (*TSum* III. 191. 1042–46). Having begun with arguments based in
dialectic, Abelard concludes with those based in worship. In one sense,
then, Abelard does close the circle of theological speculation, returning
from theological speculation back to prayer and liturgy. But it is a smaller
circle than Boethius's, one whose circumference does not include or even

reach for contact with the divine nature, striving only for images and verisimilitude in the service of what human beings can understand, not in the service of showing what God is.

Abelard does try to move beyond merely verbal analogies into what he calls "philosophical" analogies for God. He gives two: first, the analogy between genus and species and the Trinity, and, second, between a bronze seal and the Trinity.[42] What Abelard enjoys and exploits in his analogy between the Trinity and a bronze seal, however, is its linguistic properties, the way in which it supports a pattern of predications similar to the Trinity, an identity in essence or being that allows for difference in limited and nonreciprocal fashion. Hence, he explains, though "the bronze seal is nothing more than the bronze so formed," and "the bronze which is the matter of the bronze seal is essentially the same as the seal itself of which the bronze is the matter; however, in their properties they are distinct, so that the property of bronze and of the bronze seal are different" (*TSch* II. 463. 1653–56). "The bronze seal is from bronze and the bronze is not from the bronze seal, and bronze is the matter of the seal, not the seal the matter of the bronze" (*TSch* II. 463. 1657–60). Similarly, the Son is from the Father but not vice versa, nor is God the Father *causa sui* any more than the bronze is from itself. The propositions true of the bronze seal show how things can be completely identical yet within that unity have different and nontransferable properties and predicates in ways which mirror the statements made about the Trinity. The analogy, even though "philosophical," that is, about things rather than words, still functions on the level of words: we can say these things without falsehood of the bronze seal; hence, we can say the same sorts of things about the Trinity without falling into absurdity.

On freedom versus determinism, Abelard also makes rather narrow verbal arguments. So in discussing the problem of future contingents bequeathed to him by Aristotle via Boethius, Abelard opts for his own variation on Boethius's distinction between simple and conditional necessity, renamed absolute and determinate necessity. While it is necessary that what God has foreseen should occur, Abelard argues, that event is not itself absolutely necessary, but is only necessary given the determinator that God foresees that event (*TSch* III. 542. 1351–55). In order to consider whether or not there are limits on God's power, Abelard asks whether God can save someone who ought not be saved. He argues that it is possible that "the man who ought not be saved might be saved by God" at the same time, he contends, it is impossible that "God might save a man who ought not be saved." The first refers to the possibility of being saved to human nature, which can change and can consent either to salvation or damnation, while the second refers the possibility of saving to God's nature, to whose nature it is repugnant to do something inappropriate or something other than he has done or will do (*TSch* III. 520. 657–521. 679). In the same way, Abelard explains, we can say that a voice is audible, that is, able to be heard by someone, without also saying that someone is able to hear that voice (*TSch* III. 521. 680–88).

On the problem of evil, Abelard seems to offer a more substantive solution but still leaves a gap between words and reality. As Marenbon explains, Abelard takes from Plato the idea that "God's creation and providence are the best possible and could not be different" and from Augustine the notion that providence reaches into the material world and into the lives of individuals.[43] Abelard understands this to mean that God could not have made the world better than he made it (*TSch* III. 512. 402. 404–15).[44] Providence extends so completely into the lives of individuals, it even turns the evil human beings choose into part of the best possible plan for the world. Abelard is willing to accept the most difficult of the consequences that follow from this stance. Because everything is for the best, he argues, there is nothing which needs to be mourned (*TSch* III. 547. 1557–48. 1579). Not only is the suffering of the good improperly mourned, but even the evildoing of the evil has to be accepted as part of the good. For, Abelard argues, if it is good for Jesus to have died to save humankind, then it is good for him to have been killed. Hence, it must be good for someone, in fact for those particular people who did it, to have killed him (*TSch* III. 549. 1602–23). God himself wills these things, wills even his own suffering, and it can be for no other reason, Abelard insists, than that it is good that it be so.

This is what has prompted the labeling of Abelard's theology as "optimistic."[45] But it is only optimistic in a very general sense, offering none of the emotional satisfaction optimism should bring. For unlike Boethius, who holds a similar view of providence as both universal and particular, Abelard does not try to bridge the gulf between human suffering and the absolute goodness of everything and every event. He does not attempt to understand providence or even explain why we cannot understand it. Boethius's *Consolation* is dedicated to finding some sense in and solace for his suffering, some explanation of how providence can be at work in the suffering of the good and the prosperity of the evil. Abelard simply asserts the inappropriateness of grieving for martyrs (or anyone, for that matter). So we are stuck with the paradox that everything occurs exactly as it must, in the best possible way, but that goodness is completely and painfully opaque to human beings. Thus, though Abelard asserts the reality of providence, not just the truth of carefully crafted propositions about it, a gap like the one between words and things on the Trinity remains—that between the universality of providence and human understanding and experience of suffering, a gap the weakness of human insight and will is unable to cross.

In the end, Abelard engages in the battle on the ground rather than in reaching toward the heavens because that is the only project that is available to him. While it is true that Abelard famously boasted that he could produce "human and philosophical reasons" that would rewrite theology and proclaimed that there must be understanding before faith, his account of understanding in the *Theologia "scholarium"* aligns understanding with this humbler, less ambitious project for theology (*HC* 82. 690–83. 701). Abelard argues that "understanding [*intelligere*] and believing [*credere*] are different from knowing [*agnoscere*] and being manifest [*manifestari*]" (*TSch* II. 432. 788–89). Faith and understanding are concerned with the nonapparent and the invisible, and knowing, with the apparent, with "the experience of things through their presence" (*TSch* II. 432. 790–433. 796). He punctuates his remarks with long passages from Corinthians in which Paul chides the church at Corinth for being more interested in the ecstatic experience of tongues than in understanding, extols interpretation, and, failing that, silence over babble (I Cor. 14). The project of theology does not move toward knowledge, direct access, or experience for Abelard; all it can be is the continuing elaboration of the ever absent things it lives in hope for.

Thus, Abelard grimly and defiantly dwells in the gap between what we say and what is, and he draws attention to the failure of faith and understanding to bridge the gap between words and things. Describing his own project, he does not promise truth but the similitude of truth, and, moreover, does not promise similitude as a step on the path toward the possession of truth. What he offers, he says, is "a shadow, not the truth, a sort of analogy, not the thing itself." "That which is true God knows," he continues, but "that which has verisimilitude and is more congruent with the philosophical reasonings by which they attack us, I am going to say" (*TSum* II. 123. 241–46).

In his study, "La Conception de la théologie chez Abélard," Cottiaux argues for a development in Abelard's conception of theology from "conceptualism" toward "realism."[46] For the theological conceptualist there is a difference between objective reality and concepts, a multiplicity of concepts mapping onto the single reality, while the theological realist works toward a one-to-one mapping of term and reality.[47] Thus, for Cottiaux, Abelard's views develop from a theology whose method is purely dialectical and whose conclusions rest on the surface toward one whose use of reason goes beyond the limits of dialectic to achieve some grasp of the reality of things.[48] Cottiaux cites as evidence Abelard's claim in the third book of the *Theologia "scholarium"* that he will go beyond dialectic, but in this passage Abelard only claims to offer reasons going beyond dialectic which aspire to verisimilitude and fittingness, not necessity (*TSch* Praef. 313. 11–17).[49] Thus even this part of the last theology remains "conceptualist," in that it still does not claim to go beyond the surface of words to penetrate the reality. What does change late in the last version of the theology is that Abelard makes the support and amplification of belief by reasoning—rather than simply defense against attackers—an explicit goal of his theology. Thus I would describe the shift in Abelard's theology in somewhat different terms from Cottiaux. The gap between language and reality remains throughout, but Abelard comes to see that gap and the unending battle to close it as one which can become the dwelling place of faith rather than simply the abyss the believer has at his back as he fights off the attackers of faith.

The Experience of Faith in the Absence of God

Since no one can achieve complete knowledge of the truth for Abelard, one can only orient oneself toward that achievement. As a result, for Abelard the clearest sign of "true religion" is in the moral life common to pagans, Jews, and Christians rather than in an explicit belief in Christianity. Socrates is the example illustrating this life. Socrates's moral life was, Abelard quotes from Augustine, a direct result of his search for the truth about first and supreme causes, a search that requires a purified soul and prepares it to rise to join eternal things (TSum I. 111. 697–112. 728).[50] Thus a life that reflects true virtue is one that reflects "the rule of the true religion" (TSum I. 112. 729–31). This model of life and true religion is found in the integration of act and thought, not explicit belief or external practice. Philosophers striving to know and teach about God, Abelard continues, have ultimately exhorted their students more toward right living than right words because what matters is the interior spirit rather than external words (TSum II. 120. 155–57). This is all the more correct as a strategy since God does not manifest himself per se, and human nature could not grasp his nature even if God did; human beings, filled with their own sinfulness, cannot study even their own nature, let alone the incomprehensible God (TSum II. 121.179–83).

Abelard makes these comments as a gloss on Augustine's notion of the "inner teacher" who teaches while words and external teachers cannot. For Augustine, faith and the "inner teacher" provide the links between words and things, providing entry into the hermeneutic circle of understanding.[51] For Abelard, faith is expressed primarily in the living of the moral life; it does not so much join words and things as stands between them as a substitute for the full knowledge we cannot achieve. The shape of understanding in Augustine is a spiral in which understanding fortified by faith progresses toward, though never quite reaches, completion. Abelard conveys no strong sense of movement or progress in understanding. Instead the believer (the morally good person) lives in a kind of holding pattern between ignorance and knowledge. This does not mean that the pursuit of understanding is abandoned; it does, however, mean that it is undertaken more to map what we do not know than what we do.

The moral life that mirrors the desire for knowledge must be completely focused on the spiritual things it seeks but cannot possess. As a result what most seems to characterize the moral life for Abelard is abstinence. We can see this in Abelard's account of charity and faith. Abelard's brief discussion of charity, derived from a notion of love, is arrived at by contrasting virtuous (*honestas*) and vicious love. They are opposed as love of self and love of other are opposed; one is characterized by the seeking of our own interests, the other, those of the beloved. Charity, simply described as virtuous love having God as its object, is fitted into the stark choice Abelard creates between love of self and God. In charity, all things must be done for the love of God over self, so eating is for sustenance, sleep for vigilance, and sex for reproduction (*TSch* I. 319. 17–321. 89). Abelard's is a bleak picture of the life of the lover of God, one that not only commands complete rejection of the world and its pleasures for God, but also one in which all consummation seems to be postponed.[52] This view is also reflected in one of Abelard's hymns for Heloise's community. This one, unlike the others, is not a new version of a traditional hymn. It is a mealtime prayer for restraint of the desire for food and complete subordination of eating to the requirements of health, work, and prayer. Abelard depicts the vices of gluttony and drunkenness in grotesque terms and asks the community, "Why in exile do you desire delicacies when empty you must exit this world?" (*Hym Par* I. 14). Abelard's emphasis in the hymn, as in his theology, is on the present emptiness, not on any future fulfillment.

To illustrate the nature of faith, Abelard uses the example of doubting Thomas. Even doubting Thomas does not have his doubt replaced with knowledge, Abelard claims; he does not believe what he *sees*, but *sees* the body of Jesus and *believes* in God hidden within the body (*TSch* I. 322. 121–324. 166). Hence, the absence in which faith dwells is irremediable, one which can never in this life be supplanted by immediate knowledge and certainty.

The Project of Theology

Just as Abelard's theodicy may lead some to label him optimistic when he is in an important sense anything but, so his bravado about his superior rationality has led many, including influential contemporaries, to the conclusion that he pretends to complete comprehension of the Trinity and other matters of faith. But this is an incomplete reading of Abelard's theology. Abelard ends book II of the *Theologia "scholarium"* with the same two claims that close the *Theologia "summi boni."* The first is that there is a kind of natural knowledge of the Trinity common to Christians, Jews, and pagans in the recognition of God as powerful, wise, and good. If, as Abelard argues, the claim that God is Father, Son, and Holy Spirit is equivalent to the claim that God is power, wisdom, and goodness, then all, Jews and gentiles, have access to the divine nature (*TSum* III. 200. 1336–201. 1342). This optimistic and rationalistic claim is quickly counterbalanced by very pessimistic reflections on the lack of utility and substance of such knowledge. Abelard cites Augustine's account of his discovery of everything about the Word in the philosophy of the Platonists, except the mystery of the Incarnation. "In [the Incarnation]," Abelard comments, "consists the whole of the salvation of human kind, without which it is useless to believe the rest" (*TSum* III. 201.1350–51).[53] Although the natural knowledge of God extends to an intimation of the Trinity, that knowledge is not of a saving truth, and Abelard's arguments do not conclude in a saving truth; they only insure the failure of the project of the enemies of faith. The gap between the requisites of salvation and the achievements of reason, Abelard tells us, has not been closed by his work.

Abelard justifies his foray into the "incomprehensible philosophy of the divinity" as a battle with enemies of the faith rather than a search for truth. He explains that he has taken up the weapons used by the enemies of faith, thereby accomplishing "the judgment of the Truth, where it is said, 'I condemn you by your own word, you wicked servant' " (*TSum* III. 201.1363–67; Luke 19: 22). The quotation is from the parable of the pounds or talents, spoken to the servant whose fear of the master kept him from earning on or trading with the pound left in his care.[54] For Abelard, the wicked servants failing to trade or earn with the capital given by the master are the attackers of the faith, using the weapons of reason and dialectic. They are condemned by their own words insofar as Abelard takes up the challenge on their terms and wins. But on another level, Abelard's response to the dialecticians is no more fruitful, for he does not claim to increase the faith of the faithful but simply to protect them from further attack. Hence, Abelard offers the following blanket disclaimer: "we affirm nothing which we have said, we do not try to teach the truth which we affirm cannot be known, not by us either" (*TSum* III. 201.1352–58).

Clanchy describes this as a disclaimer "more to St. Bernard's liking" than Abelard's claim to have shown the universality of belief in the Trinity, but Clanchy adds that such an admission "had the potential to undermine Abelard's whole endeavor."[55] That, of course, depends on how we construe Abelard's endeavor. Clanchy, like Abelard's critics, Bernard of Clairvaux and William of St. Thierry, contends that Abelard "lived in perpetual hope of coming up with the answers, even to the paradoxes of the Trinity and the Redemption."[56] Like Clanchy, Cottiaux finds something of a contradiction between Abelard's claims that God is unknowable and Abelard's claim to have constructed theology as a well-founded science.[57]

With Jolivet, I have to disagree with Clanchy and Cottiaux. As Jolivet writes, "Abelard affirms multiple times that we cannot really think or name divine things, and that in treating the Trinity, he wanted only to defeat pseudo-dialecticians with their own arms, without flattering himself into thinking that he had explained what God was in reality."[58] If there is a science, Jolivet responds to Cottiaux, "it pertains not to God but to terms"; it has as its object "the letter and logical structure of propositions."[59] Thus, the rational science of theology is a science of words; the realities in which faith believes are not penetrated by theology.

This may save Abelard from the charges brought against him by Bernard and William of St. Thierry but it raises another question about what such a theology offers. Consider Abelard's responses to the problem of the consistency of freedom and foreknowledge and his verbal analogies for the Trinity. They are, I think, unsatisfying because they are so precariously perched on razor thin logical distinctions. Such arguments do not give much access to the nature of God except in marginal comments served up along with the main logical/linguistic response. Instead they make distinctions so that contradiction can be avoided, but just barely. These answers are in the end too clever by half, offering verbal but not substantive insight into theological matters.

But what if Abelard's goal is not to offer satisfying answers? Abelard takes up his project, he says, "in the hope that we will have already convinced [nonbelievers] to have the common sense of our faith, which they might not have confessed orally as we do, because of not knowing the significance of our words. This faith, however, they hold already in the heart just as it is written, 'It is believed in his heart and so he is justified' " (*TSch* II. 498. 2693–97; Rom. 10: 10). The rest of the verse from Romans runs, "and he confesses with his lips and so is saved." Paul ultimately unifies interior belief and exterior expression, but Abelard, who clearly knows the end of the verse and whose readers probably did too, does not give it. He thus signals that his attempt to make it possible by the use of reason and dialectic for non-Christians to confess with their lips the beliefs they already hold in their hearts, to persuade them that these are one and same creeds, is not a complete success. More importantly, Abelard signals to believers hoping for a thorough rational justification of the faith independent of support of faith that he cannot match up what is based on proof with what is believed. For Abelard, it is clear that fully satisfactory answers are not available; rather he tries to make enough space for belief, so that it will not be crushed in the onslaught of objections. All he can do is point to the unity of reason and faith in principle, in their interior meaning, not in their outward expression.

In the end, Abelard's theology does not attempt to stretch human understanding toward the divine in the way in which Augustine, Boethius, and Anselm do. Instead he constructs analogies to the divine nature in ordinary language and ordinary things. He sees God in ordinary things rather than attempting to transcend creation to give an intuition of the creator. Abelard saves the language of the Trinity but leaves the metaphysics behind; he ultimately works on finding God in the world rather than God in himself. Failing to reach understanding, Abelard falls back on the moral life as the surest sign of true belief, expressive of the only type of unity of inside and outside that human beings have any a chance of achieving.

A certain melancholy accompanies these lowered expectations of theological speculation, the sense that faith dwells in the absence rather than the presence of God. Where Abelard's theology breaks off, his laments begin, with an all-too-human perspective on evil and suffering, focusing on the reality of sorrow and struggling (without any success) to find the reason for suffering.

The Laments: Rejecting/Rewriting Allegory

Abelard's impatience with the received forms of liturgy and prayer is just as strong as with those of theology. He writes in the preface to his book of hymns that his ambition is to rewrite completely the words and music used in monastic prayer. He seeks to create a unity between words and music, song and season, time and tempo. He wants a coherent as well as simple and direct form of worship, replacing the flowery and artificial language of traditional songs with something purer and more authentic (*Hym Par* I, Praef. 5–9). One commentator speculates that the reason why the complete cycle of Abelard's hymns does not seem to have been used outside of a few years at the Paraclete by Heloise's community is because the hymns did not, unlike other hymnals, make use of traditional melodies.[60] Abelard's hymns were too complete a rewriting, leaving nothing of the comfort of the familiar, to be popular.

We have no preface justifying the composition of the *planctus* as we do for the hymns. Many readers have associated the themes of the laments with events in Abelard's life, for example, Jacob's loss of Joseph and Benjamin with Abelard's loss of Astrolabe, Jephtha's daughter's self-sacrifice with Heloise's entry into the religious life.[61] Doubtless, some version of this must be true, but what interests me is what Abelard finds (and shapes) in these complex and ancient stories that makes them appropriate vessels to carry and express the meaning of his losses and loss in general. The laments are unusual not so much for their themes, the characters and stories of the Old Testament (they were well known and often mentioned), or their genre (laments were a traditional form). What is unusual is Abelard's combination and shaping of this form with this content. First, as Peter Dronke notes, the figures and stories of Hebrew Scripture were most often allegorized in medieval texts, made into examples (or counterexamples) of moral conduct or figures for Christ, but Abelard steers clear of allegory and draws no moral from these stories.[62] Second, the most common settings for laments were the death of contemporaries or conditions of exile, and, by the later twelfth century, laments of Mary and laments for lost love, rather than the Old Testament settings Abelard uses.[63]

Janthia Yearly speculates that laments not composed for liturgical drama, such as Abelard's, were intended as stimuli for meditation; hence, they form part of a shift to a more personal and affective spirituality.[64] This supposition is supported by the fact that the kind of material found in the laments is similar to that found in the later Book of Hours, which was aimed at stimulating meditation, especially on the Passion.[65] Yearly's claim is also supported by what we know of Abelard's spirituality. What Abelard eschews across the board are easy solutions, or solutions that are merely received rather than autonomously achieved. These laments are, then, both sign of and stimulus for the project of spiritual integrity as Abelard conceives it. The goal of Abelard's laments is not a merely affective connection with suffering but an intellectual engagement with the moral and theological dilemmas posed by these stories.

Abelard also avoids the temptation to resolve the losses he confronts into a "happy ending," or indeed into any sense that good is brought about by the evil suffered. Lament, as a form of lyric, tends to stop time and narrative progress. The focus in all the laments is on the immediate and devastating loss and the past out of which it has arisen, not on any future. Thus Abelard breaks down the narrative of Scripture at two levels. First, he abstracts these moments of grief from their immediate context, taking minor, more or less self-contained narratives, such as those of Dinah, Jephtha, and Samson. Or he chooses less significant moments within larger narratives, such as the story of Joseph, in which the lament of Jacob for Joseph and Benjamin is set, or the story of David, in which the lament for Saul and Jonathan and the lament for Abner are set. Second, he disjoins these stories from their place as part of the larger narrative of salvation history culminating in Christianity.

The work of Richard of St. Victor, *The Twelve Patriarchs*, stands in striking contrast.[66] For example, Richard allegorizes the Joseph story in two ways. First, Joseph's brothers represent abstract concepts (the virtues), and, second, the events that befall them represent successive stages of the journey toward experience of God. Further, Richard finds in the Joseph cycle of stories an allegory for the events of the Transfiguration. Abelard's setting of these stories rejects both the assumption of continuity and coherence in the narrative as well as the possibility of representation that Richard takes for granted.

The Lament of Dinah

Jewish and early Christian interpreters of the Dinah story differ over its allegorical significance and the moral to be drawn from its tragic outcome. Dinah and Sichem were allegorized as the embodiments of both good and evil.[67] Interpreters also disagree about whether to assign blame in the story to Dinah, her brothers, or Sichem. Most Jewish and many Christian interpreters exonerate the brothers and see the slaughter of Sichem's people as justified; most blame Dinah for going out among foreign people.[68] A few of the Christian exegetes both blame Dinah and find her brothers' acts to be excessive.[69] One even makes of Sichem the unwitting victim of Dinah's womanly wiles.[70]

Abelard refuses to allegorize Dinah but still manages to reflect the moral issues implied by earlier accounts of Dinah in his setting of the events. His most obvious innovations are two. First, Dinah is silent in Scripture, but Abelard makes her the focus and interpreter of her own story. Second, as Peter Dronke notes, Abelard's Dinah changes her perspective on the events of the story several times in the poem. Thus, she shifts her attention from her own violation at the hands of Sichem, to Sichem's violation at the hands of her brothers, to the suffering of herself, Sichem, and his whole people.[71] She begins from a sense of her violation as a violation not just of her own purity as a virgin but of her race, of her being made into an piece of plunder not just by one man but by an enemy people (*Pl Din.* 1–6). But she changes her point of view to pitying Sichem for her family's blaming and disgracing of him, for his forced and useless circumcision. By the end of the poem, she refers to the people of Sichem not as impure adversaries but as a great people unjustly slain. Thus Abelard takes not just different perspectives on Dinah's tragedy but also exaggerates each of them. Dinah is not just raped by Sichem but violated by a whole people; Sichem is not just the victim punished too severely by her brothers but a noble leader of a noble race massacred.

The first verse consists in a series of oppositions between Dinah's origins and race and those of her violators, her purity and their impurity, her origin in the holy race of Abraham and her enemies' view of her as plunder and plaything. This is a more or less traditional way of setting up the issue. The verse ends, however, mourning her own suffering as a self-betrayal. She reproaches herself for her desire to go and live among these foreign people, recognizing her own desire to "mix" rather than remain pure. She thus blurs the opening distinction between her pure blood (*sanguine clara*) and the impure men (*hominis spurci*) who raped her (*Pl Din* 2, 4). The lamentation of self-betrayal becomes the repeated refrain of the first two verses as she cries, "Woe is me, by my own hand betrayed!"

In verses three and four, she grieves for Sichem's misery and his betrayal of and by himself. Thus the repeated refrain for Sichem becomes, "Woe to you, lost through your own act!" Taking Sichem's perspective on the tragedy, she describes his disgrace as greater than hers. His circumcision, seen from her perspective as a member of the people of Abraham, should have transformed him into one of her race, holy and pure. Nonetheless, she describes the circumcision as vain, as an occasion for shame for him (*Pl Din* 14–15). But Sichem is not the innocent victim of feminine wiles any more than she, Dinah, is the pure victim of evil; he too has been an instrument of his own destruction. Dinah concludes by describing Sichem as "driven" to rape her because he was "rapt" by her beauty (*Pl Din* 17–18).

Dinah then moves to her brothers' actions. She sums up their act as both "too cruel and too pious" (*Pl Din* 22–23). On the one hand, she accuses them of cruelty in "equating the innocent and the guilty" (*Pl Din* 24). On the other hand, she recognizes the real wrong that has been done to her and her family, as well as her brothers' obligation under piety to address the affront to their sister. Nonetheless, for Abelard's Dinah, they have gone too far. Unlike many commentators, this Dinah makes reference to Jacob's disapproval of his sons' actions in Scripture (*Pl Din* 25). Her lines attempt to capture the dialectic between the Hebrews and foreign peoples, exemplifying the tension between, on the one hand, positive and frequent cooperation and connection to non-Jewish peoples, and, on the other, the emerging need to keep an embattled and vulnerable people separate from "the nations." She ends by pleading for the mercy that should have been shown toward the young, for the diminution of fault through repentance and love (*Pl Din* 26–29). Moreover, she takes up the perspective of Sichem and his people for whom *she* is the foreigner, not him. As a leader of his own people, his offer to exchange his identity for hers by becoming Jewish is a mark of honor for her (*Pl Din* 31–32). This last shift in perspective brings the poem full circle, from its opening characterization of her pure race defiled by a foreigner, to one of herself as the foreigner in relation to Sichem, from Sichem's act of rape as a dishonoring of her and her people, to his acts of conversion and marriage as an honoring of her and her people. Dinah concludes by calling the massacre "communal," not only in the sense that all of Sichem's people were killed but also in the sense that it is a slaughter of *her* community (*Pl Din* 33–34).

This strategy of bringing out different and conflicting points of view and emotions within a single narrative returns in the other laments. There is in such a presentation, I think, something on the emotional and spiritual level akin to Abelard's approach to and analysis of questions of logic and speculative theology. Thus, Dinah relates her "arguments" for her position not only as an innocent victim of Sichem, but also as a complicit victim of her own desires, Sichem's as a victim of her beauty and his own desires, her brothers' actions as both pious and cruel, and of her race as both one opposed to and in common with Sichem's. In a succession of perspectives, Dinah condemns her act, that of Sichem, and those of her brothers. She also considers the possibility of tolerance of the other, and of forgiveness and integration of the erring Sichem. I do not mean to suggest a facile reduction of the poems to a kind of poetic *Sic et non*. Suggesting the contrary is closer to my aim, that is, that the model of analysis and exposure of conflict developed by Abelard in the *Sic et non* has something in common with his deeply felt, creative, and complex lamentations. What appear as disembodied quotations stripped of emotional content in the *sic et non* of scholastic disputation are the fragments of different responses to a single problem.

Dinah's lament is more for the failure of reconciliation once wrongs have been committed than for the wrongful act per se. She seems overwhelmed by the inability of human beings to avoid the destruction of themselves and others, and she envisions a resolution to these oppositions only in the mode of a counter-factual. Dinah is not looking toward a future armed with a neat moral about "learning from" such tragedies. The poem gives the opposing points of view without a synthesizing response, the grief without a comedic resolution. Thus we are offered a *sic et non*, forcing the reader to struggle with the conflict on his own.

There is development in Dinah's perspective; her views become more reflective and complex as she sees her own guilt and Sichem's virtue.[72] She looks beyond the surface of the actions to the more complicated depth, both of her acts and her own soul. Abelard's Dinah is thus ethical, embodying "Justice" and "Judgment" (her allegorical meaning according to Philo and others). But it is Abelard's notion of those virtues she models by engaging in self-examination and focusing more on intention and commitment than on external acts or rules.[73] In contrast to the allegory of Philo, then, Abelard's version of the story does not put forward the model of inviolable purity as the nature and moral task of the soul.[74] Rather it assumes the soul's impurity as a fact with which we must come to terms, rather than a fate that can be avoided. It even recognizes, I think, that the desire to maintain a specious purity is yet another form of unexamined impurity.

Jacob's Lament for His Sons

Traditional interpretations of Jacob make of him a model of human wisdom and virtue. Philo makes this point by focusing on the change of name from Jacob to Israel; "Jacob" means "the supplanter" while "Israel" means "the man who sees God." As the supplanter, Jacob is the symbol of the man of virtue who supplants and defeats passion; hence, Jacob is the human achievement of virtue who struggles to achieve prudence. But Jacob when renamed "Israel" receives virtue and never forgets or slackens in his practice.[75] The focus throughout Philo's interpretations is on the difference between divine and human perspectives; "Jacob" for him represents human achievement and a human point of view, while "Israel" represents divine power and the divine perspective.

Ambrose devoted an entire treatise to Jacob entitled *De Iacob et vita beata*.[76] In it, Jacob symbolizes the man who achieves happiness in spite of exile and danger. Jacob wrestles with God, symbolizing the struggle for virtue; he has compassion for the people of Sichem, anticipating a universal church drawn from all peoples.[77] Moreover, Jacob in old age represents the achievement of virtue and wisdom, having lived his life as a model of prudence, anticipating difficulties and providing remedies in advance.[78] Even Jacob's blindness in old age symbolizes spiritual discernment.[79] In sending Joseph to check on his brothers (the event that precipitates Joseph's being sold into slavery), Jacob foresees the Incarnation; Jacob's mourning for Joseph anticipates the events following the Passion of Jesus.[80] Lastly, Jacob's favoring of Joseph and his attachment to Benjamin are anticipations of the relationship of God the Father to his Son, a son whom he knows will be sacrificed but will also be resurrected. Ambrose, then, looks at the story of Jacob from the end of the story, focusing on his prosperous old age and his recuperation of his sons; thus, the story prefigures not just the Crucifixion but the Resurrection as well.

Abelard, by contrast, composes his lament for Jacob in the darkest moment in the middle of the saga of Jacob and his sons. This is the moment when, believing Joseph to be dead and having left Symeon behind as hostage, the remaining brothers prepare to return to Egypt to hand over their youngest brother, Benjamin, to the Egyptians in order to avoid starvation. Although the moral of the Joseph cycle is that providence truly controls events so that everything happens for the best, at the moment at which Abelard chooses to place his lament, there is no hint of the providential guidance.

Unlike the lament composed for Dinah and Jephtha's daugher, which radically shift the scriptural perspective, Jacob's lament does have a clear scriptural basis. In Genesis, Jacob expresses his grief over the loss of three of his sons as the remaining sons prepare to return to Egypt (Gen. 42: 36; 43: 14). Abelard's lament is unusual, however, because he constructs a lament for Jacob, for a man whose story has a happy ending and a figure who almost proverbially represents good fortune. Moreover, Abelard gives this lament to Jacob, not, as had been more traditional, to Rachel.[81] Rachel's death in childbirth means that she will never experience the restoration of all she has lost, while Jacob will. The paradox of Abelard's lament is that Jacob laments the loss of Joseph, who is not lost, and laments how he was lost, which is not accurate. This moment of sorrow and anguish is cut out from the middle of a comedic, not a tragic narrative. None of the anguish is necessary, for Jacob and his sons have been deceived, not just, or even primarily, by Joseph (who could, after all, clearly justify his treatment of his brothers) but also by God who has staged this drama.

Jacob, of course, does not and could not display any anger at any of this, since he does not know it, but this background gives Jacob's sorrow and bafflement more poignancy. Abelard has him express a sense of bewilderment at such a present emerging out of such a past; he mourns, in addition to the loss of his sons, the lack of any knowledge of how providence might be working in his life. As he turns to the loss of Joseph, Jacob focuses on Joseph's ability to interpret the future through dreams. He fumbles blindly for insight, asking what in the past pointed to this (misinterpreted) present: "What mystery did the sun, the moon, my sons, the stars and the sheaves . . . hold in themselves?" (*Pl Jac* 11–12). The reference is to Joseph's dream of the sheaves, the sun, the moon, and eleven stars bowing down to him (Gen. 37: 7–9). The brothers and Jacob himself all quite correctly interpreted the dream as Joseph's coming to rule over them, but even the correct interpretation gave way to a false inference from that interpretation—that the dream was a product of Joseph's desire for power over them. Having lost not just Joseph but Symeon, Rachel, and now Benjamin, Jacob asks for the interpretation of Joseph's dream that would have foretold such a present. The irony is that Jacob is misinterpreting the present; he compounds the irony by looking into the past for a sign of it. The story of Joseph and his brothers is, as Abelard tells it, the story of the suffering of human beings ignorant of providence, of human inability to read the signs correctly and, even when they read signs correctly, to take the wrong action in the face of them.

Jacob continues to misread the signs as he mourns the loss of Benjamin. Benjamin, Abelard takes care to note in his poem, is the son whose significance was understood in opposite ways by his parents. Rachel, dying in childbirth, named him "the son of my sorrow (Bennomin)" and Jacob, seeing in his survival the survival of Rachel and Joseph, named him "son of my right hand (Benjamin)." Benjamin for Jacob "displays the consolation for both greatest of losses," "representing both [Joseph and Rachel] with equal beauty" (*Pl Jac* 25–27). Jacob concludes that Benjamin "returns him to himself" (*Pl Jac* 28). The interpretation of Benjamin as the sign and instrument of their survival and of the restoration of Joseph and Rachel, is, of course, correct. But Jacob is convinced that he is losing that link to God and to Rachel and Joseph, believing that Benjamin will be lost forever to him in Egypt. So Jacob speaks true words, but he understands and means them in an opposite way, taking this moment as marking the loss of hope rather than as the one directly preceding and making possible its fulfillment.

The articulation of Benjamin's role in terms of restoration and mediation between God and human being in a medieval Christian text cannot help but bring to mind Benjamin as a figure for Christ. But the Christ we meet in Benjamin is one mourned, one whom no one believes will return or, indeed, even survive. Jacob is giving up his last hope, and he sits in grief and ignorance, like the disciples in the moment of loss and confusion after the Crucifixion and before the Resurrection.

The complication of perspective in this poem is not so much between different human points of view but rather between divine and human points of view. Jacob's only consolations are the childish songs sung by Benjamin, both "sweet" and "deformed" but some how "transcending . . . eloquence" (*Pl Jac* 21–24). The contrast is between Joseph's dreams, which have a divine perspective Jacob cannot begin to make sense of, and the children's songs whose words are not even clearly spoken but which somehow tell a truth or least give consolation beyond what sophisticated language can do. Jacob finds comfort not in attempting to see from a divine perspective but in the altogether human perspective of a child's song. Somehow these touch what no one should suffer or even imagine suffering—the loss of a child; they manage to speak in the midst of a grief too awful to be named.

The Lament of the Virgins of Israel for Jephtha's Daughter

The lament for Jephtha's daughter recounts Jephtha's encounter with his daughter on his homecoming from a victorious battle. Jephtha, having promised to sacrifice the first thing he saw on his homecoming, sees his daughter emerging from the house in a victory dance (Judges 11: 29–40). The lament describes this encounter and the preparation and sacrifice itself. It is framed by a dramatic setting of the annual liturgical practice of the maidens of Israel memorializing the death of Jephtha's daughter.

This poem does not so much shift perspective as it shifts moods between sorrow and joy, between the language of celebration and lamentation. The virgins of Israel are asked to engage in the self-contradictory act of singing laments "as celebrations" (*Pl vir Is* I. 1. 4), just as the handmaids at the baths later in the poems are asked to prepare for the death of Jephtha's daughter "as they would her marriage" (*Pl vir Is* III. 26. 119–20). The metaphor they are asked to act out is one in which tenor and vehicle are opposites. At the beginning of the poem, they are called to assemble in the dress of mourning to sing elegies; nonetheless, the first chorus ends with a call to admire rather than mourn and to marvel at a virgin who surpasses even the best of men. The same abrupt swing characterizes the first scene of the drama. For as Jephtha returns in victory, he applauds her victory dance while inwardly groaning in anguish. His speech to her makes clear his feeling of betrayal, describing himself as being placed in a position of unbearable grief *in* his triumph, and surrender *in* his victory (*Pl vir Is* II. 9. 31–34).

Alexiou and Dronke cite a tradition of wedding laments, probably existing even in ancient times, on which Pseudo-Philo might have drawn for his lament on the Jephtha theme. In these "marriage songs," they explain, "the language of wedding was suffused with that of lament—lament by the parents for the loss of the bride, lament by the bride at leaving her parents' home."[82] Both are forms constructed of mixed emotions. The traditional form focuses on the sadness that mixes with joy at the wedding. Abelard instead evokes the sadness of the young girl's impending death mixed with desire and joy (both on the part of the chorus and the victim herself). So Abelard mixes two paradoxes: the sorrow of the wedding and the pleasure of self-sacrifice.

The rituals that follow Jephtha's daughter's persuasion of her father to keep his vow repeat the pattern of alternation between joy and sorrow. First, she takes up the clothes of mourning to grieve the premature curtailing of her life and the emptiness of her womb, going alone to face the fear that her sacrifice might be a curse rather than a remedy (*Pl vir Is* II. 20. 76–21. 84). As the next scene opens, we see her secret return and entry into the baths; she discards the robes of mourning, just the virgins of the opening chorus were asked to abandon their luxurious robes and jewelry for the somber robes of mourning (*Pl vir Is* III. 22. 87–90). The ritual continues, carried out by the handmaids exhorted by the bride/sacrificial victim to prepare her for death as they would for marriage (*Pl vir Is* III. 26. 119–20). So she is washed, anointed, robed, and adorned with jewelry, reversing the transition from celebration to mourning in the opening chorus. Yet, the handmaids signal the conflict inherent in the situation, staining the silk and linen, the robes for the celebration of a wedding, with their tears (*Pl vir Is* III. 28. 121–29. 124).

Abelard's heroine has a complex emotional response to the dilemma she faces. While she is unequivocal in her view that her father must sacrifice her, her speech to him still moves between joy and sorrow, between excitement and dread at the role she has been asked to play. Her words in favor of the sacrifice contrast with the demand for two months of lonely mourning (*Pl vir Is* II. 19. 74–78). The same is true in the next scene, in the baths, on her return from the wilderness. She sits passively (in contrast to her very active role in designing her fate) as she is washed, anointed, and dressed by her handmaids. The *domina* as Abelard calls her, no longer young and virgin but a mistress of her fate, goes from initiating to passively undergoing, to, finally, rebelling against the wedding parody (*Pl vir Is* III. 24. 102). Thus, unable to bear the weighing down of her body with more robes and jewels, she suddenly jumps up and throws off the robes, declaring, "These things are enough for a bride, too much for one who is to perish" (*Pl vir Is* III. 30). With that she grabs the sword and hands it to her father. Her very act to hasten the sacrifice after throwing off the wedding robes in spite of, or rather because of its very decisiveness, points to her inability to tolerate the ritual, which is both funeral and wedding, taking place around her. She acts out her ambivalence by shifting between hesitation and decisiveness, alternating between accelerating and delaying the sacrifice. Her resolution of the conflict comes in a sheer act of will, handing her father the knife with which he is to kill her. But this is, of course, a resolution in name only. She does not choose and face her fate with equanimity, rather she both rushes toward and backs away from it, alternately attracted and repelled by it.[83]

When the chorus returns in the final stanza, they open in mourning, with a remembered picture of her last moments. Lamentation is their ritual commemoration of her death, but they turn from this almost as suddenly as the victim did from her ritual preparation. They turn to Jephtha just as his daughter did, but to utter a triple curse: "Oh demented mind of judge! Insane zeal of a general! Father but enemy of your race!" (*Pl vir Is* IV. 32). Lastly, they turn again almost as suddenly to Jephtha's daughter with a final note of praise and admiration, concluding, "through her we are greatly ennobled!" Thus Jephtha's daughter's response is mirrored in the chorus caught between sorrow for her loss, repulsion at the bargain made by her father, admiration for the heroine, and elation at the glory of her act, which filters down to them as inheritors of her gender.

The heroine's long speech encouraging her father to carry through with the vow expresses only her desire to be sacrificed, an apparent exception to the mood of ambivalence that surrounds it. As Abelard portrays her, she does not hesitate to accept the obligation to sacrifice herself (*Pl vir Is* II. 10. 34–37). Comparing herself to Isaac, she envisions her fate as a great honor for her sex (*Pl vir Is* II. 12. 44–13. 46). Her father, she contends, opposes both his own glory and her own by placing her life above his word to God.

Thus she argues that her father mistakenly places his relationship to her above his to God; if he persists, she argues, he will lose both God and his people (*Pl vir Is* II. 16. 54–59). She redescribes her sacrifice as "piety" rather than "cruelty," quickly disposing of any uncertainty about the divine will and its justice: "This is not cruelty but rather piety toward God, who, if he did not want sacrifice, would not have given victory" (*Pl vir Is* II. 17. 60–64).

Though she claims that there is no conflict between her glory and her father's, she nonetheless seems to assume, as Abelard does in his theology, an exclusive choice between love of self and other, love of human being and God. This is exactly the same view, of course, Abelard expresses in the *Historia* about his relationship to Heloise. It is either her or God, either the life of the philosopher or of husband and father. It is an either/or with a price Jephtha's daughter recognizes; he must give her up, she argues, or lose her unequivocally. In the terrible mathematics that governs this bargain, if he tries to keep her, he loses everything.[84]

Abelard refers to Jephtha's daughter in a letter to Heloise as "the greatest lover of truth," and in one of his hymns considers how she would have borne up had she been faced with Christian martyrdom (*Ep.* 7. 270; *Hym. Par.* I. 125. 4). The "truth" she loves is that the religious life she desires and chooses is superior to a secular life, yet she also recognizes the truth that that life has conflicts and difficulties. She is forced into martyrdom, the form of religious/spiritual life most at odds with natural inclination. But for Abelard, virtue is not the perfection of nature, in tune with one's deepest inclinations, but it is enduring what is against one's inclination or desire for the sake of something else (*Eth.* 10. 2–9; 12. 14–15).[85] For Abelard, then, conflict and ambivalence are basic to moral and religious life and characterize the most holy and heroic human acts.

In this, Abelard rejects both Aristotelian/Platonic and Stoic models of virtue. To achieve Aristotelian or Platonic virtue is to desire the good, not to struggle against one's desires in order to choose the good. Stoic virtue, which, like the act of Jephtha's daughter, aims at giving up the world for virtue, forbids what she also displays: passionate attachment to the things of the world. Lady Philosophy in the *Consolation* makes use of both Aristotelian and Stoic models. Lady Philosophy first, like the Stoics, counsels the abandonment of emotion. In the end, she argues that to return to God is to return to one's nature; it is to be released from a kind of captivity and to satisfy one's deepest desires. Boethius comes down from these heights to the reality of human struggle for virtue and against evil as the *Consolation* ends, but he articulates those ideals. Abelard does not make this ascent; instead he dwells in the struggle, in the moment of choice between God and the world. He invests this choice with emotion and conflict, emphasizing pain at the rejection of the world as much as joy in the spiritual good chosen.

This conflict is what the poem's vacillating emotions are about. Jephtha cannot have both God and his daughter and must choose between the leadership of family and community. His daughter too cannot have both glory and life and must choose between married and spiritual life. Jephtha's daughter does not pretend that the goods of marriage and children, not to mention life per se, are negligible, nor that the choice of self-sacrifice is selfless. It too has its satisfactions, both erotic and heroic. Though she expresses no hesitation about which side of the dilemma she chooses, she nonetheless sees them as irresolvably opposed to one another; she must give up her gender by dying childless in order to glorify her gender by being a worthy sacrifice.[86] This woman described by Abelard as the "greatest lover of truth" achieves no synthetic grasp of the truth that would draw her toward it in love; rather she leaps toward it in agony. While Boethius's *Consolation* depicts the steady steps of the prisoner toward God, here the distance is traversed only by a desperate leap, the leap of the heroine for the knife.

The Lament of Israel for Samson

In Samson's lament, as in Joseph's, no allusions are made to providential purpose or to any saving effect of human sacrifice. Instead Abelard presents Samson's humiliation as complete; moreover, his act of destroying the place of his humiliation and killing his enemies is not, for Abelard, an act of victorious revenge but simply of despair. Abelard's version of the story barely mentions what takes up most of the scriptural account, Dalila's early and failed attempts to trick Samson into revealing the secret source of his strength. Instead, Abelard moves directly to Samson's loss of his hair and sight (*Pl Sans* I. 2a. 13–16). We never see Samson strong but only blinded and toiling in darkness, his once strong body stooped by the monotonous work of milling (*Pl Sans* I. 2b–3a). Samson is "weighed down [*oppressus*]" dwelling in "twin darknesses," the loss of his superhuman strength compounded by the debilitation of his enslavement, the loss of his eyes compounded by the darkness of his environment (*Pl Sans* I. 3a. 24–25). These doubled losses may correspond allegorically to the loss of both inner as well as physical sight in Samson, a theme, Dronke notes, Abelard might have found in Gregory the Great.[87]

In the second half of the poem we see Samson regaining his strength but only to destroy both himself and his enemies. Samson is moved from "play to serious matters," to "put an end to all suffering." Samson uses his strength to bring down the pillars on which the house stands, motivated by the "sorrow" that "unites [*miscet*] his and his enemies' death" (*Pl Sans* II. 1a. 52–2a. 54, 58–59). In the *Theologia* "*christiana*," Abelard describes Samson as having received a divine command (to pull down the temple on himself and the Philistines) that goes against natural law (*TChr* 166. 1123–67). Like Jephtha's daughter, he must choose between nature and God. Unlike Jephtha's daughter, however, he does not leap toward God but acts in a kind of affectlessness. This Samson does not triumph in revenge (as he does in the biblical account in Judges 16), or even in his weakness (as a figure of Christ). Dronke notes that since Augustine and Jerome, Samson's death had "*meant* the deliverance of his people, the sacrificial act by which he fulfilled his destiny, the greatest deed in which . . . he foreshadowed Christ."[88] Abelard, by contrast, presents Samson and Israel in despair, without any sense of any higher good that might be achieved through Samson's losses and humiliation.

The complexity in this lament comes from the frame in which Abelard places Samson's suffering. One part of that frame consists in the opening strophe, which intones a theme that connects this lament to the previous ones: the inscrutability of divine judgments. "A great abyss are your judgments, God, the more formidable, the more they are hidden" (*Pl Sans* I. 1a. 1–4). This opening brings to mind Jacob's incomprehension of the divine plan and extends it to the difficulty of complying with the divine will even when it is known. The poem ends with a misogynistic diatribe blaming Dalila for Samson's undoing and also, more generally, "woman" for the destruction of man in an unbroken line since Eve. The diatribe culminates in a predictable warning not to commit oneself to a woman lest one wishes to follow these men into disaster (*Pl Sans* II. 3c. 86–94). The providential plan for Samson, the same as that for David, Solomon, and Adam, according to the poem, is that he be destroyed by a woman. Woman was "created" to be "supreme destroyer of the mighty"; she, according to the poem, "brought down the father of all [Adam]"; she "offers the cup of death to all" (*Pl Sans* II. 2a. 64–67, 2b. 68–76). Thus, the narrative in which the poem places Samson's suffering and death is one of necessary defeat, not ultimate victory.

One response to apparently senseless human suffering is not simply to deny providence, but to project a world controlled by a force whose aim is not good but evil. The lament for Samson, then, explores the human tendency not just to doubt the existence of providence but also to see suffering as caused by malevolent plans and motives. One kind of blindness that sees itself as perceptive is the blindness of thinking one has penetrated the plan behind human events. Like a phobia so overwhelming it makes its subject counterphobic, here we have vision so weak it creates a false picture. Just as the counterphobic looks brave, so the conspiracy theorist looks knowledgeable; both are in fact extremes of the opposite variety.

Here Abelard uses a popular medieval conspiracy theory, that women are the cause of man's downfall. The question is *how* does he use it? The evidence for Abelard's misogyny is a bit mixed. In his letters, he not only reject Heloise's placement of herself in the long line of women who caused the destruction of great men, but he also argues at some length that women have a higher spirituality and more perfect virtue than men.[89] As Peggy McCracken points out, Abelard praises Heloise both as a woman and as transcending mere womanhood.[90] In the twelfth century, however, it would not be inconsistent both to engage in misogynistic diatribe and to exalt the spirituality and virtue of woman. Abelard seems, like many in the Christian tradition, fundamentally ambivalent about women, vilifying them in one context, praising them in another. He is simply, as we might expect, more extreme in both attitudes. Thus Abelard goes further arguing for the dignity, equality, and even superiority of women, yet his exposition of the Fall is more negative on Eve and women than even was traditional.[91] My suspicion is that Abelard cannot be cast either as feminist or misogynist because he is by turns both (at least by modern standards). Rather, he makes use of misogynistic themes just the way he might make use of others for his own purposes. It is, however, very much Abelard's wont to reject simple and accepted positions and to look beneath the surface for a different reality.

In this poem, I want to argue, he takes a different look at the theme of man's fall at the hands of woman. In this setting then, misogyny represents a temptation, a false alternative to providence. For while the standard use of tales of man's falling prey to a woman's charms was as a warning against the power and evil of women, Abelard sees another, deeper moral. For Abelard, the stories of Samson, Adam, David, and others are not only about the dangers of women but also about the weakness of men, about human reason and will unable to resist seduction. George Sarton interprets another commonplace of medieval misogyny in just this way. The story, often depicted in religious as well as secular contexts, is of Aristotle, the paradigm of human reason and wisdom, being ridden by Phyllis, the young wife of Alexander.[92] The story illustrates not only the dangers of women but also the vanity of philosophy, Sarton argues, in order to teach men a kind of humility: "If the infallible Master failed as ignominiously, any excess of confidence in ourselves is mere foolishness."[93] Using the Samson story, then, I think Abelard makes this point and takes it one step further: men can hardly be counted on to grasp supernatural truth given their inability to know and act on a natural truth about the evils of submitting to one's passions. Samson is too weak to control his own passion and thus his own life. Samson's story illustrates that male weakness suffers from a double blindness, first, a blind trust in its own (illusory) strength to overcome temptations and obstacles to control its own destiny, and, second, its inability to see the workings of providence in what it suffers. Because human nature cannot be counted on to resist temptations of the flesh, much less to grasp and hold onto more difficult truths, human beings must give up the illusion of their own strength and surrender to the mysteries that render them weak, giving up the illusion of strength to take up genuine weakness.

Samson's weakness is connected to human weakness in the face of divine actions from the very outset of the poem. The lament, as I noted above, opens with the characterization of divine judgments as "the more formidable the more they are hidden," and, continues, "the more facing these, is any power whatever weakness" (*Pl Sans* I. 1a. 1–6). Similarly the account of the depth and mystery of Samson's suffering ends thus: "Who among the strong is not like the mightiest Samson unstrung?" (*Pl Sans* II. 3a. 74–76). Men are undone by feminine wiles just as all are undone by divine mystery. Using Samson, Abelard portrays the weakness of human strength and recommends that the believer give up this apparent strength for the true strength of weakness before God. I suggest that Abelard portrays Samson's final act not as the taking of power but the abdication of it as a way of portraying the embrace of one's own weakness before God. If this is so, Abelard's portrait of Samson is doubly bleak, not only portraying the only real human strength as weakness but also showing Samson (unlike Christ) as utterly devoid of any sense of the strength in his weakness.

According to Dronke, Hrabanus Maurus and Isidore of Seville find in Samson a figure for the church, more particularly "those in the Church who take pride only in the mere name of Christ, and are constantly involved in wicked deeds."[94] Abelard's Samson is less a figure for the wickedness of believers than of the weakness of their will and insight into providence, in a "fall" unable to see itself as "happy," in the dark abyss of divine mystery not yet bathed in the light of revelation. If Abelard instead or in addition uses Samson as Christ figure, a traditional allegorical reading, his Samson is a representation of Christ at the darkest moments of the Passion: the prayer to be released from the divine plan at Gethsamane, and crying out his forsakenness from the cross. At those moments, thoroughly inhabiting his humanity, Jesus himself becomes weak before the mystery of the Passion.

David's laments

The last two laments are given to David, one for Abner and the other for Saul and Jonathan. Like Dinah's, these laments are for losses which are morally ambiguous. David mourns the killing of Abner, his former enemy. Abner was murdered by one of his own soldiers for making peace with David. What we expect is a lament for Absalom not Abner; the death of an innocent child taken for the sins of the father has simpler and more complete pathos than the complex and heroic story of the death of Abner.[95]

According to Annelies Wouters, Jerome claims that the name "Abner" means "father of light."[96] For Bede, Wouters continues, Abner is a figure of John the Baptist and other defenders of the church; he is the virtuous man and the defender of truth.[97] For Wouters, then, Abner stands for Abelard himself, who identifies with Abner's masculinity, his pursuit of truth, and his faithfulness.[98] But Abelard, as is typical in these laments, complicates the picture of the noble soldier betrayed by focusing on David's response to his death and with the paradox of Abner's death itself. David's part in Abner's death is more complex than, for example, in Absalom's death. David in one sense causes Abner's death by begging for the truce Abner granted, but he did not do the killing and did not cause it by his own sin. The irony is that David is and sees himself as innocent of the death of his enemy, but as bearing a kind of guilt, having caused a death by doing good. In David's lament for Saul and Jonathan, the situation is reversed. Though David does not cause the deaths of Saul or Jonathan, in Abelard's setting, they are mourned by a morally compromised David who alludes to his disproportionate love for Jonathan and a guilt (homoerotic or patricidal?) shared with Jonathan that is never explained (*Pl Saul/Jon* 3c). What is striking is the way Abelard presents David as such an emotionally and morally complex mourner. These are stories of grieving in which the mourner experiences himself as implicated in causing the losses he mourns.

The complexities of David's position and mourning are mirrored in the circumstances of Abner's death. There is no sin for which Abner's death is payment; on the contrary, he dies as a result of his virtuous rejection of violence and for keeping faith with David. The contrast Abelard emphasizes all the way through the poem is between Abner's invincibility as David's enemy and his complete defeat once he joins David in peace (*Pl Ab* 9–11, 21–22). This contrast makes the crime more heinous, because it is committed by stealth rather than in direct and honorable battle, and makes the irony of Abner's death more complete (*Pl Ab* 3, 6). Abner protected himself while at war, when all the while he was safe; he let down his guard once hostilities ended, only to be killed, not by an enemy but by one of his own (*Pl Ab* 17–20). The poem is a tribute to Abner, David's enemy, and an act of mourning for an enemy killed because he became a friend. The paradox reaches its climax as Abner is called both greatest enemy and greatest friend (*Pl Ab* 14). David is baffled by the complexity and unpredictability of human behavior and fate's response to it.

This lament, then, like the others, is a commentary on providence. What comes through is the senselessness of Abner's death and of the impossibility of protecting oneself from harm, either by arms or virtue. The lament depicts the senselessness of suffering that occurs when someone does the right thing. Here is evil, not as repayment for evil, but for good. If Abner is a model for conversion, here the convert is not, as we would expect, embraced and welcomed into new life but prevented from joining his faith community; it is a conversion not rewarded with everlasting life but death.

The poem concludes with David crying, "May the princes of justice take zealous action to avenge such wickedness!" (*Pl Ab* 27–28). Wouters notes that in the biblical text David prays to God to punish the crime, while Abelard appeals to human agents to perform revenge.[99] Like the others who mourn in these laments, David sees his loss from a totally human perspective; he does not address God because at this moment of grief he cannot imagine a God who could allow or right the wrong. His appeal to human princes does not seem like a realistic plan for avenging the death, nor does it seem to stem from any faith in human agency. Rather it is a cry for vengeance that comes from overwhelming grief and anger.

The last poem, David's lament for Saul and Jonathan, offers no consolation, even in the form of vengeance.[100] The "princes of justice," Saul and Jonathan, appear not to right wrongs but as the dead who are now in their turn mourned. The deaths of Saul and Jonathan mark the triumph of enemies and the mockery, even annihilation, of God: "The people of the enemy have come to the highest honor, God's people meet the derision of all. The mockers say, see in what manner their god, of whom they babble, has betrayed them, seeing that he has perished, laid low by many gods" *Pl Saul/Jon* 2b–2c). Thus, David not only fails to see providence in these acts, he also imagines his victorious enemies celebrating the defeat of the one God by the many gods. The last lament leaves off in the midst of sorrow as David, unable even to go on singing cries, "I give rest to my harp strings; would that I could do so to my lamentations and tears. My hands are sore with striking, my voice is hoarse with lamenting and breath fails me" (*Pl Saul/Jon* 6a–6b). The laments end not because there is any end to grief but only because there is an end to the ability to express it further. The cycle of six laments, then, has no real conclusion except in sorrow that exceeds the capacity of language.

Sorrow without Consolation

The focus in all the laments is on the immediate and devastating loss and the past out of which it has arisen, not on any future. The laments explore the sadness that overwhelms any faith in providence, the despair that seems to crowd out any hope in the reemergence of goodness, love, and harmony in the human community. There is no trace of the "happy ending" of the story in the coming of Christ and reunion in heaven. The drama Abelard creates in his laments, his empathy for his subjects, the immediacy and intensity of the emotions of grief, despair, and anger he evokes bring to mind classical tragedy. Like tragedy, the laments seem designed to explore the frailty of human beings, their losses and lack of understanding of their fate or the future, and the irresolvable conflicts in which they are caught.

Abelard's settings of these stories offer not just one understanding of the characters and their sorrow but a multiplicity. Thus not only is the narrative of Scripture broken down, but the singularity of perspective on a single story is also fragmented and complicated. The poems grapple with the losses in question by empathizing with different characters and moving between conflicting emotional responses in the same character or event, leaving the conflicts they expose unresolved. Abelard increases rather than resolves tension and conflict by presenting a different perspective than that given in Scripture and multiplying perspectives within the same lament, using what has been called an "aesthetics of irresolution."[101]

The implications of such a project on language are complex; they change from one lament to the next along with the nature of the losses, the bereaved, and their grief. They turn around double and opposing meanings of key notions like kinship, leadership, strength, and friendship. They raise reflexive questions about their ability to represent grief or offer consolation. In this sense, the laments are a kind of inversion of Boethius's *Consolation*. Boethius transforms the worldly understanding of good fortune, power, abundance, and honor into a truer and deeper grasp of their real referents; the classical stories of struggle, conflict, and tragedy are woven into it in counterpoint recognition of the incompleteness of the prisoner's moral and intellectual conversion. Abelard's laments concentrate on ill-fortune, powerlessness, loss, and dishonor in earthly terms, refusing to effect a transformation to a heavenly perspective on them, and touching on the story that will right these wrongs only in the most oblique terms. For Boethius the ending of the story, though projected rather than achieved, is ultimately of the return of all things to the One. Abelard has difficulty even projecting such a conclusion. While Boethius offers consolation, what these poems express is suffering that eludes consolation.

Abelard's setting of these stories is tragic and not comic, and he does not allegorize but complicates the characters and narrative. Both are strategies that run contrary to the tendencies of the period and are connected to each other. The presupposition of the allegorization of Hebrew Scripture is the unity and forward progression of salvation history toward its comic conclusion. Events in this story are not just linked in time, but are causally and formally related. Allegory is a product of hope about things being able to serve and read as signs of one another. Abelard's laments, however, are about the inability to read signs. They point to moments in the Christian story in which Christ could not be seen as fulfillment of the promise any more than Jacob could see in Benjamin the fulfillment of the promise of the survival and flourishing of the chosen people. Nor any more than Israel can see victory in Samson's death, Dinah, in the union of foreign peoples in one religion, nor Jephtha's daughter, in the joy of divine union on the other side of her sacrifice. In the end, a type of the redeemer to come, David, concludes the laments not with victory but with mourning those who are his precursors and models, Saul and Jonathan. If Abelard's laments are in any sense allegories for the Christian story, they occupy the holes in that story, asking the reader/hearer to meditate on the theology of the Crucifixion not that of the Resurrection.

But none of this means that the laments are nontheological or even nonallegorical.[102] Abelard does not avoid allegory so much as engage in an inversion of it, engaging in a different kind of theological reflection and a different use of typology than that which would, for example, immediately reinterpret Samson's suicide as prefiguring the Christ who died to be resurrected. Instead Abelard attempts to dwell in the "abysses of divine judgments," to occupy the human perspective on suffering. Abelard attempts to roll back the retrospective knowledge about Samson, Jacob, and Israel as a whole, to dwell at some of the darkest moments in the history of the chosen people. Crucial to the divine mysteries are their abysses, their inscrutability to human understanding, he seems to be saying. A sense of their greatness is increased by remaining with suffering and loss, just as in the following centuries the sense of the greatness of the mystery of the Incarnation is increased by dwelling empathetically in the experience of the Passion.

These laments offer no consolation for the losses they describe, even though they were written by the same thinker whose theology forbids mourning and thoroughly encompasses evil within the circuit of providence.[103] One might argue that Abelard displaces the mourning for his own and Heloise's losses into the context of Hebrew Scripture as a sign of an exhortation to place their own losses in a larger spiritual and scriptural context. Those deeply felt losses are now from Abelard's point of view part of salvation history, redeemed in the Incarnation; so too, Abelard might be saying to Heloise, will ours be. But if that was Abelard's intention, it seems he has failed. Instead of salvation history—providence absorbing and resolving private grief, the opposite seems to happen, grief seems to overwhelm the hope that salvation history offers.

In the end, then, the view of the theologies and the laments are not opposed but complementary. The theologies assert the universality of providence, encompassing the particulars without descending to the details to offer explanation or consolation. The laments follow and thus evoke the

entire narrative of salvation history but are so immersed in the losses they
describe that their connection to the larger comedic narrative from which
they are drawn is obscured. In neither the laments nor the theologies is
there any mediation between the power and goodness of God, on the one
hand, and the weakness and finitude of the human being.

Abelard, thus, sets out to explore grief, anger, and fear in the *planctus*
without integrating them into the faith and hope in providence in the
mode of Boethius's *Consolation* or Augustine's *Confessions*. The extent of the
fragmentation of genres in the work of Abelard—the definitive split of
poetry from philosophy, of prayer from philosophical reflection, of autobiography from emotional expression in lyric—is a measure of this emotional
disjunction. Thus in the laments Abelard represents sorrow without consolation, anger without just retribution, sin without forgiveness, doubt without faith, despair without hope, and desire without consummation. I do
not offer these observations as accusations, as if they located some flaw in
Abelard's writing. Abelard's laments make the point that attempts to
resolve negative into positive emotions, to look at loss and sin always and
only in the larger context of restoration, forgiveness, and just punishment,
may belie their reality by wrapping them up too neatly into the single and
unified perspective of providence. In the same way, for Abelard, the work
of resolution and harmonization of conflicting authorities or texts of
Scripture may produce only apparent rather than real understanding when
it fails to take account of the depth and difficulty of the problems which
makes it necessary. What these laments share with Abelard's logic and
theology is their opposition to oversimplification.

The Ethics and Letters: Living in the Wound of Exile

I have portrayed Abelard throughout his works in logic, theology, and poetry
as concerned with the gap between surface and depth, with creating rather
than resolving conflict and difference. This remains constant, in my view, in
his later writings, but what changes is that he comes to see these struggles as
being in the service of spirituality. The first step in this process is coming to
see the morality of actions as divorced from their surface appearance; this is
the argument of his *Ethics*. The second step is to make the striving for inner
truth over external appearance the core of spiritual life; this is the theme of
Abelard's rewriting of the Benedictine rule for Heloise and her community.

The "Ethics of Authenticity"

The *Ethics* was written late in Abelard's career (1139) seven or so years after
the *Historia calamitatum*. In it I think we see the theme of the *Historia*,

(*Eth*. 38. 22–40. 3). These examples illustrate the gap between what Abelard calls the "pure equity" by which God operates as opposed to the "government" by which the human system of justice operates (*Eth*. 44. 3–12). What is striking is that Abelard does not try to narrow the gap between real and human justice by reforming the standards by which human beings judge guilt or innocence. He simply presents it as a fact that human beings do not see, judge, and act according to true fault but must judge based on the surface they see in order to serve the more approximate utilitarian (external) good of the whole community.

Abelard carries his principles beyond punishment to repentance. First, Abelard argues that true repentance comes out of love of God rather than fear of penalties (*Eth*. 84. 27–29). True repentance, proceeding from love of God, is "sorrow and contrition of heart" (*Eth*. 88. 4). At the moment of this interior "sigh" of contrition (and not in the act of confession to a priest or his granting of absolution), sin is forgiven because with it contempt of God ceases (*Eth*. 88. 6–10). These are all views that fall directly out of Abelard's original definition of sin as contempt of God, but they lead him to a complicated position on the need for confession.[109] Since for Abelard inner contrition is identical with remission of sin, he can only ascribe the obligation to confess to other factors. Hence, he argues, one confesses in order to obtain the help of the prayers of those to whom one confesses, and because in the confession and the humility it brings, part of the satisfaction for sin is made (*Eth*. 98. 12–15). Also he notes that it is helpful to be corrected by the judgment of others because sin originally consists in the rejection of God's judgment and replacement of it with one's own (*Eth*. 98. 19–24). All these are good reasons to confess, but they clearly separate the act of confession from forgiveness.

Abelard's account of emphasizes the internal and the individual aspect of religious life, something we also see in his rule, yet he does not do away with individual confession to a priest. Abelard requires contrition as well as confession and absolution, but without joining them. Words and external actions, though required, do not bring about or even coincide with the interior changes penance brings about. Just as we are stuck with the gap between human justice and divine equity, we are stuck with the gap between interior contrition and the external words of absolution. Abelard does not heal the rift either by bringing inner and outer together or by getting rid of the outer altogether.

The Letters and the Authenticity of Relationships

The most important and obvious context in which issues of intention and authenticity arise is in Abelard's relationship with Heloise, or, more precisely, in their differences over the meaning of the past and the hopes for a future relationship expressed in their letters.[110]

Heloise insists on the complete disjunction between intention and act, appearance and reality in her own case. She was innocent, she insists, in her fornication with Abelard, punished by separation after the marriage, which should have been the external redemption of their union. She argues that her present state is completely hypocritical, her outer serenity, holiness, and chastity barely covering her overwhelming sexual desire for Abelard, revealing her commitment to Abelard instead of God (*Ep.* 3. 80–81).[111]

In his response, Abelard notes that on the intention-based ethics they both share, Heloise's rejection of praise would make her more praiseworthy. That is, Heloise's sincerity about her own insincerity might save her; her recognition of her own inability to repent might be the saving recognition of sinfulness, which then would merit forgiveness (*Ep.* 4. 87). But Abelard adds that she must be careful lest her own claims of unworthiness, sinfulness, and incorrigibility, her own rejection of the praise of Abelard and others, might themselves be simply more sophisticated ways of taking pride in her own self-knowledge and the seeking of the very praise she pretends to eschew (*Ep.* 4. 87). As Abelard points out, she now separates them more by her persistent dwelling on their former relationship and by rejecting God for Abelard. "Can you," he asks, "endure me to go on [to beatitude] without you—I whom you declare yourself willing to follow to the fires of hell?" (*Ep.* 4. 87–88). Unless Heloise gives up her sexual attachment to Abelard, it will be impossible for them to be together in God, so physical and emotional (i.e., superficial) separation will result paradoxically in their greater spiritual and eternal (i.e., authentic) union.

Abelard uses the figure of the black bride from the Song of Songs to extend his reversal of Heloise's reversal of reality and appearance. For while Heloise has claimed that she is outwardly pious but inwardly sinful, the black bride is ugly on the outside but beautiful on the inside (*Ep.* 4. 83–84). As Brown points out, the bride from the Song of Songs, like Heloise, "chooses the heady pleasures of a whorish secrecy over the public honors of an acknowledged wife."[112] Abelard uses the allegory not just to transform Heloise's vision of herself but women in general. Like Heloise, he argues from the weakness of women but unlike her, concludes from this their superiority. He looks beneath the surface of the apparently less worthy "blackness" to find a deeper worth and humility about that worth, describing, for example, black skin as less beautiful to look at but softer to the touch (*Ep.* 4. 85). Women in their less powerful position in this life exemplify more perfectly the position of the Christian in relation to Christ (*Ep.* 4. 83–84). His elaborate arguments can be summed up in the thesis that the logic of Christianity gives primacy to that which is secondary, reversing the values of secular society. Because woman is created second and within Paradise, her creation is in a way more perfect; the concealing and safeguarding of her precious charms, like the blackness of the beloved in the Song of Songs, makes her more pleasing and her virtue more authentic (*Ep.* 6. 268, 4. 83–85). Throughout, Abelard's "feminist" arguments take a form of finding the true reality beneath a misleading surface.

Abelard analyzes Heloise just as he does the examples in his ethics. The morality of an act may be completely other than it appears, contrary to both the appearance of the outward act and desire. The consequences of this extreme emphasis on the internal element makes it possible (or even likely) that the actor will be ignorant of his or her own moral state. Heloise's attempt to adopt a sincere insincerity and Abelard's response shows that there is no end to the ways in which real and apparent value, surface and depth can be reversed.

The letters move on to their shared project of directing the community of nuns at the Paraclete still conscious of but without resolving the gap between surface and reality in their acts and relationship. Heloise changes the topic, she explains, out of a kind of inability to keep picking at the wound that gave her so much pain, clear that once again the depth of her feelings will be belied by the surface of her words (*Ep.* 5. 240–41). Hence, Heloise simply shifts the nature of her entreaty to Abelard from the personal and erotic to the communal and spiritual, asking for Abelard's guidance in the reformulation of the Benedictine rule for her religious community. She makes very clear that her shift is not, or at least not yet, an act of conversion, not a sign of transformation of her affections or perspective on her loss, so much as it is a diversion for those affections.

Linda Georgianna argues that with this concession Heloise has "quit the battle for perfection" Abelard remained committed to, opting instead to "struggle on in weakness without any definitive victories or signs of spiritual progress."[113] In my view, neither Abelard nor Heloise abandons the ideal expressed in their ethics of authenticity. Rather both recognize and critique their own actions in accord with that ideal and live very self-consciously in that gap between the model of authenticity and their imperfect matching of surface and depth. Heloise asks Abelard to address her questions about the religious life of the community as a way of directing her thoughts away from her loss to her community, using, she says, "one nail to drive out another" (*Ep.* 5. 240–41). Morgan Powell notes that Heloise wishes only that her pain be *alleviated* rather than completely *removed* by Abelard's agreeing to correspond with her about a rule for her community.[114] Abelard too is looking for palliation rather than cure. Abelard's hope is not that they be made whole again but simply able to continue to function. He advises Heloise to think of herself as a "widowed bride" (*Ep.* 5. 83–84). It is a condition which manages to preserve her love for Abelard, now lost, and her love for God, not yet consummated, but gives her neither the happiness of marriage nor even the joyful anticipation of the young bride.

Questions have often been raised about the genuineness of Heloise's conversion and similar questions could be raised about Abelard's conversion, but I think that Heloise's and Abelard's apostasy has been exaggerated by those taking their own rhetoric too literally.[115] Both Abelard's and Heloise's self-portraits, in which the search for the disjunction between outward practice and inward reality figure so prominently, give an exaggerated sense of the possible incompleteness of their own conversions.[116] They self-consciously pursue the lowest vision of themselves and the highest vision of the other as part of the complex rhetoric of their exchange, which pits them in a contest to become the victor in the Christian hierarchy of "the last shall be first and the first shall be last."

Abelard's rule

In the revision of the Benedictine rule written at Heloise's request, Abelard's intellectual predilections for criticism, for questioning authority, and for elevating his own *ingenium* over tradition or his teachers' wisdom find a spiritual home and become part of a compelling spirituality.[117] Following Heloise's lead, Abelard formulates a spirituality that focuses not on outward practice but on the inner transformation. It is a spiritual life to which doubt and inquiry are integral, doubt and inquiry not as means oriented toward the finding of solutions but as spiritual practices in themselves.

Heloise asks Abelard to rewrite the Benedictine rule in a way suitable for her community of women, for, as she puts it, "our weak nature, so that we can be freer for the offices of praising God" (*Ep.* 5. 252). The point, Heloise explains, is to arrange their lives not to offer sacrifices, outward actions to God, but rather thanksgiving and honor (*Ep.* 5. 252). A rule that is not suited to women will be impossible to conform to; a rule that is too strict will invite laxity and hypocrisy. "We must therefore be careful," Heloise advises Abelard, "not to impose on a woman a burden under which we see nearly all men stagger and even fall" (*Ep.* 5. 246).

The problem is on one level a literal one. The Benedictine rule is used for communities of women as well as men, but women cannot even in principle conform to it, for it prescribes practices appropriate only to men, for example, one concerning clothing that women do not even wear (*Ep.* 5. 242). Other female houses did not worry about this discrepancy but Heloise did, and such questions begin in both Abelard and Heloise a process of rethinking the rule in more substantial ways. Questions about diet and drink bring Heloise to quote Romans: "The Kingdom of God is not eating and drinking, but justice, peace, and joy in the Holy Spirit. . . . Everything is pure in itself, but anything is bad for the man who gives offence by his eating" (*Ep.* 5. 248–49).[118] Heloise concludes, "Those who are true Christians are totally concerned with the inner man so that they may equip him with virtue and purge him of vice." She continues, "it is not so much what things are done as that which is in the soul when they are done that must be considered" (*Ep.* 5. 250–51). This is the principle around which Heloise and Abelard agree that spiritual life should be organized: that inner spirituality should drive exterior practice. Thus Heloise begins her letter as if she is asking for small changes in the rule but ends up requesting a charter for a new kind of religious life, one which will prioritize inner life over outer works.[119]

Abelard's reply begins with the basic principles of monastic life: continence, poverty, and silence (*Ep.* 7. 243). He thus attempts to rethink the nature of monastic life from its foundations, guided by principles we recognize from his theology. First, in the midst of his ordering of the practical life of the community he stops to consider the inevitability of "irregularities," that is, failures to conform to the rule. Just as Abelard composed theology for human beings (with all their attendant limitations), he constructs a community for human beings, not angels. He quotes from Augustine's description of his own community: "However vigilant I am about the discipline in my house, I am a man and live among men. I would not dare to claim that my house is better than Noah's Ark, where among eight men one was found to be a reprobate. . . . It is not better than the company of Christ himself, in which eleven good men had to endure the thief and traitor Judas, nor better, lastly, than the heaven from which angels fell"(*Ep.* 7. 264).[120]

The principle articulated here and worked out in the specific recommendations for adjusting the rule is not, as Marenbon argues, moderation, except incidentally.[121] First, moderation in Abelard's rule is in the service of human weakness, not because moderation is commensurate with human excellence as it is for Aristotle, Cicero, and Seneca. So Abelard counsels, "It is sufficient for the weak if they avoid sin, although they may not rise to the height of perfection, and sufficient also to reside in a corner of Paradise if you cannot be with the martyrs"(*Ep.* 7. 274).[122] Moderation serves the ends for which the community is composed because it allows the community to match its practice to its principles by not choosing a rule that is too difficult or ill-suited to the community.

Second, and more importantly, a more moderate rule allows the community to focus not on outward practice but on the inner transformation, which the outward pattern of life structured by the rule is supposed to make possible. Concern with "works," the external behaviors of monastic life, is for Abelard equivalent to involvement with the business of the world; it is to be distracted from true spirituality. "Many," he writes, "afflict themselves more in outward things but make less progress according to God, who looks to the heart more than works"(*Ep.* 7. 274). Following Heloise's lead, then, Abelard clearly makes the focus of the rule the inner state, not outer works. To sin is to go against conscience, that inner guide of moral action, Abelard argues (*Ep.* 7. 268). What is sinful is not the particular food but the way it is desired (*Ep.* 7. 276, 278). "We might," he explains, "be without fault when we take more sumptuous foods but be held responsible for eating more lowly food"(*Ep.* 7. 278).[123] Sin, he concludes, is a disorder of the soul, not the body (*Ep.* 7. 276).

Abelard attempts to prevent a kind of fetishization of the practices of the community; they serve its spiritual ends, not the other way around. The standard by which to judge whether those spiritual ends are served by a given practice, Abelard asserts with great vehemence, is not tradition. "A practice must never be defended on grounds of custom but only of reason, not because it is usual but because it is good"(*Ep.* 7. 224). He quotes Augustine with great approval: "In the Gospel the Lord says 'I am Truth'. He did not say 'I am custom' " (*Ep.* 7. 266).[124] Here is the same rationalism that led Abelard to write his logic and that recoiled from the demand of his opponents that he recite without interpretation the words of the creed, now put firmly in the service of his spirituality.[125]

This is even clearer in the account of the place of reading and learning in Heloise's community. In the rule, a rule for *women* we must recall, Abelard argues for the same primacy of inquiry and the search for understanding he does in the *Sic et non* and other systematic texts. Inquiry is necessary for spiritual life because it is connected to spirituality through self-knowledge. He writes, "Whoever looks at Scripture which he does not understand is like a blind man holding a mirror before his eyes in which he is unable to see what sort of man he is . . . ." (*Ep.* 7. 285). Continuing this theme, Abelard quotes Origen's extended analogy between the wells dug by Isaac and understanding the deep and hidden meanings of Scripture.[126] The faithful are not only to drink from these spiritual wells but to dig their own: "Therefore you try too, my listener, to have your own well and your own spring, so that you also when you take up a book of the Scriptures may begin to bring out some understanding of it from your own judgment. . . ." (*Ep.* 7. 291). He contrasts this model of drinking from the deep well of spirituality with the practice in other monasteries, where monks are thought literate if they simply know the alphabet and are trained to sing rather than understand words from the Scripture. These monasteries "glory in the multitude of their books but have no time to read them. . . ." (*Ep.* 7. 286).

Only with understanding can one pray for, teach, and do the right things, Abelard argues; even more, Abelard continues, if the faithful do not seek to understand God, they cannot be united with him. "For the beginning of withdrawal from God," Abelard warns Heloise, "is scorn for doctrine" (*Ep.* 7. 288). Eileen Kearney argues that Abelard reshapes prophecy and meditation into forms of discursive reasoning, not in order to separate reasoning from religious practice, but to transform religious practice.[127] The transformation is in informing the outward words and practices with meaning and life. Thus an important theme of Abelard's complaints against Anselm of Laon and others in the *Historia* returns in the rule—the need to give substance to the external word and deed, to inform them with the logic and clarity that produces understanding. Mary's pondering of the words of the annunciation in her heart for Abelard signifies that she "carefully [*studiose*] examined each word separately and compared them with each other, seeing how closely all of them agreed with one another" (*Ep.* 7. 292). Only after the separation of topics and comparison of authorities can the crucial connection between belief and action be made. This itself is always further questioned, so he follows this account of Mary with the question, "who can observe the words or precepts of the Lord by obeying them unless he has first understood them?" (*Ep.* 7. 292).

This approach to theological issues and texts is behind Abelard's infamous assertion that it is impossible to believe what has not been understood (*HC* 83. 697–98). There is in this, as Clanchy claims, something of a challenge to the Anselmian principle of "faith seeking understanding."[128] Abelard's emphasis on understanding before belief is an emphasis on the need for authentic belief rather than on the repetition of mere verbal formulas, and authentic belief requires intellectually working through the verbal formulas by the individual, in order to make those principles his own.

Between Scylla and Charybdis

Abelard's *Soliloquium* is a dialogue (perhaps unfinished) between "Peter" and "Abelard" on the model of Augustine's *Soliloquies*.[129] In it Abelard argues that the names "Christian," "philosopher" and "logician" all belong most truly and rightly to the followers of Christ (*Solil.* 886, 889). Abelard claims, however, that the names "philosopher" and "logician" do not belong to Christians according to usage, only according to their etymologies (*Solil.* 889). Thus, on the one hand, Abelard notes the deep coherence between language and things, faith and reason. For philosophers, lovers of wisdom, those who wish to know the true nature of things, are identical to logicians, those who are skilled in the use of words, and thus able to convert others to the truth, which is found in Christianity. In this Abelard asserts the ultimate unity, integrity, and coherence of his life, love, and intellectual projects. On the other hand, the gap between surface and depth, reality and appearance still remains in his distinction between the etymology (the true origin and deep meaning of the words) and the surface of use. Thus, unity is asserted only in a distant and attenuated way, in principle rather than in feeling in this little work, which is either really or in appearance a fragment rather than a whole itself.

I do not think Abelard started out with this vision of bringing together his exploits in reason and faith. Rather I think he found a way in which to bring together the strands of his own intellectual temperament into something more than a reflection of his own restless and dissatisfied spirit. It seems to have developed over time and with Heloise's help. Abelard's restlessness and discomfort do not, however, disappear in a synthesis of faith and reason. The fault lines remain visible. They are as visible in Abelard's confession of faith as in the *Soliloquium*. He begins with what others had said about him, that he is "outstanding in logic but limps not a little in Paul" (*Conf.* 152. 2). Taking up that opposition, he continues, "I do not wish to be a philosopher if it means conflicting with Paul nor to be an Aristotle if it cuts me off from Christ"(*Conf.* 152. 3). Here and in the rest of his confession, Abelard professes his unambiguous faithfulness to Christianity, yet he expresses that commitment in terms of conflict on two levels. First, he describes his choice as one of Christianity over philosophy, as if, at least in fact if not in principle, philosophy and Christianity could conflict. Second, he presents his own rock solid stand as one taken in the midst of storm and conflict around him. Thus, he writes, "Safely anchored on [my faith], I do not fear the barking of Scylla, I laugh at the whirlpool of Charybdis, and have no dread of the Sirens' deadly songs. The storm may rage but I am unshaken, though the winds may blow they leave me unmoved; for the rock of my foundation stands firm"(*Conf.* 153. 15). While Burnett describes the *Confessio* as "progress[ing] from uncertainty to confidence, from concern about worldly reputation to security in heartfelt belief," I read Abelard's final stance less as one of confidence than of continued defiance.[130] He stands firm but not on stable ground, sure of himself but in the face of extreme conflict, within and without.

What we have seen throughout this chapter is that Abelard's desire for integrity, for the coherence between word and deed, inside and outside, leads to a kind of dwelling in the absences, disjunctions, and separations. He will not belie the reality of the distance between himself and God, between word and meaning and between intention and act. Hence, his criticisms make these gaps obvious, and his solutions, in their formality, their very explicit "de-reification," repeat that absence more than they fill it.[131] The laments, in their exquisitely crafted thematic of loss, absence, and separation, emphasize the distance between the present state and the life of and with God. Abelard's sharp criticisms are directed against the false appearance of immediacy and union; hence, he scolds Heloise, saying that she should prefer him to be "happy in absence" rather than "present and unhappy" (*Ep*. 4. 86). His solution to the lack of immediate union and full presence is not to propose what he accuses others of, a pretense to immediacy. Rather it is to recognize and live in the gap, orienting himself toward, without tasting, future union.

Waiting, in the sense of not having but looking toward the time one will have the union desired, is of course a traditional mode for Christian consciousness and common to any number of Latin medieval thinkers. In Boethius, however, waiting is imbued with more *eros*, anticipation, and impetus toward that end, more feeling that some part of its promise has already been fulfilled, than in Abelard or, as we shall see, in Alan of Lille.

CHAPTER 3

ALAN OF LILLE: LANGUAGE AND ITS PEREGRINATIONS TO AND FROM DIVINE UNITY

The Paradox of Form: Fighting Fire with Fire

The standard view of Alan's theology fits him into the line of twelfth-century humanistic thought. On this view, Alan embraces the study of the arts by making them stepping stones on the road to theology and models for the construction of theology as an academic discipline. For most scholars, Alan's theological and poetic writings make a real but somewhat eccentric and uneven contribution to this project.[1] Alan is often named in different contexts as the precursor of many important later developments in theology and poetry: he is noted as a forerunner in the development of a so-called "scientific" theology leading into the thirteenth century,[2] as the daring architect of an "axiomatic" theology admired by Leibniz, as an important figure on the way toward the systematic study of the Bible and the development of the complete concordance,[3] and as the poet of allegories influencing and anticipating the work of Chaucer and Dante.

Alan himself sends mixed signals about how he sees his own work in relation to the tradition. On the one hand, Alan describes himself as the protector of Theology against the untoward advances of arrogant theologians, characterizing his own work as utterly traditional, a mere theft from the work of the fathers (*SQH* 120). On the other hand, unlike Bernard of Clairvaux, for example, Alan indulges gladly in novelty, choosing the newest forms and vocabularies.[4] But he does so with a certain ambivalence. Alan writes of the *Anticlaudianus* that it ought not be denigrated though it smacks of the "rudeness of the moderns." This justification has been read by some as endorsing and by others as rejecting "modernity."[5] On the one hand, Alan clearly views the arts, in their newest configurations, as necessary tools for the theologian; he also quite liberally uses nature as a vehicle to carry the mind toward God. On the other hand, Alan stresses the dissimilarities between nature and God and the discontinuities between the arts and theology. His primary targets are the humanists and rationalists who overestimate their achievements and underestimate the limitations of nature and language.

How do we make sense of the combination of innovative form and conservative content, especially as it is mixed with other unusual combinations—poetic and scholastic methods, mystical and rationalist approaches to God, sophisticated irony and earnest apologetics? There is an answer, I think, in reading the major poetic and theological works of Alan's corpus as constructed on the model of fighting fire with fire. He uses this model to understand the saving activity of the Christ, which he describes as different modes of defeating weakness with weakness (wounds with wounds, death with death, and so on). In the Incarnation, "Heaven adapts itself to earth . . . light to darkness, rich to poor, well to ill, the king to the slave," taking on darkness, poverty, illness, and slavery in order to defeat them (*AC* 5. 155; 521–39). Alan also uses it to describe a divine strategy of strength rather than weakness, portraying God as the sun that warms our sun, who counters the flame of anger and the heat of Venus with his heat. He concludes, "thus heat subdues fire, flame is repelled by flame, heat by heat, the coal by the glow" (*AC* 6. 165; 261–69). It is also the model for theology in the apologetic mode, in which each enemy is fought with a tactic dictated by the form of attack.

Alan's adherence to the model of fighting fire with fire explains, I contend, the literary genres in which he chooses to write. Thus, I will show that in his allegories, Alan writes poetry to fight poetic falsehood and composes new myths to correct old ones; in his theological works, he offers arguments against those who think they have found necessary reasons (*SQH*), and axiomatic principles to supersede those placed as the highest and most universal (*Reg.*). Lastly, we shall see that he transmits a "properly" theological vocabulary to those attempting to find one for theology analogous to the technical language of the other sciences (*Dict.*).

Alan takes up these literary forms, we shall see, not as new pieces of technology that might deliver a science of God; though Alan is attracted by their novelty, he is skeptical of their promise to deliver truth. Thus, my contention is that Alan does not take them to be transparent and unproblematic means of transmission of his ideas; they are structures he self-consciously *uses*, with a complex sense of their limitations as well as the limitations of the general strategy. As we shall see, most explicitly but not exclusively in Alan's witty and self-referential introductions to a number of his works, he takes up these diverse forms partly because the challenge and complexity appeal to him and partly because it is a defensive and apologetic strategy, addressed not to those outside the faith but those within, that is, theologians.

Just as Alan uses the most innovative literary forms for theological investigation of his age, so he adopts the newest, most complex, and obscure vocabulary of the twelfth century, that of Gilbert Poitiers, also with a similar ambivalence. Gilbert takes up and complicates Boethius's theological vocabulary. Alan shares Gilbert's attempt to trace out the consequences of Boethius's transformation of the categories when applied to the divine nature. However, we shall see that Alan gives this terminology a self-conscious, self-referential, playful, almost baroque elaboration, pushing its consequences to stress the paradoxes and otherness of theological discourse in much more radical ways than Gilbert. While Alan revels in the transformation of language in theology, Gilbert takes his task to be to "restore transposed words to order" and "subject novelties to rule."[6] While Gilbert "believes that with aid of the liberal arts human reason can penetrate the mysteries," Alan works to "emphasize the stupefaction of human reason and the arts of language."[7] D'Alverny puts Alan's relationship to the arts in these terms: the arts are "servants of God in the world, whose nature is to prepare man for the perfect knowledge which only faith can attain."[8] What D'Alverny does not quite bring out is that for Alan what this means is that the arts work toward their own obsolescence. Moreover, Alan does not portray the "perfect knowledge" of faith but rather the failure of the arts in theology, both their failure to comprehend the subject of theology and to portray whatever it is that faith knows. Compared with Gilbert's, then, Alan's is a much more negative, almost mystical theology, showing the influence of Pseudo-Dionysius. Alan was among the first to exploit the negative theology of Dionysius, another instance of Alan's fascination with the new. Dionysius, however, is a novelty that serves rather than stands in tension with Alan's theological project.

Alan's work is another rewriting of Boethius, but it is not just a complication and elaboration of it the way the work of Gilbert of Poitiers is. Alan's is an original, speculative theology produced by the alchemy of combining Boethius with the newest in the trivium arts of the twelfth century and Pseudo-Dionysius on theological language. Thus, it is a reworking of Boethius's notion of language as the tool for theology, of the ways in which theology requires the shifting of the most important and most elemental metaphysical and moral vocabulary. But Boethius's goal is integration, carried out by careful stages of expansion of the field of vision, working toward the transformation of perspective, while Alan's goal is disorientation. Thus Alan speaks in unmistakable tones the same truth the Boethian corpus does *sotto voce*: that he does not and cannot understand God (or Fortune).

Boethius struggles to catch a glimpse of the divine and to see all else from a divine perspective. Alan struggles against the tendency to bask in the supposed light of human understanding, making it his task to create disequilibrium instead of a sense of sure-footed progress. Alan, we might say, fills the old wine skins of the liberal arts with the new wine of theology, showing how it bursts the skins, not because he does not know that that will be the result, but rather because he thinks his contemporaries need a demonstration.[9]

Regulae caelestis iuris: Order in Mystery and Mystery in Order

Alan begins the *Regulae* with the claim that theology is not "cheated [*fraudatur*]" of the rules or axioms the other sciences have; those in theology, Alan claims, are even more worthy in their obscurity and subtlety than those in the other arts (*Reg.* Prol.). Alan's introduction draws parallels between the other sciences and theology, showing the rigorously scientific character of theology but also emphasizing the peculiarly hidden and elevated character of theology. Alan fills the prologue with Greek words for various kinds of axioms for which he gives positively fanciful meanings and etymologies. He comes up with many parallel rules in other disciplines, showing his own knowledge of those disciplines and giving credibility to his claims about theology. When he turns to alternate terms for the *regulae* of theology, the meanings (all untrue) given to the Greek terms emphasize the esoteric character of the discipline.[10] As Jolivet writes, we are in an atmosphere both "axiomatic and initiatory," where the rules of theology are "*éclatantes* et *cachées*."[11]

The *Regulae* claims to derive the whole of Christian theology—including the Trinity and Incarnation—from a single axiom on the unity of God. It is as if Alan has taken the form of Boethius's *De hebdomadibus* and tried to see how far it can be pushed.[12] The sense of exaggeration is only increased by the fact that the axioms are stated in the most paradoxical form Alan can manage. The work is ultimately Alan's comment on Boethius's distinction between principles that are self-evident per se and those self-evident only to the learned. Even though the axioms of theology are the most intelligible principles about the simplest, most intelligible being, they are, Alan insistently reminds his reader, infinitely far from being accessible to the human mind.

The tension between the rationalist demand for technical correctness and the paradox demanded by the divine nature is heightened by terseness. So while Boethius writes in a way that requires decoding and a grasp of his technical vocabulary, Alan writes in a way that seems to make decoding impossible. Here are a few examples: "Only the one is alpha and omega without alpha and omega" (*Reg.* 5); "only simple being is form without material subject and substance without formal predicate" (*Reg.* 13); "of that that is the to be (*esse*), nothing is the to be (*esse*)" (*Reg.* 15); "only form is formless, since of form there is no form" (*Reg.* 16); "any name given from form said of form, falls from form" (*Reg.* 17); "any simple being properly is and is improperly said to be" (*Reg.* 20); "it is not the case that if it is true in being (*essentia*), it is possible in nature" (*Reg.* 59).

If the form of the *Regulae* is a rewriting of the *De hebdomadibus*, the content of the *Regulae* is, like Alan's *Summa quoniam homines*, a rewriting of the *De trinitate*. The *Regulae's* obsessive concern is to trace in detail the shifts that occur when God, rather than creatures, is the subject of discourse. Boethius traces this change through Aristotle's categories and describes a different kind of predication appropriate to the simplicity of the divine nature, but the changes Boethius maps out are not so radical as to preclude any similarity between theology and the other disciplines. Most see the *Regulae* as a product of a certain kind of rationalism, a project that assumes a substantial amount of continuity between theology and the other sciences. Alan accepts, I think, that to have knowledge or science is essentially to be able to express something in language, a language that must be governed by rules. However, what becomes increasingly clear as Alan draws out more consequences from his original rule is that the changes necessary to accommodate God as subject are much more significant and consuming than any continuity with the other disciplines.

The Rules of Theological Propositions

Boethius's twelfth-century commentators did not just comment on the changes Boethius argues for in language when God becomes subject, but added more changes and technical rules for theology. The first fifty rules or so of the *Regulae* extend this project almost to the point of parody. Alan begins, traditionally enough, with the denial of any composition or parts in God. This leads, as it does for Boethius and his twelfth-century commentators, to the conclusion that all predicates of God are identical with his being (*Reg.* 8). Alan also takes from Boethius and Gilbert the notion that this changes the nature of the predication, making it copulative or conjunctive rather than divisive.[13] For Gilbert this means that nothing is "left over [*reliqua*]" or "divided off [*dimittat*]" from God by applying a predicate to God.[14] That is, since God is wholly and essentially God and just and wise, and so forth, his divinity is his justice and wisdom, and so forth. When, by contrast, we predicate justice or greatness to a human being, these attributes are not identical to one another, and do not contain in themselves any other properties the person might have.

Where Alan parts company from Gilbert is not in changing the principle but in drawing a somewhat disconcerting conclusion from it: "Since
God has no diversity of parts or properties, by any term whatever God is
shown to be something, one and the same thing is predicated. For one and
the same is predicated by these terms when it is said God is 'God,' 'strong,'
'patient,' or 'merciful' " (*Reg.* 8). In other words, terms said of God are
synonymous, and when one has predicated one of them, one has predicated them all. Hence, Alan concludes, "For I say just as much when I say
'God is good,' as if I had said 'God is God, good, holy, and strong' " (*Reg.* 10).
Alan asserts this conclusion, but not, I think, in the sense that he wants to
put a stop to applying diverse predicates to God because the others are
given with any single one. He is attempting rather to provoke his reader to
try to imagine the completeness and unity that would make this predica-
tional structure appropriate, and to sense the distance between that and
ordinary things. It is clear that one cannot gather up all of the diverse
concepts of God into any one of them, which is, in a way, Alan's point.
Alan's goal in embracing such apparently problematic corolaries is to keep
alive the tension between what one says and what one is trying (and failing)
to mean about God.

We see a similar strategy in Alan's handling of the application of abstract
terms to God. Gilbert, commenting on Boethius's *De trinitate*, argues that
one cannot mix concrete and abstract terms in the same proposition.[15]
Thus Gilbert bans using concrete terms as predicate for a form, for example,
calling the category "place" a place, or "time" a time. Gilbert's rule is general, not only for God; it is an attempt to prevent the infinite regress of the
"third man." Alan takes it in an exclusively theological and paradoxical
direction. Thus, Alan bans the application of formal (i.e., abstract) predicates of God even though, or rather because, God is the source of all form:
God is, Alan writes, "without formal predicate since no formal predicate is
predicated of itself, i.e., [divinity] of divinity" (*Reg.* 13).

This conclusion falls under a rule describing God, who, because he is a
simple being, falls outside the guidelines for both concrete and abstract
predication: "only simple being is form without material subject and
substance without formal predicate" (*Reg.* 13). The model proposition of a
concrete thing is, of course, the application of formal predicate to it as
individual subject (e.g., Socrates is a man); on the other hand, a pure form,
because it is not a substance, cannot function as subject for a form. But God
is both pure form *and* substance. This leads Alan to articulate some of the
highly abstract and paradoxical rules I mentioned earlier: "of that that is the
to be [*esse*], nothing is the to be [*esse*]" (*Reg.* 15); "only form is formless,
since of form there is no form" (*Reg.* 16), "any name given from form said
of form, falls from form" (*Reg.* 17). Gilbert, I suspect, sets up the distinction

between concrete and abstract predication exactly to avoid such paradoxical outcomes; I take it that if, for Gilbert, form cannot be predicated of
form, place of place, neither can formlessness be predicated of form or
placelessness of place. Alan, however, embraces the paradox caused by the
combination of the principle of excluded middle with the divine nature.

These conclusions about the transformation of names applied to God
lead Alan to a general principle concerning affirmative and negative
predications: affirmations of God do not signify the inherence of some property in God; instead they signify "incompositely"; negations, however,
predicate "truly" (*Reg.* 18). Alan explains, "Hence Dionysius, attending to
what is said of God as cause, attending to the sense from which words
[*verba*] are made rather than the sense which words make, considering that
from which they are said rather than that about which they are said, says,
'God is just, holy, and strong' " (*Reg.* 18). The claim that the sense *from
which* "just" comes can be affirmed of God seems to attribute the original
sense to God, in the form of *esse justicia*, while the derived sense applies to
creatures in the form "*justus*," which inheres in them (*Reg.* 18). Alan goes
on to embrace Dionysius's negative theology: "[C]onsidering what is not
appropriate to God as a property rather than what is said of God as cause,
Dionysius says, 'God is not holy, strong, or merciful,' removing the
propriety of the saying [*proprietatem dicendi*] rather than truth of being
[*veritatem essendi*]" (*Reg.* 18).

Consistent with the emanative and axiomatic form of the text, Alan
places the origin of the meaning of words in God, the derivations in
creatures. But even though the origin of properties such as justice is in
God, because they have come to mean the inherence of the property
in creatures, their *proper* sense is applied to creatures, and they can be
applied to God only as the cause of the creaturely property. In this way
Alan shows himself to be less sanguine than Gilbert seems to be about the
possibility of disengaging syntax, the structure of predications, which carries
with it the metaphysics of creatures from semantics, the pure meaning of
terms. For Alan, we cannot, ultimately, signify pure or abstract qualities
because we cannot remove the creaturely shadow from predications. In
this, Alan is also rejecting Prepositinus's solution, which claims that terms
signify the same thing when predicated of God and creatures but signify it
differently.[16] This view simply does not adequately take account of the
difference between God and creatures for Alan.

Having made the distinction between the propriety of being and saying,
Alan's next group of rules draw the consequences of the gap between being
and saying. Alan writes, "Any simple being is in one way and is said to be
in another," (*Reg.* 19) and "any simple being is properly and is improperly
said to be" (*Reg.* 20). Even the statement of such rules involves a paradox,

for they make the absolutely simple being the subject that receives an additional predicate, introducing the diversity of predicate and subject into the perfectly simple. As Irène Rosier notes, others, like Peter the Chanter, tried to reverse completely the perspective from which some terms are said of God, arguing, for example, that God is properly said to be while creatures are improperly said to be.[17] Thus, Peter simply declares language proper to God and goes on to use it normally. This is, in a way, the position one expects from Alan, given his emphasis on the otherness of theological discourse, the uniqueness of its principles, and the axiomatic form in which he writes this text. And sometimes Alan does talk this way, but in such contexts, and indeed here, his point is to emphasize the gap between creatures and God, making it clear that, even in a theological context, language cannot throw off its limitations. Once again, as in his account of copulative or conjunctive predication, Alan gives the reader a glimpse of the radically different syntactic and semantic structure that would be appropriate to God if we could manage it. But, he also makes it clear that no one *can* manage such a radical shift in perspective.

For Rosier, Alan's distinction between saying and being is a precursor of the distinction between *res significata* and *modus significandi*; rather than articulating an opposition and "irremediable devaluation" of the linguistic compared with real being, it is, she argues, a distinction internal to language.[18] In one sense, of course, she is right, for there is nothing *other* than language through which to express the failures of language, and Alan does indeed write "God is properly," predicating the *sensum ex quo*, the later *res significata*. However, this statement never stands alone in Alan as it does in Peter the Chanter. For Alan, the impropriety of saying must be immediately added—that God *is properly* but *is improperly said to be*, negating the sense that what one wishes to say of God can be said. In this sense, Alan's bald statement of the gap between being and saying is indeed an "irremediable devaluation" of the linguistic. Alan would, I think, see the later distinction between *res significata* and *modus significandi* as a domestication and, therefore, as an invitation to forgetfulness of the radicality of the problem.

The Names of God

At the end of a group of rules governing the application of nouns and adjectives to God (rules 21–35), Alan concludes by constructing a hierarchy of all names of God. Nouns are "less improper" than adjectives (we have already heard that abstract or "mathematical" nouns are more proper than concrete nouns in rule 30), positive nouns are more proper than comparatives or superlatives, and names of incorporeal things are "more usually" proper than those pertaining to the corporeal (*Reg.* 35). Moreover, God, said to be not body but spirit, is called "mercy, holiness, merciful, and holy," but not whiteness or blackness, lined or line (*Reg.* 35). Alan explains this distinction, "For although these [whiteness, body, line, etc.] can be said of God as cause, in order to remove any suspicion from God [*propter amovendam suspicionem a deo*], they are removed because of idolaters who imagined [*fingebant*] the natures of things to be gods, and because of meta-morphosing heretics who believed God to be distinguished by corporeal features [*lineamentis*]" (*Reg.* 35).

As a hierarchy of the names of God, Alan's has some unusual features: it has no real *archē*, no truly proper origin, because its highest member is merely "less improper" and "more usual" than those falling below it on the ladder. The hierarchy is also almost without a last member. The lowest members are only *more* improper than the higher members, and if these names are not to be used of God, it is only on pragmatic grounds, as protection against heresy, in keeping with custom, and as not too dissonant to the human intellect (*Reg.* 34).[19]

When names are said of God, Alan explains, we transfer the name and not the thing. Alan explains, "When we say 'God is just,' this name 'just' is transferred from its proper signification to that which is appropriate to God, but the thing of the name is not attributed to God; rather divine justice itself is attributed to God, not that from which [*a qua*] this name 'just' is given" (*Reg.* 26). Thus, what is predicated, on the one hand, is divine justice, a pure, perfect, and substantial justice. On the other hand, we predicate what we know of God, the effect of justice in creatures, which does not belong to him. So when we say God is just, we *predicate* divine justice, Alan explains, but we *co-predicate* the effect of justice in creatures. The predicate is identical to the divine nature; the copredicate is, like God's effects, plural.

Though more in my explanation than in Alan's text (which is terse to the point of obscurity), this distinction sounds like the later one between the *res significata* and one *modus significandi*. However, it is important to note the ways in which Alan's distinction is different in aim. The distinction between the thing signified and the mode of its signification attempts to mediate the gap between ordinary and theological language, trying to find a way of speaking about God that is not merely metaphorical. But in Alan's scheme, the type under which divine predication falls, the transfer of word and not thing, is clearly the least proper of the three types of *translatio* Alan gives. Further, though Alan distinguishes between divine justice, which is what is predicated when the *name* "just" is given to God, and the *res nominis*, the quality of being just, which is not applicable to God, he does not allow us to think we can predicate the former of God without the latter. If we could, it would mean we could separate out the metaphysics of creaturehood and make the predication of a pure quality of God. Instead, Alan insists that one is predicated and the other co-predicated.

Grammar of Theology

Alan not only considers the many ways in which the rules for the construction and interpretation of propositions change with God as subject, but he also traces the repercussions of God as subject on the different parts of speech. In redefining the different parts of speech for God, Alan is following once again in Boethius's footsteps. Aristotle's *Peri hermeneias* presents definitions of noun, verb, and adjective, and Boethius comments on these definitions and attempts to connect them with the categories and the metaphysics of substance and accident. This "logicized grammar" as it has been called, becomes the obsession of the twelfth century. Alan takes up this obsession but in relation to God as subject, taking the Boethian/Aristotelian account of the parts of speech and showing how those accounts must be reshaped when applied to God.

Alan begins with the verb. The standard account is that "every verb signifies either that which is action or passion or something else in the manner of act or passion, that is with tense, in a verbal termination and *as it is said of another.*"[20] This last clause, that verbs signify something as said of another, we recognize from Boethius's commentary on Aristotle's definition of the verb.[21] The clause is added in order to distinguish the signification of verbs from that of nouns, which signify substance. For Alan, however, any verb said of the divine "is not a sign of that which is said of another or that which is another, but rather that which it itself is" (*Reg.* 38). Alan once again asserts the identity of all predicates with the divine nature following from its absolute simplicity, but in terms that take away from verbs said of God their specific difference.

In the same mode, Alan states as a rule that demonstrative pronouns said of God "fall [*cadit*] from demonstration" (*Reg.* 36). Though he contends that possessive pronouns are most improperly said of God because they posit a distinction between possessor and thing possessed, he seems most concerned to note the impropriety of demonstrative pronouns applied to God because they signify a kind of presence of the thing to the senses or intellect, neither of which can be the case with God. Alan even worries about how to understand scriptural passages in which God speaks, wondering whether this "*prosopoeia*" is accomplished by God taking on human characteristics, or a human being taking on divine properties. The "*ego sum qui sum*" of Exodus 13 must be, Alan reasons, spoken not by God but by an angel "as if reciting what he read in the divine mind" (*Reg.* 36). The direct and unmediated contact suggested by the demonstrative pronoun and the first person singular, Alan contends, is improperly applied to God.

Similar changes from ordinary language take place in the account of adverbs. Adverbs of place predicate the immensity of the divine, showing how God is *not* contained in a place, or they predicate the effect of God in the creature (*Reg.* 41). Temporal adverbs signify not time but eternity when used of God (*Reg.* 43). Adverbs of similarity may signify similarity, but also may, again contrary to their usual sense, predicate "essential truth," "impropriety," or adjunction (*Reg.* 44). Terms such as "*quasi*," "*sic*," and "*sicut*" are exactly the terms that, while linking subject and predicate or proposition and proposition, also put a space between them and assert something less than the complete correctness or correspondence of the predicate. Instead of using these terms to show the gap between what we say and what we mean about God, Alan subjects them to the same analysis. So these terms, which ordinarily signal likeness and not identity or absolute difference, Alan asserts, can signify both when transferred to God. These terms seem uncontaminated with the assertion of presence or the metaphysics of creatures, yet even they require a radical shift in their meaning in theology.

From Divine Unity to Incarnation and Sacrament

The analysis of particular concepts as applied to God allows Alan to make the transition from a discussion of God's unity to one concerning God as Triune and Incarnate. It begins with a discussion of omnipotence. God is called omnipotent, Alan argues, not only because he can make all the things that can be made but because he can also make "those things which cannot be made" (*Reg.* 56). From this it follows that "it is not the case that if it is true in being (*essentia*), it is possible to nature" (*Reg.* 59). This rejection of a basic rule of modality, *ab esse ad posse*, is necessary to accommodate the Resurrection and virgin birth (*Reg.* 57). Thus Alan takes these matters into the heart of divine metaphysics. Alan might be criticized for failing to do what Aquinas did, that is, drawing a sharp distinction between the nature of God, on the one hand, and the Trinity, the Resurrection, and virgin birth, on the other hand, the former accessible to reason alone, the latter known only by revelation. But Alan draws no such line because he wants to remind his readers that the mysteries of theology are its center, given in the nature of God per se. Hence, they cannot be put to one side while considering the metaphysics of God as one.

At this point, Alan seems to lose the axiomatic structure of the work, prompting Evans to argue that Alan's project is a failure "for the very good reason that he presses the method beyond the point where Christian doctrine lends itself to philosophical methods."[22] I think that the work is only incomplete rather than a failure; moreover, I think Alan intended to press the method into areas for which it seems inappropriate. There are hints about how Alan might have intended to complete it. For example, Alan takes up the practice of explicitly noting the derivation of later rules from previous ones again at two important points, first, as he turns to the nature of divine providence and an account of possibility and necessity, and, second, as he considers the relation of creaturely to divine goodness (*Reg.* 64–66, 68–69). These rules are crucial because they attempt to construct an axiomatic transition from God to creation. So power leads to a discussion of providence, which leads to a discussion of the relation between the natural order and the divine (discussed in terms of the differing meanings of possibility and necessity seen from a divine versus a natural perspective), to a discussion of the goodness of creatures based on the principles of Boethius's *De hebdomadibus*.

The next important transition is from the discussion of morality, arrived at by means of the consideration of goodness, to the Incarnation. Here Alan does not state that one rule follows from another, but he does attempt to connect the issues. After a discussion of charity, Alan states the following rule: "Just as the human being through charity ascending from the thesis of his nature to apotheosis by grace is deification, so God through charity descending from the apotheosis of his nature to hypothesis of our misery is humanity" (*Reg.* 99). A structurally parallel transition marks Alan's turn to sacramental theology: "Just as the creator is made creature through reception [*susceptionem*] of the creature, so is the creature made the body of the creator through the transubstantiation of the creature"(*Reg.* 107). I do not think Alan means to suggest that Christ divests himself of his divine nature in the Incarnation, literally becoming *only* a creature; rather he wishes to emphasize the paradox of God becoming human. Thus, Alan's phrase "body of the creator [*corpus creatoris*]" is, I think, purposely provocative; it stresses the link to the Incarnation, "creator becoming creature," and makes the parallel paradox of "creature becoming creator" in the Eucharist its corollary. We have in effect Alan's axiomatic version of a *Cur Deus homo* in these rules, given a formality and brevity so audacious that it is scarcely imaginable that Alan could have intended it to be taken as "science" in an unnuanced and straightforward sense.

Seeing from a Divine Perspective

Alan's rules for theological language seem designed to refute a spectrum of contemporary views that Alan contends underestimate the gap between ordinary and theological language—Prepositinus's view that terms are univocal when used of God and creatures, and Peter the Chanter's view declaring theological language to be proper and ordinary language transferred to God. Even Gilbert, who insists, following Boethius, on the shift of all terms applied to God, speaks consistently of a *proportional* transfer or adaptation, implying that if one is very careful and makes the requisite changes for the divine nature, divine predication can be relatively successful.[23] For Alan, by contrast, the crucial feature of divine predication is the *disproportion* of the shift required.

There is in Alan no attempt, then, as there seems to be in Gilbert, to distinguish and control the shifts necessary to make the transfer from the other sciences to theology. If Gilbert's insight is, as Sten Ebbesen summarizes it, the view "that you cannot simultaneously change semantics and syntax," Alan's is that to remain faithful to the model of science and to construct a language that corresponds to the object of the science of theology, you must make any and all changes required.[24] When that subject is God, in effect *nothing* remains of the language with which one began, since the language we have is, Alan maintains, only appropriate to creatures. Ebbesen does not explain further, but I take it that for Gilbert the reason one cannot change both semantics and syntax is that if all the rules are abrogated, language becomes utter nonsense and any standards about what can and cannot be said truthfully and meaningfully become impossible to invoke. Mystics and mystical theologians, like Dionysius, see this problem and try to approach this limit without crossing it.

However, I do not want to place Alan's *Regulae* in the category of mysticism. In deriving the whole of theology, down to the Incarnation, morality, and the sacraments from a single principle, Alan is imitating the divine activity of emanation, looking at the world from a God's eye view. If, as Kenneth Burke argues, hierarchy seen from above is order but seen from below is mystery, Alan wants to create a sense of order.[25] But like Dionysius, he also wants to create a sense of the mysteriousness of the theophany, to emphasize the complete otherness of the perspective he attempts to represent. On the one hand, as attempting to simulate a divine perspective, Alan's project is to create an axiomatic and, hence, scientific system of theology. On the other hand, he wants to show that the air is in effect too thin at these heights for mere mortals, that they can only *imitate* (imperfectly) a divine perspective.

The goal, both to create order through science and to undermine it by presenting mystery, is reflected in the *Regulae*'s form and style. Its form is academic, scientific, and technical, promising a clear understanding of its subject and an ordered grasp of the interrelation of its principles. But its content breaks those promises in the process of making every attempt to keep them. While the spare, technical style of the axioms reflect the work's scientific pretensions, they are so terse, they become cryptic and paradoxical, hiding in mystery as much or more than they reveal by their order.

Alan takes the project of seeing the order of things from above, tracing the transformations on language consequent on this shift of perspective in every grammatical category—nouns, adjectives, verbs, pronouns, adverbs, gender, number, tense, case. The multiplicity of the distinctions and modes of predication becomes dissonant with the clear and overarching insistence on the unity of God. The project of ordering from above results not in the clarity of Euclidean demonstrations but in a tangled web of paradoxes. Such a pursuit only makes sense if we take it that Alan simultaneously accepts the project of imitating the divine perspective in language and recognizes the impossibility of it. As Alan remarks on a number of occasions, when speaking of God there is a plurality of signifyings but a single signified. He himself seems to want to set out a maximum number of signifyings thereby approximating both the completeness of the divine being and the infinite distance between our perspective and God's.

What Alan achieves by the combination of these strategies is a sense of the gap between these two perspectives, one looking down from above (God's) and one looking up from below (the creatures'). While one foot of language attempts to find a toehold in heaven, the other remains earthbound. The result is, I think, best described neither as the order the gnostic posits nor as the mystery the mystic always fails to express, but something like vertigo. The person in a high place looking down gets vertigo, feeling that he is falling, uncomfortable at the heights because of the huge distance between his position and the ground where he belongs. The *Regulae* will not allow a language constructed for the heights (God) to settle into a comfortable, clear relationship to its signified; it always makes the theologian look at the huge drop down to creatures and feel his language falling back to where it originated. Instead of trying to make steady progress toward a divine perspective while leaving behind the human one, as Boethius does, Alan attempts to keep both perspectives in play as much as possible. Thus, the axioms he formulates have their meaning, but also their disorienting effect, only when their terms shift their meaning from a heavenly to an earthly sense (or vice versa) within the same sentence. Unlike Boethius, Alan refuses to mediate the abyss (one of his favorite words) between these two perspectives.[26]

Summa quoniam homines: Disputation as Defense and Diversion

The Prologue: Joining the Battle to Defend Theology

The differences between the *Regulae* and *Summa* follow from their differences in form. Here, instead of breathing the thin air of the heights, looking down from a perspective of purity and simplicity, Alan is on the ground fighting to defend the honor of theology from the theologians who have assaulted and betrayed her. The motif of the knight-theologian fighting for truth is one we recognize from Abelard. But Alan goes a bit further (too far, quite possibly) with this conceit. In a parody of the *Consolation* depiction of Lady Philosophy, Alan depicts Theology as a lady in distress, her castle beset by those attempting to make improper entry, her suitors/attackers insufficiently screened by her doorkeeper, her robe ripped, her dignity offended, and her unity pulled apart by diverse errors.

The errors are the result of ignorance of the liberal arts and a rash attempt to do theology armed only with the arts. Alan describes this combination in highly inflated terms: a bacchanalia of drinking from the river Lethe has turned the "miraculous signification of divine words" that is theology into something "monstrous." "Those who are ignorant of the virtues of words quickly paralogize," Alan explains; "they go over into theology, ignorant that, just as divine things, preeminent over nature, are miraculous, so also do its names not naturally but miraculously signify" (*SQH* 1. 119). When the ignorant attempt to mount up to the "ineffable" things of theology without even having found the right path to the arts, they "ineffably fall" into various errors, and their entry into the palace of theology ends in a shipwreck of heresy. Having gotten past an imperceptive gatekeeper at Theology's castle, they attack Theology in a bacchanalia of false teaching and errors (*SQH* 1. 119).

Theologians are cast as the knights of Lady Theology. They are called to defend theology with the protection of divine authorities and the equipment of necessary reasons, in order to "drive out errors along with the erring" (*SQH* 1. 120). The method of disputed question is thus described essentially as a defensive tactic against error. "We [the theologians fighting error] who declare ourselves in the army of Theology, taking our support from the authority of the holy fathers, place our boundaries [*terminus*] with the holy Moses around the mountains of holy scripture" (*SQH* 1. 120). His role, then, is largely negative, surrounding the "garden" of sacred Scripture, guarding against the sowing of weeds, lest any of the "flowers" of sacred Scripture be "deflowered" (*SQH* 1. 120). He asks indulgence for his work, which is, he says, more a theft from the ancient fathers than something new.

Alan's contribution is, moreover, dedicated to the protection of great secrets rather than their revelation. "The understanding of our tractate is closed off to the unworthy," Alan claims, adding the traditional warnings about diminishing great secrets by divulging them to the unworthy and casting pure and invisible pearls before swine. Thus he concludes, "By this work of demolishing rivals [*demolientium emulorum*] access might be prevented, lest by their venomous objections the little fire of our work suffer eclipse" (*SQH* 1. 120). The "demolition" work is refuting the false theologians, thereby preventing the unworthy from gaining access to the secrets of Theology.

This is just my paraphrase of Alan's prologue; it is his rhetoric, his metaphors. In contrast to the academic project of argumentation on abstract topics that is to follow, he writes the prologue in this highly inflated prose, characterizing the present situation of theology as a crisis and sounding a call to arms. The repeated motif is not of revelation but protection, not of offense but defense, not of consummation but indefinitely prolonged courtship (from quite a distance indeed). Theology must be protected from untoward advances, and Alan sees himself as preventing these advances by imitating their militant and aggressive form. His own work, like that of his enemies, is a battle of reasons. He thus proposes to defeat them on their own terms, taking this form not because it grants him true access to theology but because it constitutes a kind of diversion preventing their approach to theology.

There is, for Alan, an equally large gap between logic and the super-logic of God as there is between illogic and logic. Thus every attempt to do theology inadequately educated in the workings of the arms of necessary reasons (of the liberal arts) or armed *only* with the weapons of nature or logic turns into a betrayal of Theology. The result is a fall not simply below the heavens but below nature altogether. Alan's disputations are designed to demonstrate this failing.

Alan's project here is refutation of arguments by arguments on two levels. First, his aim is to refute particular theological errors (this he has in common with his fellow theologians). Second, he works to undermine the more systematic error and constant temptation of theologians to *philolobia*, the overestimation of human abilities to understand and speak truly about God (*SQH* 2. 122). There is also a positive project and positive view of reason in all of this. For Alan the use of reason and education in the arts is required to begin work in theology; without it, one can have no sense of how reason and the arts are brought up short by theology. Only reason, in other words, can show what reason cannot know.

Defending the Incomprehensibility of God

Alan begins, as he does in the *Regulae*, with the unity of divine essence. In this text, however, he arrives at it negatively through necessarily composite creatures, which can only be brought into being from an absolutely simple source (*SQH* 3. 122). This is the occasion for Alan to describe the divine nature by a series of privative terms: immense, incomprehensible, untraceable (*investigabilis*), unintelligible, unengendered, incorruptible, immortal, immutable, and eternal (*SQH* 3. 123–24). He ends his series of arguments about the divine nature by citing an unnamed authority, "And this only we claim to know of God, that we confess to know nothing of him" (*SQH* 8. 134).

After numerous arguments for the simplicity of God, the identity of God and divinity, of *esse* and *in quod est*, Alan concludes, "just as out of the above it is clear [*liquet*] that God is simple, so, as was said, [it is clear that he is] incomprehensible" (*SQH* 8. 134). Alan then proceeds to offer a long and complex disputation supporting the conclusion that God is incomprehensible, beginning by offering authorities on both sides. The leading contrary citation is one of the most important Scripture verses for the whole project of medieval theology, Rom. 9: 11: "The invisible things of God are perceived from the things that are made" (*SQH* 8a. 135). Alan agues *against* the view expressed by this verse, a favorite of Augustine's, Abelard's, and later of Aquinas's, and *with* the arguments supporting the incomprehensibility of God, arguing in effect that God cannot be perceived from the created world.

Alan supports the Pauline view only once he has distinguished between "the knowledge [*scientia*] of faith," by which "the invisible things of God" may be known from and in the created world, and "the knowledge [*scientia*] of certitude," by which they cannot. This reading essentially robs the text of its sense since Paul's point is to equalize the knowledge of God given to the Jews through revelation and the knowledge of God achieved by the Gentiles through reason. Alan adds, "Although the intellect comes upon that which is [*id quod est*], it does not however follow that that which is more truly [*quod verius est*] is more truly understood" (*SQH* 8b. 136). This is a restatement of Boethius's distinction between that which is self-evident per se and that which is self-evident to us. In Alan's hands it becomes an understated reminder of the limitations of an understanding that does not correspond to and grow in proportion to its object. The understanding one may have of God is for Alan only by remotion, distinct from understanding properly speaking. He even raises questions about the possibility of a true understanding of God in heaven. In the end, he gives no positive account of how such understanding will work in response to arguments that it is impossible, but simply affirms his belief that it will occur (*SQH* 8c. 137–8e. 139).

It follows, Alan argues, that if God is incomprehensible, he is unnamable. Alan's arguments for this proposition sound like those he offers in the *Regulae*. God is form without form because he is the form of forms, cause without cause because he is the cause of causes. Since names are given from form, no name can be appropriate to God (*SQH* 9. 140–41).

Moreover, he argues, all terms created for and proper to natural things must be transferred (*translate*) to God and are thus improperly applied to God. So there is the gap between saying and being, like that between understanding and being (*SQH* 9. 141). For, more is in the thing than can be captured by the understanding, and more is in the understanding than can be explained in words (*SQH* 9. 140). This relationship between being, understanding, and saying seems to hold for Alan regardless of whether the object is natural or divine. But, Alan notes that the disproportion between simplicity of God and the multiplicity of names and effects of God exacerbates these gaps (*SQH* 9. 141).

God is unnamable to the degree that God is not even named by the name he gives himself, "*ego sum qui sum*" (Ex. 3: 14). Alan does concede that *est* is "least improperly" applied to God, but he claims that *est* is said of God "not by reason of the signifying, but by reason of the signified, not from a propriety of saying but a propriety of being" (*SQH* 9b. 143). This is the same distinction found in the *Regulae*, that God "is" or "is just" properly but is improperly said to be so. In both contexts Alan invokes the distinction to leave the worlds of saying and being far apart even while arguing for a kind of appropriateness of this name of God.

An objection tries to align God and the names of God by arguing that those names are proper to God which cannot truly be said of anything other than God, for example, eternal (*SQH* 9a. 142). Alan answers this by making a distinction between proper and true names. True names are those that follow the truth of being (*veritas essendi*) while proper names follow the propriety of saying (*proprietas dicendi*); names such as "eternal" are "proper" without being "true" (*SQH* 9c. 144). Alan thus rejects the notion that proper names, in which one name maps onto one thing, are the paradigm of successful language. He rejects it, firstly, because the giving and using of proper names is more about conventions of naming than the nature of the objects named, and, secondly, because naming, even proper naming of God, still tells us more about the being of creatures than the being of God.

Having rejected the possibility that common or proper nouns might properly signify God, Alan goes on to consider whether demonstrative pronouns might correctly signify God. The objector argues as follows: since demonstrative pronouns signify substance without qualities, such pronouns do not, as other nouns do, attribute to God the possession of properties as qualities distinct from his substance. Moreover, the mutability of corruptible things makes "demonstration" of them impossible (the "that" one points to is constantly changing into something else), but God is immutable and, hence, supremely there to be named ostensively (*SQH* 9a. 142). Alan's response lets stand the contrast between God and creatures in terms of stability and substance but argues that there is nevertheless no demonstration of God because he cannot be shown either to sense or intellect (*SQH* 9c. 144). Creatures cannot truly be called a "this" since they are always changing from this to that. In the case of God, the problem originates from the side of the human knower, who can have no immediate and present connection to God as a "this."

The third objection Alan constructs is one which tries to bring the world of being and language into symmetry by arguing in the opposite direction, from a kind of nominalism. If words are instituted to signify *ad placitum*, the objector argues, names could also simply be instituted to signify the creator properly (*SQH* 9. 142). Alan replies, "Where there is a failure in understanding the signified, there is also a failure in the power of signifying" (*SQH* 9c. 144). Thus, we cannot for Alan simply obviate the difficulty by re-conforming language and declaring victory. There must be a link between language and being, between what we say and what we understand. Like Boethius and many others, Alan seems to fall into some kind of moderated realism. But I think he does so not so much to solve the problem as to carve it into even starker relief. It is as if Alan wants to maximize the difficulty—language is neither conformed nor arbitrarily related to reality. Thus nothing can be exactly right but not just anything will do. Words and things, like lovers, cannot be perfectly matched but are unable to lapse into complete and carefree promiscuity.

Alan intensifies the problem by stating it in its starkest terms: can *any* name by extension be attributed to both creature and creator? In the long and complicated debate which follows, Alan's consistent answer is in the negative. Taking up the language of battle from the prologue, Alan writes, "We destroy [*perimimus*] all such statements as 'creator and creature are,' or 'are something', or 'are substances', and the like" (*SQH* 10. 145). The equivocation in applying "is," "something," and "substance" to God and creatures is at least as strong as that involved in the use of the word "dog" to describe the barking animal and sea creature, Alan continues (*SQH* 10. 145).[27] One cannot, Alan claims, even say God and creatures are two since that would make the divine being part of a binary relation. Alan seems to be in direct dialogue with Prepositinus here, who poses exactly the same question. Prepositinus compiles a list of things commonly and authoritatively said about God and argues that they cannot even be said unless there is some term common to God and creatures. God cannot even be distinguished from creatures without some common term. So, for example, Prepositinus notes that Augustine distinguishes between things to be used and enjoyed, only God belonging to the latter class, but, he argues, saying this requires that "thing" or "*res*" be applied both to God and creatures.[28] Alan rejects Prepositinus's common sense way of retaining our ability to say anything about God, embracing the paradoxical consequences that make it then impossible to describe even God's difference from creatures.

In his explanation of place as applied to God, Alan goes so far as to imply that the transfer of meaning is so radical that the meaning of the predicate does not just change but can come to mean its opposite. Angels, because they are spiritual, cannot be said to move, Alan explains, but they can be said to move if this is understood negatively, since they are not immense and do not fill all places. Thus they can be said to move "by comparison to God." In this sense, "they are said to move from place to place, just as the stars from God's perspective are not said to be refined, however much in themselves they are refined." By way of explanation he refers to the book of Job (4: 18); in this passage Eliphaz asks Job how any human being can be just before God when "in his angels he finds deformity" (*SQH* 14. 153). Alan explains that angels are just in themselves but *unjust* compared to God. The implication is that if *angels* are unjust in relation to God, human beings are yet more radically unjust. And if angels are characterized as moving because they are finite and not present everywhere, human beings, again, are even more deeply finite. If humans are called just, then we must say that God is not just; if God is called just, we must say that humans are not just. But neither claim can stand alone; each needs the complementary negation to make clear its limitations.

"Toward the Purification of War"[29]

For Alan, then, there is no perspective from which the same term can stretch from us to God or vice versa. Thus Alan takes the outline of his discussion from Boethius's application and transformation of the ten categories to God in *De trinitate* but reshapes it radically. Boethius's project in both the tractates and the *Consolation* is to build a bridge between divine and human perspectives, to make the journey from one to the other. Boethius notes, in the end, the unfinished and unfinishable character of that project, but Alan is driven to highlight the necessity of its failure, because he thinks that this failure has gone from being understated to disappearing altogether from the work of theologians. Peter the Chanter, Prepositinus, and Gilbert claimed to have made the transition from lower to higher perspective, to have achieved a theological perspective. For them, once the distinction is made between theological use of language and that of other disciplines, there are no troubling reverberations further down the line. Alan makes clear that taking the theological perspective does not just have reverberations but creates earthquakes and tidal waves throughout the lower realms of the liberal arts.

God will not fit into the straight jacket of natural and proper language, nor can language throw off the shape of creatures, which it was originally cut to fit. The result is an asymmetry of staggering proportions between language and God. Language cannot be purged of the old associations that are fused into both its syntax and semantics; thus, it cannot be made to signify the totally other God, to whom none of these structures apply. Here, as in the *Regulae*, Alan attempts to correct both vices, joining and separating theological and natural language. He joins them so that the theologian knows whence he has come (and whither he cannot progress), but separates them by making them incommensurable perspectives. Where Prepositinus asserts univocation and Gilbert a "proportionate" transfer from the other disciplines to theology, Alan argues that there is only equivocation. There is no way of dispensing with one or the other of the perspectives, nor any smooth transition from one to the other. So, unmediated, they are placed side by side, producing, like the *Regulae*, a kind of vertigo. In the *Summa* it is, if you will, the vertigo produced by being on the ground and looking up to a great height; one cannot gaze upward comfortably for long, the urge to blink, to look away at something of more human proportions is irresistible.

As in the *Regulae*, the vertigo produced by the *Summa* is in significant part created by the form these reflections take. The disputation promises answers and the harmonization of dissonant sources; it promises further that both can be arrived at through the use of the methods, terminology, and distinctions of the liberal arts. In the *Summa*, Alan engages in disputation to argue for the incomprehensibility and unnamability of God, playing the result of his disputation off the expectations one might have of its form, using arguments to show the insufficiency of argument. Alan in effect concludes that God cannot coherently be the subject of disputation, at least not a conventional disputation that is supposed to result in a determination of the question. As promised in his prologue, he has engaged more in a defense of Lady Theology against theologians making untoward advances than in making any such advances himself. Of course, Alan is well aware that he *has* made God the subject of disputation exactly by disputing that God cannot be comprehended or named. The *demonstration* or proof of incomprehensibility is a paradox of which one cannot suppose Alan, the master of oxymoron and paradox, to be unaware. Of course, a proof of what is not subject to proof is possible, but such a proof reveals as much about the weakness of the method as about the subject considered. Alan, however, is no fundamentalist; he does not wish to stop the practice of disputation on such topics. Nor does he hold himself off to the side as a noncombatant, unsullied by the battle, even though he believes that ultimate victory, the comprehension of God, cannot be won by these means.

Most commentators have tended to underplay Alan's remarks that God is unnamable, that no terms can be transferred from nature to God.[30] Such a view, they argue, would be inconsistent with the belief Alan obviously has in the efficacy and value of trying to speak about God. But this conflates a relatively negative theology (which I think Alan's is) with the view of the so-called *nominales*, for whom the result of the failure of all language to reach God is despairing silence.[31] Ziolkowski shares this view of Alan as a negative theologian; however, though he notes many of the negative comments Alan makes throughout his allegories and theological works, he maintains that Alan's project is to show how words *can* be transferred from the arts to theology. For Ziolkowski and Evans, once Alan has issued his warnings about the need to shift natural language in theology, he has "remov[ed] a hurdle that had been holding back theologians for centuries," solving the problem of theological language.[32]

My view is that Alan's mission consists neither in advancing the techniques of grammar and dialectic to contribute to the "progress" of academic theology, nor in "solving" theological problems. It is not an *inability* to solve a problem that induces Alan, as Evans puts it, to "take refuge in a cloud of words," but rather Alan's desire to show that fully satisfactory solutions are in principle impossible.[33] The "cloud of words" is a reminder of that necessary failure, and a theology that knows and displays its limits is, like Socratic ignorance, one step better than one that is deluded about what it can achieve. There *is* a language most appropriate (i.e., least *in*appropriate) to God—language that signals its own inappropriateness. Alan does not reject the project of reason to know the truth; like Socrates, he is engaged in disabusing us of the notion that it has been completed. His contribution is neither to call off the battle nor achieve victory; rather it is "toward the purification of war." Kenneth Burke uses this epigram to suggest that instead of looking for supposed "cures" for our condition, we should learn to "enjoy our symptoms." There is in Alan a similar pessimism mixed with enjoyment that displays itself not just in Alan's disputations but also in his axioms and, we shall see, in his theological definitions and allegories as well.

Liber in distinctionibus dictionum theologicalium: The Wonder of Words

The Prologue: Wandering Words

Alan's book of *distinctiones* is a compilation of meanings of terms from scripture. It is perhaps the most neglected of his major works, but it is, in my view, as creative and significant as any of them. The neglect is partially due to the genre of *distinctiones*, which even those who study the development of methods and textual forms for Scripture study find puzzling. Richard and Mary Rouse argue that distinction collections formed a crucial stage in the movement from the tradition of gloss and commentary on Scripture to the development of a full-blown verbal concordance. The distinction collections were among the first alphabetically arranged texts, beginning the process of replacing memory with "artificial finding devices" and making possible the "thematic" sermon, whose popularity in turn fueled the demand for more distinction collections.[34] While conceding that such collections were in demand and being made for at least a century, the Rouses nonetheless find the form "an oddity of quickly passing importance, one of those ideas whose time has come and, long since, gone."[35] I concede that Alan's book is odd, but I would like to consider that oddity in terms of the rest of Alan's work and in terms of the larger development of academic theology.

Alan's prologue to the dictionary makes a very strong statement about the context in which the work is to be understood. It begins with the citation from Aristotle that he who is ignorant of the power of words will quickly fall into paralogy, a danger exacerbated in theology. In theology, Alan writes, words "wander [*peregrinantur*] from their proper signification"; "nouns are made into pronouns, adjectives become substantives, verbs are no longer a sign by which something is said of another, where predicates no longer inhere in subjects, subjects are without matter, affirmations are improper, negations true . . . ." (*Dict.* 687B–C). The characterizations of noun, adjective, verb, subject, and predicate in this passage are specific denials of the standard definitions from the grammar of Priscian and early speculative grammarians.[36] Thus nouns, which signify substance with a quality, lose their particular form or determination and become content-free pronouns. Adjectives come to signify substance and not just quality because God is his qualities substantially.[37] Verbs, which ordinarily name the act but not its subject, signify both of God.[38] In theology the predicate does not inhere in the subject, and the subject itself is not material.[39] Thus, theological propositions contradict the most basic structure of ordinary predication: the inherence of the predicate in the subject and the reception of form and definition by the undetermined material subject from the predicate.

The prologue also makes broad claims about the limitations of the arts of language when transferred to theology and applied to Scripture. In Scripture, "where constructions are not subject to the laws of Donatus," "metaphor [*translatio*] is alienated from the rules of Cicero," "the proposition wanders [*peregrina*] from Aristotle's schema [*documento*]"; "in faith argument is far from reason" (*Dict.* 687B–C). The contradiction of the standards of the *trivium* in theology not only refer to *the* author who represents these arts in each case, but also, Alan puns, on the nature of the transgression in each case. *The* construction of grammar is the "subjection" of subject to predicate, yet this specific hierarchy is denied in theology. All tropes or *translations* involve the "alienation" of a name from its proper subject, but here *translatio* itself is alienated from the rules properly governing such transfers.

Lastly, propositions in theology are estranged from the *documento* of Aristotle. By "*documento*" Alan could mean the Aristotelian schema of the categories or syllogistic figures. Thus, for the three verbal arts Alan reiterates the principle that he applies to all seven of the arts in his well-known poem, "De incarnatione Christi," concluding for each one, "In hac Verbi copula/ Stupet omnis regula."[40]

We can easily trace each of the broken rules concerning the parts of speech and sentence structure back to the rules of theology in the *Regulae* or the arguments about the divine names in the *Summa*.[41] Alan thus links the project of the *Distinctiones* with his works in systematic theology. But this work also has a specific task—the correction of three types of error: false interpretations, which could confirm the errors of heretics, literal understandings, which prevent the conversion of the Jews, and, interpretations of which the theologian might become proud. His antidote to these errors is this work, dedicated "to distinguish[ing] the significations of theological words" and bringing to light hidden and metaphorical significations (*Dict.* 687C–688B).

Moreover, the dictionary is designed to provide different benefits to those with different needs, much like Scripture itself. It is offered "to invite the less intelligent, inspire the sluggish, and delight the more experienced" (*Dict.* 688B). In the *Summa* and *Regulae*, Alan is writing for his fellow theologians; here he writes to attract others to the study of Scripture, both those who find it too foreboding, and those who find it insufficiently sophisticated and challenging for their skills. Thus if the *Summa* is for correction and the *Regulae* to create a sense of awe and distance, the *Distinctiones* is to allure. Unlike the *Regulae* and *Summa*, this work is explicitly exoteric; it offers access "so that a freer introduction for sacred scripture might be extended," so that Scripture "might be understood in an easier way" (*Dict.* 688B). As we shall see, Alan's invitation is a genuine one, but the world to which he invites his readers is one they will find strange indeed. He does not need to hide a world that will itself put off the unworthy.

The Entries: The Abyss of Meaning

Even a cursory look at the entries in Alan's collection shows the same kind of variety as he saw in the readers he hoped to attract. Some entries are short and clear explanations of difficult or rare words. Some are tremendously long and complex entries for rather simple words. Some of these complex entries seem constructed to emphasize the broadly different, even contradictory meanings a term can have. Some are constructed largely around moral rather than doctrinal themes; others are almost scholastic in tone, making "distinctions" of the type with which we are more familiar.

Most keep Alan's opening promise: that words stray from and "wonder at" their new meanings in theology.

While many entries begin by giving the meaning Alan describes as *proprie*, often that meaning is figurative by our standards. For example, the first and proper meaning of *frumentum* is Christ (*Dict.* 799C), of *fumus*, prayer (*Dict.* 800C), of *nidus* (nest), the sanctified body of Christ (*Dict.* 874A). As Gillian Evans notes, Alan's use of the designation *proprie* in this way "turns much of contemporary opinion on its head."[42] For Alan's contemporaries, the "proper" meaning is the technical meaning circumscribed by the arts, but for Alan, theology has its own propriety radically different from, and even contradictory to, the propriety of the arts.

The entries under *agere* show a breadth of uses which tends strongly toward equivocity. "To act" encompasses everything from God's activity, where it means something like "authority," to human activity which is really a kind of passion (*Dict.* 695C–696A). For the last meaning, Alan quotes Paul's lament, "I do not do the good I want, but the evil I do not want is what I do" (Rom. 7: 20). Thus God's action follows the model of Genesis—God spoke and it was so, without any intermediate effort, motion, or struggle, while human action can only be done in great struggle and the effort is often utterly ineffectual.

The entry for *coelum* (the heavens) lists as meanings everything from the firmament to celestial judgment, the pride of hypocrites, sacred Scripture, God, the apostles, and the human mind (*Dict.* 744B–745B). The entry for *caro* (flesh) is a minisermon against various forms of a life of the flesh, while the entry for *concupiscere* offers Alan the opportunity to construct a minischolastic account of the place of desire in the path toward sin (*Dict.* 748C–749A). The length and detail of some entries, like that for *abyssus*, reflect the words for which Alan has a special penchant. For *abyssus*, Alan begins with the standard "proper" meaning but spends almost two columns describing the different ways in which things may have a depth beyond human penetration. Thus, it can mean everything from the depths of sin, the depraved human body, the cunning of the devil, to the depths of meaning and coherence between the two testaments (*Dict.* 689D–691B).

The diversity of the entries does, then, correspond to the different needs of his readers. Alan gives clear and short explanations of difficult or rare words for the beginner or less intelligent reader, and complex and diverse entries for more ordinary words to combat the pride of those who think they understand everything. Others serve to provoke the interest of those lacking it, and the admiration and delight of every reader of Scripture. But the diversity of types of entries leaves the reader a bit dizzy, increasing the sense that perhaps indeed anything goes in theology as words take on a baffling set of new meanings and uses.

The Many Definitions of Nature

Most entries are constructed around scriptural passages rather than the writings of other theologians. However, Alan does include entries based on Boethius and uses scholastic distinctions alongside those tied to Scripture. Both are signs that he does not draw a sharp line, as later theologians do, between the books of the Bible and writings of later church fathers and masters, and between a biblical and scholastic or philosophical use of language. The entry on *natura* is a much expanded version of Boethius's numerous definitions of nature from the *Contra Eutychen et Nestorius*.[43]

The form and context in which Alan places these Boethian definitions and examples makes them seem almost perversely chosen, more designed to illustrate the inadequacy of the definitions than to display the order and intelligibility of a family of concepts presented by Boethius. Boethius lays out these definitions in order to distinguish and relate different senses so that he can use the term, once carefully defined, to argue for and explain his account of Christ's nature and person. Without the Boethian context we notice in Alan's account, for example, that God and matter, given under the definition of nature as what is intelligible, are exactly what we *cannot* understand. We realize that God, mentioned under the definition of nature as what can act or suffer, surely does not suffer and acts in a way peculiar to himself. And, we see that the definition of nature as giving specific difference is applied to Christ, who has two natures, neither of which is born in the natural way.

Alan also makes his own additions to Boethius. Nature can mean origin, for which he cites the angels' original nature capable of sin, that is, having free will to do good or evil. But the original nature of angels is exactly what has changed and stands now in an irreversible state dividing the angels into those that fell and those who did not. Nature can mean the nature of physical things as assuming diverse forms and as complex, and so in this sense is the opposite of the indissoluble natures just mentioned. Nature can mean that into which one grows, that is, that which is *not* original; in this sense, custom is second nature, and mortality and vice are natural to human being. Next Alan notes the "heat of nature" (fever), "which is said to be the fight between sickness and nature." He lists "the reason of nature," the natural law of reason written on the hearts of the gentiles, but also cites the "natural instinct" according to which St. Paul writes, "I only do that which I do not want" (Rom. 7: 15–16). And, lastly, Alan adds, nature can mean the natural potency of things to reproduce their like, to be made according to nature. For this sense he cites not an example but a counterexample: the creator being made creature in the Incarnation.

Alan's definitions added to Boethius's list construct the narrative of fall, sin, and redemption. We are told of an original nature having freedom before being changed by sin, and of a nature acquired through sin, that is, mortality. The law of reason or nature can mean both the law inclining nature toward virtue and the law inclining nature against one's will toward vice. The story ends with the account of the non-natural transformation of creator into creature. Alan thus adds more tension to a line of definitions stretching from God to matter in Boethius. He constructs it to tell the same story, that of the Incarnation but tells it in an entirely different way. In Alan's entry, things seem to be struggling to break away from nature, sometimes for ill (the fall), sometimes for good (the Incarnation), and the concept of nature can barely contain the story it is supposed to tell.

The entry as a whole and in its parts, placing side-by-side the most diverse "natures" and definitions of natures, strives, I think, for diversity and breadth of meaning, brought so far that the unity of the term "nature" threatens to shatter into equivocity. One might object that Alan did not intend such an outcome but merely searches for the senses of *natura* insofar as they have a role to play in theology. But this is exactly my point (and, I think, Alan's): within theology, the meanings and uses of the term "nature" are radically different from its uses in the other disciplines. And if my suspicion about the story Alan's definitions tell is at all plausible, then Alan is also saying that the definitions, heterogeneous as they are, do form some kind of whole, some coherent and related set of meanings. They tell *the* story, the one told by Scripture, a story in which the natural view of nature is completely destroyed.

Gilbert of Poitiers takes up a very different strategy. His commentary on Boethius's *Contra Eutychen et Nestorium* painstakingly explains and expands each one of Boethius's definitions. But he also attempts to order them. Gilbert argues that there are three different classes of things that can be said to have natures in different ways; we may use nature in one way to designate subsisting beings, in another way to designate bodily things, and in still another, to designate specific differences.[44] Gilbert's point is to put the brakes on the slippage of the term by dividing off the senses from each other, because if he lets them stand together, the result would be exactly the paradoxes Alan's juxtaposition of uses points to. Alan's way of placing these meanings seems to create or at least emphasize slippage, adding to the list and omitting any attempt to order the many meanings.

I have spent so much time on this one entry because, first, of all the entries it has aroused some interest in the secondary literature perhaps because it sounds more scholastic than the others.[45] Second and more importantly, "nature" is a key notion philosophically and for Alan. It is key, of course, for the discussion on which Alan's entry is based, Boethius's *Contra Eutychen et Nestorium* and its account of the two "natures" of Christ. But it is key in a deeper sense. Alan's additions to Boethius's lists of definitions make clear that Christianity redefines nature, breaking down a single human nature into different natures defined by their relationship to the double-natured Christ, nature before and after the Fall, nature before and after salvation through the Incarnation. In the same way, Alan's two allegories are both concerned with nature, with the descent below nature into vice and with the ascent above nature to God, and with nature herself as unstable enough to break down and as insufficient enough to require transcending.

Distinction collections and theological language

For Richard and Mary Rouse, distinction collections embody the transition from one notion of order, a rational one based on logical and content-based connections, to another notion, based merely on the alphabet.[46] The form is characterized by the at least partial alphabetizing of entries as well as the juxtaposition and confusion (at least to modern sensibilities) of proper and figurative meanings of terms.[47] What are compiled are not *meanings* in some ordinary sense at all, but *uses* that are both very different from each other and from non-biblical uses, uses which are the elements of allegorical readings of Scripture.

What is especially interesting is the tension between these two models of order, the rational and alphabetical. For the rational (i.e., logical and content based) order on which these collections are based is the polysemy of Scripture: words and the things named in Scripture have many meanings. While we might tolerate such an order within the context of, say, a sermon of Bernard of Clairvaux, in the context of the more modern, scientific form of the encyclopedia, the *distinctiones*' system of order seems fanciful and even perverse. For modern readers of Alan, the rational order organizing his text no longer seems either rational or ordered.

Both orders operating in *distinctiones* collections are linguistic; it is linguistic in terms of the ordering principle given, the alphabet, and it is also linguistic in terms of the ordering principle that grounds the symbolic reading of Scripture: that material things are signifiers of God. But the two linguistic modes clash with each other because the encyclopedia form, like the Aristotelian categories, has as its *telos* classification *tout court*. The medieval practice of reading Scripture allegorically has *meaning* as its *telos*, not an understanding of the thing in itself, but the thing as a sign of God. It was, Louis Mackey notes, Bonaventure's conviction that a view of the world as classified or sorted into genera and species à la Aristotle is incompatible with a view of the world as signifying God that led him to reject Aristotle.[48] Because he pre-dates the recovery of the full Aristotelian corpus, Alan did not face the dilemma in that radical a form. Nonetheless,

Alan seems aware of the tension between this more atomistic and analytical way of thinking embodied in the dictionary form and the allegorical reading of Scripture. Alan uses the analytical order to subvert it and subsume it under the ordering dictated by Scripture.

The distinction collections mark a transition not only in the development of Scripture commentary but also of scholastic theology. Chenu argues that there is an "epistemological continuity between the biblical type of symbolic imagery used to name God or describe his mysteries and the purely conceptual type of analogy used as a technical instrument for coming to know transcendent realities and truths."[49] The different meanings of terms listed in distinction collections are the precursors for more hierarchical, ordered, and controlled shifts of meaning, like that found in Aquinas's theory of analogy. Distinction collections are also part of the development of the scholastic technique of solving difficulties by making a distinction, usually and probably originally, by making a distinction between two or more meanings of a word. Chenu's point in linking *distinctiones* collections and thirteenth-century developments in scholastic distinction and analogy is to show a trajectory moving from the twelfth century toward a scientific theology in the thirteenth. But those links can and should be read backward as well. Notions of analogy and the making of distinctions are linked to the fertile, even overgrown, verbal garden of the distinction collections, and more generally to the tradition of the polysemy of Scripture. These "scientific" developments are linked, then, to uses of language now viewed as literary or improper rather than philosophical or scientific. They form a link between what Newman calls "imaginative theology" and scholastic/analytic theology.[50]

Richard and Mary Rouse report that we have no information on how Alan's or other books of *distinctiones* were composed, whether Alan, for example, had other kinds of related collections to draw from.[51] D'Alverny surmises that Alan's collection is elaborated notes from his courses.[52] If so, this would mean that Alan rearranged his own work, taking from courses on various parts of Scripture and turning them into an alphabetized list of terms. Such an origin would explain the unevenness of the entries in terms of length, tone, and detail. The resulting dictionary reads like a free composition based on Alan's memory of passages and terms and gives the impression of a *tour de force*. Alan clearly enjoys the challenge of rearranging his biblical knowledge and Scripture itself according to the completely arbitrary categories of the letters of the alphabet. He also revels in the way in which terms are used in Scripture in one place in a way that bears little or no relation to their use in other passages.

Alan's collection, in contrast to that of the roughly contemporary Peter the Chanter, strives for maximum tension between the different uses and interpretations of terms, pushing the words themselves to the point where the list of meanings seems almost to embrace contradictories.[53] As Evans puts it, "the two masters agree upon exactly what was important and must be included, and entirely disagree on what was to be said about it."[54] Peter's task is to master ambiguity, to show the commonsense rules by which the language of Scripture and theology can be mastered; Alan's is to illustrate the destruction of all such rules in theology. The fabric Alan weaves ("*textetur*" is the word he uses to describe the composition in his prologue) from these arbitrarily thrown together threads resembles a quilt rather than a tapestry. Often no pattern, no single or family resemblance of meaning emerges from the juxtaposition of different uses of the same word.

The presupposition of Alan's virtuoso performance is the Augustinian principle that Scripture tells one story overall and in all its parts. Augustine's hermeneutical theory and practice for Scripture is that every passage has multiple meanings. These multiple meanings, like the many roads to Rome, all lead to the same single truth told over and over again in different ways in all the parts of Scripture.[55] Taken to its logical conclusion, this comes to a view of Scripture as synecdochic, that its whole meaning is expressed in each one of its parts. Alan takes this principle of Augustine's hermeneutics and exaggerates it to become the conceit of the *Distinctiones*.[56] Because of the underlying unity of meaning, Scripture will not break down into babble even under the pressure of a form that breaks it down into separate words and whose account of those words gives them wildly different "proper" theological meanings.

In Alan's *distinctiones* collection, the multiple meanings for words with which we have been concerned since beginning with Boethius reach a kind of breaking point and with it comes the kind of vertigo produced by Alan's *Regulae* and *Summa*. Alan gives his reader the experience Reason and Prudence entering heaven in the *Anticlaudianus* have, a sense of being in a totally new place in which up and down, proper and improper are reversed. Alan's *distinctiones* collection echoes the view of theological language he expresses in his other theological works. For the *Summa* and *Regulae* argue that there are no terms that can be extended from creature to God. Alan's dictionary goes to the proof of such a view.

The prologue to the *distinctiones* describes theology as a place where all the rules of language are broken. Alan introduces every clause describing the deficits, transformations, and contraventions of language in Scripture with *ubi*, and sets as his task the undermining of all ordinary notions of how that linguistic and rational space is constructed. So Alan's prologue describes the destruction of the linguistic categories marking all other disciplines, and the text which follows constructs a totally new and different space, imitating the omnipresence (and omniabsence) of God in the way the things of

Scripture signify God. Place is the conceit of Alan's favorite definition of God as "an intelligible sphere whose circumference is everywhere and whose center is nowhere" (*Reg.* 7). Alan's *distinctiones* create of the sense of God as being signified everywhere, just as the *Summa* and *Regulae* make the point that God is signified nowhere. Both the distance between the thing and the thing *as* sign of God, and between the thing as sign of God and God, are, to use one of Alan's favorite expressions, an abyss. Alan reminds his reader constantly of these abysses. He does this, firstly, to counteract the repression of them he sees taking place in the work of other theologians. He does so, secondly, to produce delight at the way the distance is both traversed and widened by the myriad ways in which the creature represents God, calling to mind the metaphor paradoxically become true in the Incarnation.

The Allegories and the Proper Impropriety of Theology

The traditional way of reading allegory is to see it as the tool of the moralist, asserting the correspondence of words and things and, thus, the rules of right action and signification. This has been the dominant way of inter-preting Alan's allegories, putting down their eccentricities to the excesses of their overzealous author.[57] Even Jan Ziolkowski, whose concern is the background and significance of Alan's use of grammar as a metaphor for sex, insists on the seriousness of moral purpose in Alan (as opposed to the playful, erotic, and satirical uses of such metaphors in antiquity). He con-cludes that *De planctu* "warns of the retribution that verbal decadence receives, while [the *Anticlaudianus*] enumerates the rewards in store for the person who refines his knowledge of grammar, logic, and the other *artes.*"[58]

Some recent critics, influenced by post-structuralism, however, have seen allegory very differently, not as moral but as radically undermining the possibility of a regulative nature and proper and stable norms of significa-tion and interpretation.[59] Rather allegory places those very norms in doubt by the very explicit artificiality with which they are asserted and the complex and unending reflexivity with which they are used and abused. A group of recent interpreters of Alan notice the way in which Alan's own use of language seems to transgress the rules he lays down; hence, they conclude, the poem's prohibitions against sexual deviance (especially homosexuality) fail, or at least do not succeed on the grounds they are supposed to: that it is against the laws of nature just as grammatical errors are against the laws of grammar.[60]

Both sets of readers, modernist and postmodernist, miss part of the story in my view. These recent critics, mostly interested in Alan's views on homosexuality and, therefore, in *De planctu naturae*, do not engage in any careful reading of Alan's theological project; only Jordan seems to have read Alan's other works, but he does so only to search for Alan's views on sexuality.[61] While they all notice Alan's playful and self-conscious language having to do with sex, they do not seem to notice that his language of God has exactly the same quality. On the other hand, those on the other side, arguing for Alan's moralism founded on nature, ignore or criticize aspects of Alan's writing—its reflexivity, playfulness, and artificiality—that seem to contradict that straightforward message.

The case I would like to make here is that, like the theological works considered above, Alan's allegories both assert and undermine the norms of morality and signification. In these poems Alan combines the seriousness of moral and intellectual purpose associated with humanism and rationalism— to know the truth and do the good—with the corrosive playfulness and reflexivity of the ironist and skeptic. Here, as in the theological works, Alan shows that he is committed to the efficacy of the project of using reason and the arts to reach God. Yet he also shows his skepticism about the ability of language to capture reality.[62] Alan's allegories cover subjects much bigger than the small island of nature, over which reason and language are designed to reign, and work to prevent human pretensions to exaggerate their own ability to understand and capture that reality.

As in the three theological works examined above, Alan uses a recognized school form, in this case, the didactic allegorical poem, and uses it against itself to show what the form cannot possibly take in and explain. The didactic poems Alan imitated were designed to show the nature of the arts and illustrate their rules in an easy, accessible way through the allegorization of the arts themselves. They were used to teach beginning grammar students the rules of the trivium. Alan allegorizes the arts and nature in his poems but spends much of the two poems describing what falls outside the arts: vice and God. Vice and God confound the rules for allegory; they cannot be straightfor- wardly represented because they do not obey the rules of nature or language. These two poems thus represent yet another instance of the tactic of "fighting fire with fire"—using poetry and myth to critique and rewrite some of the uses to which poetry and myth have been put. They appropriate a form and make its content not the material of the arts but of theology to show how the subject of theology exceeds and distorts the form that tries to contain it.

The Symmetry of Opposites: Falling Below and Rising Above Nature

Vice and Trope, Ungrammatical and Figurative Language
in De planctu naturae
De planctu naturae is a lament for the fall of human nature. Vices, most often sexual sins, are figured as improper grammatical constructions, and the

nature they violate is allegorized as Lady Nature who "wrote" the script of nature and (unwisely) turned it over to Venus to trace. The Nature we meet here is unlike Bernard Silvestris's Nature in the *Cosmographia*. Alan brings us to see Nature as she beholds her fallen handiwork, while we meet Bernard's Nature in the midst of an apparently successful creation of both universe and man.[63] While Bernard adds qualifications to his optimistic scheme just as Alan adds panegyrics to nature, the place in the narrative of creation and fall they choose to allegorize is telling. Alan thinks Bernard and others like him need a reminder that the present state is fallen, not edenic.

The problem is to find a language to tell the story of the fall from nature into vice; in order to describe what falls outside nature, language must go outside the rules of the arts. Alan finds his vehicle in the rules of grammar. Thus, Alan opens by allegorizing sexual sin as the double application of the same term, as a *translatio* of one term to that to which it does not properly belong. In homosexuality, the male is subject and predicate, Alan explains; it "extends [*ampliat*] too far the laws of grammar" (*DP* 1. 68; 20). So Alan warns, "Grammar does not find favor with him, but rather a trope. This transposition [*translatio*], however, cannot be called a trope. The figure here more correctly falls into the category of defect [*vicium*]" (*DP* 1. 68; 22–24). Ziolkowski brings the technical meanings of *tropus, translatio,* and *vitium* from Donatus's *Ars grammatica* to bear on this dense passage. For Donatus a trope is a term "carried over [*translata*]" from its proper signification to an improper one; tropical or figurative language (such as metaphor or *translatio*) falls outside of accepted usage but is excusable on the grounds of ornament or necessity. *Vitium*, on the other hand, while also an improper usage, is "an unpardonable aberration in aim, that is, in the author's purpose in writing."[64] Thus, Alan berates men for preferring trope to proper grammatical usage and, further, for letting that trope become vice, which neither supplements nor makes up for a gap in nature or language but remains an improper and pointless straying from nature/ grammar. Both tropes and barbarisms, beatitude and sin, are "extensions" of grammar and of nature, both outside of the law.

Nature bans the figurative along with the un-grammatical, she says, because of the tendency of *tropus* to turn to *vitium*, "elegance to villainy," "refinement into boorishness," and "color into discoloration" (*DP* 10. 162; 113–14). The danger of a slide from color into discoloration is created, according to Alan, when Rhetoric "embarks on a harsh transposition [*dure translationis*] and transfers [*alienet*] the predicate from its loudly protesting subject to something else" (*DP* 10. 162; 112–13). Nature responds by legislating strict marital fidelity, by banning figurative language along with vice because it creates an atmosphere of flirtation in which radical promiscuity might arise. The possibility of infidelity, the separability of signifier from signified, of subject from proper predicate is, according to the allegory, practically as original as their conjugal bliss.

Nature nonetheless concedes the *honor* of Rhetoric's metonymies, implying that improper names belong to their subjects on some level of appropriateness (*DP* 10. 162; 111). Alan's description of the *honor* of metonymy and the *honestas* of figures restates the ambiguity of Nature's law. For the "honorable" is both that which is proper and thus, we might say, natural, but it also designates a kind of beauty or grace that goes beyond mere correctness. Figure occupies a similarly ambiguous position in the *Anticlaudianus*; she is not exiled as mere mistakes are, but she sleeps outside Grammar's door asking for indulgence. She is ultimately admitted but not welcomed by Art. In verse (*metrum*), the poem notes, grammar's rules are suspended as words are transformed in ways that look very much like the mistakes of vice, for example, changing form, pronunciation, and adding and losing letters (*AC* 2. 86; 421–23, 440–48). The tropic relation of terms is a fundamentally ambivalent one; its unusual appropriateness gives delight but opens the door to more unorthodox combinations.

This ambivalence plays out in Nature's description of Desire in which she is forced to use figures. The task of "explaining Desire," Nature complains, is impossible. It amounts, she says, to the attempt to delimit the unlimited, explicate the inexplicable, and make known the unknowable. Desire is incapable of being captured by the methods of the arts—description, definition, or demonstration (*DP* 8. 148; 269–76). According to Nature, Desire, once let loose from its prescribed path, goes about joining the disparate and transforming otherwise stable natures. Desire makes man into woman, monk into adulterer; she so perverts nature that under her spell Ulysses becomes foolish, Ajax wise, and Nestor youthful (*DP* 9. 150–51; 28–34). Desire accomplishes these feats because her own nature, which is to join peace with hatred, hope with fear, and madness with reason, infects what it touches. *Amor*, here equated with *Cupido*, is described as "sweet shipwreck," "light burden," "delightful misfortune," and "pious misdeed" (*DP* 9. 149; 3, 8, 12). The first 18 lines of meter five consist of some forty-seven oxymora of this type, some of which Alan even reverses, claiming that love is, for example, both "delightful misfortune" and "unfortunate delight." The works of Desire, Alan summarizes, "effect miracles by antiphrasis" (*DP* 9. 150; 21. My translation). But Alan himself uses antiphrasis in his description of Desire's acts as "*miracula.*" Like miracles, Desire's acts are beyond the ordinary and natural, but they would be more properly called monstrous or vicious, falling below rather than rising above nature.

Nature explains that her own discourse both engages in a kind of impropriety by revealing these (improper) subjects, and stays within the bounds of propriety by concealing them in "charming diction" so as not to offend the virtuous. After giving her long series of oxymora describing Desire, she describes her own account as "theatrical," "jesting," and "lascivious" (*DP* 8. 143–44; 183–95; 10. 155; 17–20. My translation). In this case proper language, that is, language appropriate to and mirroring its subject, is improper because it is outside the bounds of appropriate usage. But equally, proper language, that which obeys the laws of the art of grammar, becomes improper because it is inappropriate to its improper subject. Nature is caught in a kind of double bind: if she tells the truth, she speaks improperly, but if she speaks properly, she lies.

There are, I think, strong resonances between the tropes Alan uses here, the combining of opposites in an oxymoron and the use of a word to mean its opposite in antiphrasis, and the transgressions and tropes Alan outlaws throughout the poem. Nature outlawed improper combinations of predicates with subjects, but she herself combines opposites in oxymora. The extraordinariness of his figurative language constructed to be "proper" to the subject of vice tends seductively toward deformity, imitating the slide from elegance to defect Nature tried unsuccessfully to forestall.[65]

The two parts of *De planctu* that have come in for the most criticism are its comparison of sexual sin to grammatical error and the long series of oxymora describing Desire. The former has often been seen as tasteless and even scabrous; the latter Wetherbee, for example, complains is "long and turgid."[66] Ziokowski defends Alan's use of grammar allegorically, noting that Alan is part of a tradition of such uses of grammar in the service of a moralist's message.[67] However, both Alan's detractors and defenders seem to ignore the self-consciously artificial character, the irony and self-parody of these poetic excesses which is, in my view, exactly their point.[68] It is also what makes the view of Alan as simple moralist unconvincing. Alan's poetry is sophisticated and exotic enough not only to be called into question but also to call itself into question.

In case we might doubt whether Alan means to suggest the likeness as well as proscribe the confusion of vice and sophisticated elegance, the persona of the poet in the poem asks Nature about this symmetry. Might not human deviation from nature, the creation of our own laws of language and love, be excused, even commended, as an imitation of divine creativity? Have not the gods, Alan asks, "translated" the human into the divine, as Jupiter transferred Ganymede both from human to divine and from boy to woman? (*DP* 8. 138–39; 117–19).[69]

Nature denies the likeness and places the blame for its plausibility on the vagaries of poets. They are known to present falsehood so boldly as to bewitch their audience, to cover falsehood with the veneer of probability, and to hide truth beneath a false or off-putting shell (*DP* 8. 139–40; 128–36).

This response maps out all possible combinations—apparent truth hiding falsehood, falsehood hiding truth, and falsehood hiding falsehood. The warnings about the wiliness of the poets to market falsehood as truth, as well as the ban on tropes, have been read as indictments of particular poetic excesses of Alan's time. Others have read Alan here as defending his own poetic practice under the description of hiding truth beneath a false shell.[70] But the only positive description of poetry that follows this description of the various forms of poetic dishonesty is very tentative. After her condemnations, Nature concedes the possibility of "more elegant" (she says nothing of their truth) combinations of history and fable the poets might construct. However, she immediately disqualifies poems that have entertained the possibility of multiple gods or sexual deviation among the gods (*DP* 8. 140; 137–39).

As an answer clearing up the apparent confusion of the elegant with the alluringly false, Nature's response is unsatisfying.[71] In lamenting the degree and types of deceit of which the poets are capable, she undermines the possibility of distinguishing between the truth and falsity of their discourse. For, Nature admits, the apparent truth or falsity of a discourse is no guide, not even a negative guide, to its real truth or falsity; what appears true is neither necessarily true nor even necessarily false, or vice versa. Thus, the poem gives no criteria for distinguishing between poetic truth and falsity, but also, since it uses figures to outlaw the use of figures, it offers no alternative to poetic discourse.[72]

Nature's inability to discern between the veneers of truth and falsity and the truth or falsity they hide beneath them is made even more pronounced when she compares herself to Scripture. Her own work is, she says, "set aside in the mystery of the second birth" brought about by God's saving act; the power of reasoning that works to discern the patterns of nature in these acts "languishes" (*DP* 6. 125; 145, 150). Hence, Nature continues, it is not surprising that theology "shows no close kinship with me" (*DP* 6. 125; 151–52). She concludes, "You can realize that in comparison with God's power, my power is powerless; you can know that my efficiency is deficiency; you can decide that my activity is worthless" (*DP* 6. 124; 131–39).[73] So not only Desire but also God causes things to merit opposite predicates. Though Nature claims that she and theology are simply *diversa*, not *adversa*, she goes on to list a number of their differences as oppositions. In theology the orders of faith and reason, assent and understanding are the opposite of that found in the arts; moreover, the intelligibility and importance of their subjects lie at opposite ends of the spectrum. Nature ends in hyperbole with a description of herself as a beast in comparison to the heavenly bearing of theology (*DP* 6. 125; 152, 154–58).

What Alan asserts here, as he does in his works of theology, is that the perspectives of Nature and Theology are incommensurable. The only analogy we are given by which to try to understand theology is a parallel incommensurability: just as Nature falls unspeakably below Theology, so Vice falls unspeakably below Nature. But since both theology and vice are unspeakably beyond nature, the question with which Nature's lesson in literary theory began is considerably sharpened: Can we be confident of our ability to discern between these two forms of unspeakability, between vice disguised as theology by the poets and theology proper?

The Incarnation and revelation solve the problem, Alan answers. "For now the nightmares of Epicurus are put to sleep, the insanity of Manichaeus made sane, the quibbles of Aristotle argued, the false arguments of the Arians falsified; reason approves the unique unity of God, [which] the universe declares, faith believes, and [to which] Scripture testifies" (DP 8. 140–41; 143–45. My translation). But such an affirmation represents only the belief that in principle these foes can be defeated by the united forces of faith and reason (which must discern the truth the universe declares) by a reading of the two books of nature and revelation. It is a battle cry, exhorting the forces of good to continue in the fight by fighting fire with fire.

Theology and Unreason, Heaven, and Fortune in the Anticlaudianus

The Anticlaudianus, written toward the end of Alan's long career, is not the sequel to the early De planctu. It is, however, often taken to resolve the negative ending of De planctu, in which fallen human nature is neither restored nor redeemed but simply excommunicated.[74] The Anticlaudianus opens with Nature enlisting the help of the Virtues to embark on a new creation of a perfect man.[75] The journey to heaven, the aspect of the poem with which I am most concerned, is undertaken to ask God for a soul for this new creation; the favor is granted and the new man is created and sent into battle against the vices, from which he emerges victorious. Despite this more optimistic plot, however, the Anticlaudianus restates and complicates the same problem De planctu confronts: the inability of Nature and her language (and Alan and his) to deal with what falls outside of her purview. In the Anticlaudianus, however, the emphasis is on the failure in the realm of theology instead of vice.

The first changes marking the transition from earth to heaven are in transformations of Prudence and Reason as they travel outside their domain of nature. Prudence loses her normal composure and her usual sense of knowing what to do, which is the substance of her being on earth. In heaven she "wavers" and "is full of doubts"; she has a real fear that "she will be led astray [seduci] by the confusion of directions," a complete reversal of her proper role (AC 5. 138; 43–47).[76] Reason also loses the power of her name. She cannot control the senses, the horses that draw their chariot (AC 5. 139; 76–78). Reason's natural role is to guide the senses and the

passions, but here she is powerless to do so. Finally, the road itself becomes
a non-road, a road that no men or birds have followed, that gives no
direction (AC 5. 138; 48–50). Even the poet is no longer a writer but the
"silent page" as "the language of earth [verba soli] will yield to and wait on
the language of heaven [verbis poli]" (AC 5. 146; 274, 271–72). For Alan to
continue to be the vehicle of the representation is for the stutterer to utter
words and the dumb to speak (AC 5. 147; 301–302).[77]

Alan extends this same kind of language of Theology, who appears to
guide Prudence toward God. Theology's robe is covered with a design
which mirrors her project: "Here a fine needle has traced the secrets of
God and the depths [abyssum] of the divine mind and with form informs
[figurat] the formless, localizes the boundless, reveals the hidden, gives limit
to the unlimited, brings the invisible into view" (AC 5, 141; 114–18). This
tracing stands in contrast to the tracing Nature assigned Venus in De planctu.
Instead of carefully following the patterns of distinct classes, correct junction
and disjunction, Theology's project can only be tracing in an equivocal
sense since her subject is without boundaries and determinations.[78]

Language is not, as it was in De planctu, the metaphor through which
this transfer (now from nature to the divine, rather than nature to vice) is
portrayed, but it is primarily on language that the effects of the changed
location are noted. All natural standards of correspondence and distinction,
those which proper language is designed to reflect, have been annulled, and
Alan's language attempts to describe and embody this unnatural state.
Reminiscent of the transformations and conjunctions of opposites in the
realm of Desire, in heaven water and fire are placed side by side, but they
neither struggle against nor mix with each other (AC 5. 147–48; 311–14).
They are, Alan writes, "bound by a dissenting assent, a concordant discord,
a hostile peace, an unreliable alliance, a fictive bond of love, a deceptive
friendship, a shadow covenant" (AC 5. 148; 316–18). Like Desire,
Theology is represented by a long list of parallel oxymora. In both allegories, then, Alan is absorbed in playing with and luxuriating in language
(cf. DP 9. 149; 4–7).[79] In this sense, language itself becomes the subject of
the text, as Alan attempts to represent the impossibility of representation.

The elements of revelation mentioned, Christ and Mary, are described in
the same paradoxical language and in a way that emphasizes the "unnatural"
character of their relations. According to the poem, Mary is the one in
whom the two names, motherhood and maidenhood, "exchange [vertunt]
the kiss of peace" (AC 5. 153; 476–77). Faced with Mary, Alan tells us,
"nature is silent, logic's power is exiled, rhetoric loses its judgment
[arbitrium], reason wavers [vacillat]" (AC 5. 153; 477–79. My translation).
"As daughter [Mary] conceived her father and as mother conceived her
son" (AC 5. 153; 481). Christ is described as both the Virgin's Father and

Son, and as he who "became sick to heal the sick, poor to bring aid to the poor, died to bring with his own hands the gift of life to the dead" (AC 5. 154; 518, 522–26).[80] The Incarnation itself is further problematized not just as the begetting of the Father by the daughter but also of "God by earthly power, the permanent by the transitory, the cedar by the bloom, the sun by a star, the fire by a spark" (AC 6. 161; 159–61). For the effect to give birth to its cause, for the derived to act as source for its source, is not just a biological but a metaphysical impossibility.

Alan thus seeks out the paradoxical aspects of the Incarnation—the disruption of relationships and coexistence of incompatible properties brought about by the conjunction of the human and divine in Christ. Such an account brings to mind the conflations, confusions, and reversals of relationships in the sexual activity Alan proscribes in the De planctu. As a consequence of the Incarnation, motherhood and maidenhood, fatherhood and sonship, come to coexist in the same individual, parallel to unnatural sexual relationships in which manhood and womanhood, active and passive coalesce. Ziolkowski compares the sexual misconduct of De planctu to the relations of the Holy Family, quite rightly contrasting the former's "offen-siveness" to reason as opposed to the latter's "passing beyond" reason.[81] But what is interesting and unusual is that Alan describes that which rises above nature in a way that suggests some likeness to what falls below nature. In this way, Alan, while remaining absolutely orthodox, even traditional, manages to show the radical character of the orthodox position.

The description of Fortune in the Anticlaudianus in contradictory terms also echoes that of Desire in De planctu. In Book VIII Fortune is depicted by a series of contradictions; her rest is described as flight, her permanence as change (AC 8, 189; 15–16). "For her," Alan explains, "method and reason [modus et ratio] is to lack reason [ratione], faithfulness is not to keep faith, piety is to be without piety" (AC 8. 189; 17–20. My translation). In comparison, God is described as "directing all things without movement," "lasting without time," "abiding without abode," and "measureless without measure"(AC 5. 141; 130–33).

Fortune's placement as counterpart to the divine has a substantive theological as well as formal purpose. In Boethius's Consolation, Fortune only appears to be perverse and disordered confusion because human beings are unable to grasp the order and its principles.[82] Boethius attempts to make both Fortune and God intelligible, to inhabit those different perspectives and see how they are united. Alan presents only the severely limited human perspec-tive on both Fortune and God. Thus instead of stretching reason, logic, and language up toward God and down to fortune and vice as Boethius does, Alan concentrates on the limits of reason, language, and logic, showing them as surrounded by that which they cannot take in on their own terms.

Having made the link between defect and trope, vice and mystical union, Alan does, however, attempt to distinguish them. Alan explains that Theology is "intoxicated" in a way that is really sobriety. Theology's "drunken sobriety," unlike the numbing intoxication of sensuality, "does not cause the mind to fall below its natural power, rather it raises it to a more noble level" (*AC* 5. 143; 170–74). Alan uses paradoxes to describe fortune and sensual desire to signify the unintelligible; paradoxes are used of God to signify not only what is beyond language and reason, but what is the source of all language and reason. God is not "unjust justice" (a contradiction of the type attributed to Fortune or Desire) but "just without justice" (*AC* 5. 141; 128). Created things are properly called just in virtue of participating in justice. However, God is the unparticipating, who is not just in virtue of justice, who is not living because of some participation in life; he is "strong without strength, powerful without force" (*AC* 5. 141; 130–31). Hence, God turns the normal justification for the application of names on its head because he is not an object who possesses certain qualities—he is these qualities substantially. So Alan writes, "[God] is called strong not only by form [*racione*] but he is subsisting strength itself flourishing in eternal strength. Only he is by rights powerful who, as the highest power, can alone do all things, from whom proceeds the power of the powerful" (*AC* 5. 142, 141–44. My translation).[83]

The solution offered by the *Anticlaudianus*, then, is that the tropes and paradoxes that would be improper in other contexts are proper in theology because they are proper to its subject. Theological language is not *un*grammatical but figurative, reflecting a divine nature in reference to whom grammatical distinctions between subject and predicate, gender, number, or case have no place. Both the laws of language and of nature are contradicted in heaven, yet the contradiction is expressed as the *overcoming* of opposition and contradiction in which naturally opposing forces are allowed to harmonize and combine.

To signal the transcendence of all mixture and opposition Alan uses the language of absolute purity. So in heaven there is "laughter without sadness, bright sky without cloud, joys unfailing, pleasures unending"; heaven is free of the mixing of opposites effected by Fortune (*AC* 5. 150; 378–91). Alan represents this perfection not with straightforward, simple predications indicating that words have finally found their true home; instead he constructs a new kind of paradox. The "extramundane" heaven is, Alan writes, "clearer than clear (*munda magis quam mundus*), purer than pure, brighter than bright, more glittering than gold;" fire in heaven burns with less heat and more light, "remaining one yet more and less the same thing" (*AC* 5. 150; 394–97, 401–402).[84]

Even though heaven is the realm of the absence of opposition, where the good is not mixed with bad and the only place where joy is truly joy, language strains to express purity because of its links to the world of mixture and ambivalence. So Alan describes the purity of heaven in a way that also evokes the impurity of earthly experience: if natural laughter were unmixed with sadness, there would be no need to add the superlative. Because language arises from and cannot throw off its origins in earthly experience, even the purity of the extramundane can only be expressed in extraordinary rather than proper language.

Here as in his theological works, Alan not only faces but exploits the paradoxes inherent in Neoplatonic realism. He emphasizes the fact that the source of perfection contradicts the normal rules of predication; God, in other words, at once grounds and contradicts nature. Hence, confronted with God as its subject, language is transformed in ways reminiscent of *De planctu's* depiction of the ungrammatical language of vice: "Language is stupefied when put to the test to speak of the divine, loses the power of speech, and desires to revert its older meaning; sounds lapse into silence, with barely the power to lisp, and words lay aside their complaints about their meaning" (*AC* 5. 141; 119–23. My translation). The resonances between Alan's representation of defective and theological language point out the fine line that from a limited earthly perspective, separates irrationality from super-rationality, babble from language which obeys the rules of a higher propriety. This way of portraying theological language and theology itself makes clear both the transcendence of its object and theology's utter failure to grasp it.

It is, of course, true for Boethius and Abelard (as well as Augustine) that God is both the ground of and radically outside of nature. However, Alan, in contrast to the more optimistic Boethius, emphasizes the aspect of God as radically other. Alan gives the reader no chance to bask in the certainty of God as the ground of nature before he brings home the way in which God confounds nature.

The Combination of Opposites: Nature, Virtue, and Art

For Boethius, nature is the path to God; it is that which, properly understood, reveals God. The liberal arts and works of the philosophers are the tools transporting us along that road toward God. In order to serve as stepping stones, nature should be a place of harmony and unity amidst the tension and opposition of the realms of both grace and vice, and the arts, reflecting nature, should be the realm of rationality, coherence, and order. For Alan, however, nature is a mean that partakes of its extremes; it is not a synthesis or true unity but only an uneasy construction placed on disparate and volatile forces. Alan does depict Nature as a guide that "unite[s] all things in a stable and harmonious bond and wed[s] heaven to earth in a union of peace," but he makes very clear that the wedding that she performs is a union of opposites, and that the opposites she rules pull against one another and against her rule (*DP* 7. 128; 10–13, 21, 37–38). This view of nature is a variation on a theme from Boethius. Alan takes from Boethius the notion of nature as the ordering of opposing forces but puts the emphasis on the oppositions in nature rather than on the order amongst them. In the *Consolation*, it is Boethius who cannot fully grasp the order of nature, not nature herself who does not have and display order. For Alan the wonder of nature, of the unities she manages to create, is always placed against the backdrop of the opposition she has to overcome.

In *De planctu* Alan writes that things are constructed by "leaguing [*federando*] together things hostile to one another by generic opposition, things whose position had placed them on opposite sides, and He changed the strife of contrariety into the peace of friendship" (*DP* 8. 145; 210–13). This marriage brings unity to plurality, identity to diversity, and concord to discord, according to Alan, but it does so through conflict, achieving "stability by instability, boundlessness [*infinitas*] by boundary [*finem*]" (*DP* 8. 145; 214–16, 219–20).[85] Bernard Silvestris, like Alan, describes Nature as creating order of opposing and chaotic forces, but Bernard presents the finished work of Nature as possessing tranquility and harmony, while Alan's view of nature is much more Hericlitean: stability is only an appearance or momentary equalization of tensions, and change is constant and frenetic.[86]

Alan's take on the *topos* of the human being as microcosm in *De planctu* is to describe human being, like Nature, as an uneasy blending of opposites.

> For just as concord in discord, unity in plurality, harmony in disharmony, agreement in disagreement of the four elements unite the parts of the structure of the royal palace of the universe, so too, similarity in dissimilarity, equality in inequality, like in unlike, identity in diversity of four combinations bind together the house of the human body. (*DP* 6. 118–19; 46–50)

The beauty and complexity of human nature, like that of nature, is achieved only at the price of tremendous fragility.

Similarly, in the *Anticlaudianus* creation is presented as the joining but not the synthesis of opposites. The new human being is fashioned by the "federation" of discordant elements, simple and composite, subtle and dull, soul and flesh (*AC* 7. 175; 57–61).[87] In the new man, Alan continues, "contraries live in peace, discordants lay aside the contention natural to them and flesh no longer threatens war, as it yields to spirit, though not without many a murmur" (*AC* 7. 175; 63–65). The "murmuring" of flesh against spirit is a signal of their opposition, and of the struggle that natural, that is, moral, behavior is. The elements composing the human being are joined but not integrated, implying a moral life and a model of virtue full of tension, in which the possibility of disintegration is always near the surface. The unions of nature, then, are "federations" in the political sense: unions of elements retaining some degree of separate existence, in which the boundaries are still visible; such unities are not seamless, and the seams are points of weakness at which the whole garment can be rent.[88]

As confirmation of this view of nature and morality, Alan goes on to describe the physical features of Nature's creation as the avoidance of or alternation between different extremes. Thus, Anticlaudianus's face is lifted neither too high nor bowed too low; he neither walks with a rigid pride nor a buffoon-like swagger; his hair is neither effeminately coiffed nor neglected "after the manner of a philosopher"; he is "counterbalanc[ed] toward the mean in all things" (*AC* 7. 177–78, 131–55. My translation). Hymen and Genius in *De planctu* also are described as this same uneasy mean. Hymen is young and old, both tall and short, neither in tears nor laughing; his hair is ordered into a truce and "bitten" by scissors; his beard is both short and long, his clothing both lowly and fine (*DP* 16. 196–97; 3–25). Genius, that "other self" of Nature, is described as neither too large nor small, and shows signs of both youth and old age (*DP* 16. 206; 188, 18. 215; 60–64).

It is a pattern Alan keeps to in his depiction of particular virtues as well. Alan's allegorical depiction of Temperance in *De planctu* shows her as a set of restraints on the abundance of Nature. Temperance achieves the mean by the restraint of forces within and without: her belt "moderating the drop of the tunic, *summoned* its undue length to *rule*," keeping it neither too short nor too long; "her necklace, *keeping guard* in the forecourt of her bosom, *refused entry* to any hand." Her concern is with that which should be "*excised* from our words," "*circumscribed* in acts," and "*restricted*" and "*reproved*" in the consumption of food and drink (*DP* 16. 201; 89–94. My emphasis and translation). This is Virtue, if not actively under siege, at least ready for the battle to keep opposing and excessive forces in check.

Prudence is also portrayed as hovering between contrary decisions, wavering, willing and not willing, swayed by her own inclinations in one direction and the counsel of reason and concord in the other. Alan portrays the decisiveness, control, and unity for which she is known as recaptured only by calming opposing forces (*AC* 1. 56; 271–76, 2. 72, 79; 163–65, 310–11). Though Alan is sometimes praised for his view of virtue as "natural," what we find on closer examination is a model of virtue as the *resistance* of opposite vices.[89] We might say that for Alan virtue *is* natural with this caveat, that nature itself is an unstable construction, a tension between opposites, possessing a good deal less than complete harmony and fulfillment.

De planctu draws another moral corollary from the principle of nature as a "federation" of opposites. Like the planets that Alan views as fighting the directions of the stars, the elements of which the human being is composed can revert to a state of disintegration in one of two directions. Sensuality may break loose and descend to the bestiality of vice, but equally reason may be apotheosized, reunited with its heavenly source (*DP* 6. 119; 58–62).[90] We are far from classical virtue in such a world in a number of ways. First, for Alan the goal of human life is not the fulfillment of nature but the surpassing of it, and vice is not the tarnishing but the eclipsing of nature. The extremes are more extreme, the depths deeper, and the heights higher for Alan than they are for Aristotle or Cicero. Moreover, the possibilities of descending to the level of a beast and of ascending to the level of a god loom larger because they lurk within a nature that is already a tension of opposites. Thus virtue, like nature itself, is a precarious and only provisional achievement. Again the contrast with Boethius's characterization of virtue in the *Consolation* is clear. Even though Boethius concedes that we experience virtue as a struggle against the world and worldly inclinations, he holds that virtue is *really* that to which human beings are most deeply and naturally inclined. Alan, again shifting Boethius's emphasis, transmits and exaggerates only the sense of virtue as struggle.

The arts, like the virtues, are supposed to be that perfection, imitation, and fulfillment of the activity of Nature herself.[91] Like nature herself, the arts are presented as an uneasy balance between extremes, struggling against opposing inclinations. Grammar is virgin mother as well as father to the child; one hand succors with milk and the other chastises with blows; and her work is that of a carpenter, a struggle against resistant matter (*AC* 2. 84–85, 89; 392–410, 476–85). Logic is a blacksmith working with fire to soften, and hammer and anvil to shape the refractory steel; her two hands attract and repel, smite and soothe (*AC* 3. 91–92, 94–95; 25–32, 79–105). It is as if the arts take up the contrary methods of negative and positive reinforcement to construct a mean analogous to the one the virtues attempt by resisting opposite extremes and nature tries to stabilize from opposing forces.

Alan portrays the content of these arts in complex and self-conscious linguistic twists and turns, resulting in poetry even Alan's most sympathetic readers find almost obsessive. The long list of rules displayed on Grammar's robe, for example, includes metaphors and other exceptions to propriety; it is remarkable for the number of times it uses and puns on *proprium* and its variants, especially in connection with the activities of political and commercial life (*AC* 2. 86–88; 419–71, 549–55). In the description of logic, Alan puns with a number of logical concepts—elenchus, topic, induction, middle term, and so forth (*AC* 3. 92–94; 42–69). All these passages on the arts pun by simultaneously using terms in their technical and ordinary and/or etymological senses. This technique is, I think, poetically defensible not in spite of but *because of* its exaggerated stylization of language. Alan attempts not just to describe but to enact the linguistic and artificial character of the arts.

The figures of Nature and Genius are cast in the same artificial and dualistic way.[92] They are represented as artists whose work is then represented through paintings described in the poem. Thus we only see depictions of what they have depicted, in an extension of the Platonic scheme in which human artists are represented as working two removes from their divine source. Second, not only is the figure of Nature doubled by Genius, but both of their works are two-fold, one set successful, the other failed. After the long catalogue of birds and animals depicted on Nature's robe, we are invited to view a mural depicting nature's human creations. The first painting shows the great figures who have created the arts and those virtuous fictional characters who have been created by that art. The second mural portrays the less successful artists and less virtuous creations of art (*AC* 1. 49–53; 119–83). The painting itself is praised in ambiguous terms— for its ability to make the false appear true, and as more powerful than logic because it is more effective in its deception (*AC* 1. 49; 122–30).[93] Genius also draws two sets of pictures on which many of the same figures reappear. The virtuous figures are drawn by the obedient right hand, the vicious by the wandering and disobedient left (*DP* 18. 216–17; 68–92). Beside Genius, presumably overseeing the two hands at work, stand his two daughters, Truth and Falsity, the first clad in clothing inseparable from her body, the second in a pastiche of rags (*DP* 18. 217–18; 92–110).

Art is not likened to nature but rather nature to art. It is an attempt to clarify the prior by an appeal to the posterior, the original by the copy. Further, the art of nature is presented as fundamentally and intrinsically flawed, resulting in vice as often as virtue. As a representation of representation, let alone nature, Alan's view is pessimistic. The cluster of images Alan uses to represent nature and her followers is full of the artificial, the doubled, and the ambiguous. Nature's creation is painting, and her compositions are the negotiation of federations, treaties, and pacts. Virtue and art, the human attempts to mirror nature, are portrayed as instruments of restraint of and as tensions between opposite forces. What is palpable in all these descriptions is the ever-present possibility of deceit, dissolution, discord, and chaos.

This is hardly the affirmation of nature, reason, and the arts one might expect from a twelfth-century humanist.[94] But this is exactly the conclusion that Alan's two poems portray dramatically. In *De planctu* Nature and Genius do not repair or reconstitute their creations, but only excommunicate (more language) those gone astray.[95] In the *Anticlaudianus*, Nature creates a "new man" once God supplies the soul, but he is immediately thrown into the battle of the virtues against the vices. Like his name, *Anti*claudianus's victory is by opposition to vice, not a matter of positive growth and fulfillment.[96]

Allegory and Artifice; Nature and Propriety

Alan's style in these allegories is not in the least naturalistic. He constructs long series of metaphors and oxymora to describe a single object or relationship. He extends his metaphors so far that the vehicle replaces the tenor as subject; the text becomes so overburdened with word play that his language creates a surface so dazzling (or at least distracting), one can only look at it and no longer through it. Language is often the explicit subject of these texts, as the protagonists protest their inability to represent not only the worlds of vice and heaven but also nature and the arts. Representation is repeatedly presented as a *re*—presentation falling short of its object.

Consider the most constant feature both of Alan's two poems and of allegory in general: the personification of abstract concepts. Alan turns the structure of the conceit adopted from Boethius to depict philosophy and repeats it over and over for every force, virtue, and art appearing in the poems. The subjects and natures of all of these are presented through allusions to further texts woven on the robes of these figures—either those written by the practitioners of the arts or by those depicting the most famous (fictional) possessors of virtue and vice. Nature's work is presented through the images on the murals and Genius's inventions are shown through the drawings he makes; both are engaged in artistic endeavors that fail as often as they succeed. The allegorized birds on Nature's robes are metaphorically re-naturalized, but even their resurrection is textual when they are described as "seeming literally" (*ad litteram*) to be on Nature's robe; Quilligan describes this passage aptly as a "Chinese box-like arrangement of self-consciousness" (*DP* 2. 94; 193–95).[97] But it is not only an unfailingly self-conscious presentation, it is also a hopelessly mediated one, in which texts are layered on other texts.

This is surely the "cold heart of the stylist" C. S. Lewis so famously deplored.[98] And Lewis has not been alone. James Sheridan remarks in the introduction to his English translation of the *Anticlaudianus* that its early books are marked by what he calls the "stylized manipulation of words," excused because they are "types of ornament that are the stock-in-trade of so many writers of his day"; his *De planctu* introduction accuses Alan of "torturing the Latin language to such an extent one is reminded of some of Joyce's English."[99] Quilligan clearly prefers the de-allegorized version of Alan's tale in Chaucer's *Parlement of Foules*, and Green's attempt to defend the *Anticlaudianus* opens with a description of "the artificiality of its language, the bloodless abstractions of its fable, the conventionality of its ornate figures, the contrived order of its ideological patterns."[100] Green goes on to refer to the "thinness" of Alan's allegory which he argues is justified in the end by the poem's goal of taking the reader away from the world of sense to the spiritual reality visited by the poem.[101]

I want to defend Alan's allegories precisely for their artifice and for their way of drawing attention to their status as products of the imagination rather than nature. This is not opposed to but is fully consistent with a more traditional reading of the poems as what Green calls an *ascensus mentis in Deum*. For Alan structures this ascent by making the world of things signifiers of spiritual and divine reality. This hermeneutic is from Augustine's *De doctrina christiana*. For Augustine and Alan, the true apprehension of the natural object is of it as *signifier*, not *signified*.[102] Allegory as a genre is one way of taking such a claim seriously (and literally) because *things* are its *signs*: persons, clothes, birds, chariots, and such, signify concepts and abstractions. *Signification* is its *subject*: its real drama is setting up the lines of signification between thing and concept. Thus, allegory reflects the relationship of God to the world as a relationship of signification. So too, then, sin or vice is fundamentally a misreading of things in the world as the signified rather than as signifier, a taking of the vehicle of transfer for the destination.[103] Alan turns this Augustinian insight into the elaborate conceit of the *De planctu* in which vice is allegorized as a literal misuse of signs.

Though for Alan and Augustine (as well as Boethius) the signification of God by the world is not one-to-one but many-to-one, Alan once again shifts the emphasis from his more optimistic predecessors. The failure of creatures to represent adequately the divine drives Alan not only to make multiple and figurative predications of God but to stress that they are all improper ones. Moreover, predication breaks down not only when the divine is its subject; what falls below nature also falls outside the arts. Lastly, since nature herself is unstable, so are the predications made of her. Thus within and outside of nature, the achievement of order and unity between sign and signified, lover and beloved, is provisional and qualified, instead of normative and absolute. The disjunction of word and thing, lover and beloved (and their conjunction with other unnatural, improper partners) is an always present possibility. It is to this possibility that the artifice of Alan's allegories draw attention. Their metaphors are non-naturalistic, obtrusive, and extended, making it impossible to mistake them for literal or proper predication. In this way we are reminded not to place too much weight or hope on the connections between word and thing, symbol and symbolized.

For many critics, any account of a poet (or philosopher) as concerned with the gap between word and thing implies his abdication of any moral and truth-telling aim. Alan's allegories, they argue, must be moral in the only sense possible, straightforwardly recommending virtue and condemning vice and its linguistic correlative by "persuading the reader of the ethical effects of interpretation," and that "right reading is ethical action."[104] If Alan admits or, worse, promotes the view that right reading is problematic and misreading almost inevitable, he cannot also intend to make of his poems an offering toward the goal of avoiding misreading and promoting right reading. Similarly, philosophical and theological commentators have argued that Alan must be worked into the narrative of progress in the development of the liberal arts and of theology as a "science." On this view, Alan cannot be understood to reject, even in a qualified way, the achievements of twelfth-century humanism, nor can his work point anywhere else than toward that of Thomas Aquinas in the thirteenth century. Alan cannot, in other words, be taken at his word about the unnamability of God without rejecting altogether the efficacy and legitimacy of theological discourse.

On the other hand, Scanlon, Leupin, Jordan, and Schibanoff notice the ways in which Alan's allegories seem to deconstruct their own moral assertions. However, instead of making Alan a deconstructionist *avant la lettre*, they conclude in different ways that Alan falls back on the legislative arm of the church to make the rules and enforce morality after having shown the insufficiency of nature and reason to accomplish this task. These writers end up attributing to Alan a kind of fideism and a reliance on ecclesiastical power. What they leave unexplained is the effort Alan expends using reason and the arts. Even if Alan is critical of the arts and reason, he does not *simply* reject them but takes them up with a great deal of enthusiasm, showing both their power and their limitations.

I think it makes more sense to see Alan's stance as ironic, both asserting and undermining the connections between words and things, nature and God, and, ultimately, the individual and God. Irony can be of two types: one that holds itself off from and above the fray because the struggle itself is unwinnable, unending and/or misguided; the other accepts the impossibility of victory but gets into, rather than locates itself above, the battle because there is no alternative to the battle, no better or higher place to be, and what is at stake is a crucial matter of life and death. Like Socrates and Kierkegaard, Alan is an ironist of this latter type. He attempts to enter *and* bars himself from the world in which the union of word and thing, human being and God, can take place.

For Alan, then, one of the important ways of promoting "right reading" and a legitimate theology is to disabuse readers of the notion that they have avoided the contrary. This is not, at least in Alan's case, the abdication of moral and veridical purpose but an attempt to remain faithful to it. Remaining faithful to it means portraying the possibility, even necessity of at least partial failure. Remaining faithful to it, then, means undermining one's own attempts and pretensions, an infinitely regressive task, achieved only partially by witty and playful self-parody, and in turn only partially corrected by earnest and straightforward purposiveness. Language is indeed for Alan, as Quilligan claims, "a force that must move society toward the Word at the center of the universe." But, as Alan's famous definition of God states, "God is a sphere whose center is everywhere and whose circumference is nowhere."[105] And as Alan, a good negative theologian, knows, neither the words of the poet nor the world can adequately capture the Word. This means Alan's words cannot move toward God in a straight line but must keep spinning around that omnipresent but unlocatable center, abjuring both progress and defeat.

All Alan's works examined here attempt to obey this double-edged imperative. Hence, Alan seriously presents the axioms, arguments, definitions, and allegorical representations of God, using all the forms and kinds of language available to try to capture the divine nature. At the same time, however, he undercuts the ability of those forms and of language in general to represent the reality they try to express. Alan makes his reader gasp in the thin air of the theology of the *Regulae*, spin in the arguments of the *Summa*, reel in the overgrown garden of the *Distinctiones*, and leaves her blinded and stupified in the unnatural environment of the allegories. In this way Alan achieves his goal, bringing the reader to sense the poverty of language in the *Regulae*, the impossibility of victory in the *Summa*, the too-muchness of the God in the *Distinctiones*, and the incomprehensibility of heaven and God in the allegories.

CONCLUSION: LANGUAGE AND THE
ASCENSUS MENTIS AD DEUM

The poverty of our human intellect generally produces an abundance of words, for more talk is spent in search than in discovery.

Augustine, *Confessions* 12.1.

Language

What is striking about the theories of language and uses of linguistic models discussed in this study is that they do not posit or attempt to create a perfect language. The shared conviction of all three authors is that words do not and cannot capture reality, that they do not map onto things in one-to-one and unambiguous ways. This is perhaps why none of these figures nor indeed any medieval thinkers figure in Umberto Eco's recent book, *The Search for the Perfect Language*.[1] I take it that different models of the perfect language such as the ones Eco explores are attempts to create an absolutely transparent language, to have it deliver, without standing in the way of the signified. With regard to the period stretching from Augustine through the entire span of the Middle Ages prior to Dante and Raymond Lull, Eco mentions only the medieval belief in the fall from the perfect language in the Genesis story of the Tower of Babel and the notion that Adam, possessed of this perfect language, named the creatures of the earth. Eco seems almost puzzled that Augustine, for example, shows no desire to return to or reconstruct this perfect language. In my view that is exactly the point in Augustine and his followers: that no language, be it Latin, Hebrew, or one yet to be engineered, is or could become a perfect language, one which can perfectly and without remainder represent the world.

None of the thinkers considered in this volume see their project as only or primarily cleaning up ordinary language with the tools of logic so that it can correctly mirror the structure of things. In the logical commentaries Boethius tries to mediate but not erase the difference between words and things, and language remains asymmetrically related to things. Even at the end of the *Consolation*'s careful steps toward transforming language and understanding, we discover that the ambiguities of language cannot be disposed of. For though in some sense Boethius reaches a higher perspective from which words more closely correspond to the reality of things, he and Lady Philosophy find that they cannot fully understand it and, thus, cannot remain there.

Abelard and Alan's rewriting of Boethius take trends in Boethius in two different directions. One strain in Boethius is the Neoplatonically inspired exploration of the metaphysics of God; this becomes Alan's obsession. Where Boethius sees the possibility of working from the metaphysics of this world (which he expresses in Aristotelian terms) to the metaphysics of God, Alan concentrates on the incommensurability of one with the other, on the impossibility of creating a transition that does not negate the reality of one realm or the other, this world or God. Boethius's pluralistic and optimistic vision is that both God and the world can be real, that words can somehow be stretched from one to the other. Alan seems to engage in the same project, but, we see in the end, only to show its failure. Alan thus focuses on the ways in which theological language breaks all the rules of grammar and logic. Alan's reflection on language is governed almost exclusively by the conviction that the project of refining language until it reaches God, its ultimate and most worthwhile object, is an irretrievably complicated and necessarily interminable one.

The other strain in Boethius is his commitment to this world and to the logic and language that describe it, to careful distinctions and step by step argument. This is the element taken over and transformed in Abelard. Abelard breaks down the narrative connecting word, thought, and thing Boethius had constructed in his account of universals. Abelard points out the difference between grammatical (ordinary) language and dialectic; while the former describes the surface of language, the latter sees beyond it to the deeper structure of things. Yet he does not propose to reform language in accord with this picture. Rather he leaves the complexity of language and of correspondence intact. In his theologies Abelard calls attention to the ambiguity of ordinary language not in order to dissolve it but to show that theological language is analogously ambiguous. Where Boethius attempts to give at least some small glimpse of God through and in words, Abelard disjoins the divine nature from the words used to describe it. Heresies are refuted and the truth of propositions describing God and the Trinity is saved but without offering access to God's nature.

Abelard and Alan are certainly more pessimistic than Boethius about language and its ability to represent God and the world, but in this they are simply extending and exaggerating tendencies already present in Boethius.

Alan's work is ultimately the exploration of the consequences of Boethius's recognition that even language transformed by the Neoplatonic metaphysics says both less than the whole truth about God and more than we can actually understand. Moreover, the distinctions between word, thought, and thing, and between the nature of God and statements about God, which become the basic principles of Abelard's logic and theology, originate in Boethius.

Boethius, Abelard, and Alan are convinced, then, though in different ways and with varying degrees of despair or hope, that language maps onto the world only imperfectly and problematically. The gap between word and world, signs and things, cannot be overcome. Indeed, they narrow the gap as much by recognition of the limitations of language as by improvements and clarifications of it. Since these authors realized that language does not and cannot be made to map on to reality in anything like a one-to-correspondence, their project was to live with the ambiguous and incomplete correspondence without denying it and without suppressing the desire to overcome it.

However, these views do not bring them to the conclusion that the limits of language are the limits of the world. Boethius keeps his faith in the possibility of progress even though the completion of the journey he begins in the *Categories* is always indefinitely postponed. Even though Abelard and Alan in a sense concede defeat, they still work on constructing a theological language that can tell us something. Abelard engages in an analysis that shows clearly and honestly where the gaps on the path from word to thing are located. Moreover, he finds a viable project for theology: it can make the problems clear; it can perform both the Socratic function of showing us what we do not know and the pastoral function of showing God in the world even though it cannot show God in himself. Alan's irony keeps him engaged in the project, experimenting with new forms even though he has moved beyond a naive view of their possibilities for success. All of these authors tell the story of the failure of language, but their attempt to succeed is as important as their ultimate failure.

Ascensus Mentis ad Deum

In the midst of a discussion of contemplation in the *Summa theologiae*, Thomas Aquinas asks whether contemplation can be described in terms of circular, straight, and oblique motion, a view which originates in Pseudo-Dionysius. Aquinas also considers Richard of St. Victor's account of the mind's contemplation in terms of the motion of different birds in the air, some flying almost straight up and swooping back to earth repeatedly, others from left to right, some going far ahead and others lagging behind, others moving in a circle, and still others almost remaining suspended in one place.[2] For both Dionysius and Richard St. Victor, these are images of reason as discursive, of human knowing as always moving from one thing to another in order to move, ultimately, to God. The conceit of my reading of Boethius, Abelard, and Alan of Lille has been that the mind's journey from word to thing, and from this world to God, are parallel movements shaped by these thinkers in different ways, just as different birds' flights from earth to sky follow different trajectories—Boethius ascending by measured steps, Abelard almost suspended in space, Alan traveling at intentionally dizzying speed from the depths to the heights and back again. The paths of these trajectories map different narrative lines, paralleling the individual soul's existential journey to God constructed by each of these thinkers.

Boethius began his task with the painstaking translation and commentary on Aristotle's *Organon*, a task he wanted to carry throughout the works of Aristotle and Plato, incorporating both into a single truth, affirming a secular or worldly perspective even while attempting to enfold this lower perspective within a higher one. This project is continued in the theological tractates' attempt to derive a Neoplatonic vision from an Aristotelian one, and in the *Consolation*, deriving a transcendent goal for human life from the worldly perspective and failed vision of the prisoner. The prosimetrum of the *Consolation* enacts this project of assimilation, tracing in its prose arguments the conversion to a Platonic ethic and Neoplatonic cosmology from a worldly one, and rewriting in its poetry the narrative of Greek myths and tragedy to accommodate the Christian story. So too in his logical commentaries, he maps careful steps from words to things, only tentatively uniting them in the understanding and carefully distinguishing different meanings and uses. In Boethius, in contrast to Augustine, the "things" of this world are not only treated as signs pointing toward God; they are first accorded autonomous reality and then argued to have as a condition for their possibility dependence on God. Care, measure, and moderation are the hallmarks of Boethius's writing; they should, Boethius shows by example, be the characteristics of Christian discourse and map the pattern of Christian life.

If Boethius makes distinctions in order to make connections and constructs arguments to make steady progress toward certainty, Abelard makes distinctions in order to prevent false identifications and constructs arguments which hold the believer in place, staving off both the lie of premature union and the absolute failure of separation. Abelard's criticisms of realism, like the criticisms of dialecticians and of his critics, concentrate on pointing out the non-identity of word and object, mind and world, and his theologies make a point of distinguishing between the truth, which is God's to tell, and the "verisimilitude" he can offer. If Boethius's Lady Philosophy sometimes produces surprise and skepticism in the prisoner at the paradoxes her chain of arguments produce, Abelard enjoys the puzzlement he produces that result from the distinctions apparently without differences he continually constructs and deconstructs.

Instead of looking toward the salvation and union with God promised in the New Testament, Abelard's laments stop the story at moments of extraordinary loss and grief in the Old Testament. Thus he breaks down the unity of salvation history, emphasizing the differences and distance between human beings and God, concentrating on the failure of signs to make present the signified. Where Boethius's *Consolation* tries to make sense of his own suffering by placing it in the context of providence, Abelard's account of his own life and retelling of losses in Hebrew Scripture concentrates on the lack of intelligibility in human suffering. For Abelard, spiritual discipline in this life does not consist in reaching for God but in constituting oneself in the position of waiting for God. He does not seek to know God but to live as a lover in the absence of his beloved; he does not achieve union between word and deed, intent and act but examines them and himself for discrepancies and self-delusions. Where the *Consolation* attempts to construct a path of transition from life in the world to life with God, Abelard envisions a life without consummation or vision. Abelard's lamentations in effect break the links of the chain of meanings, refusing to read the Old Testament stories as prefiguring the Christian completion and fulfillment, just as his logical and theological works seem to be constructed wholly to erect roadblocks between word and thing.

The literary forms Alan takes up—axiom, disputation, dictionary (scientific forms promising certain and systematic knowledge of their subject), and allegory (a form whose governing conceit is that everything is a signifier)—seem optimistic about delivering things through words and bringing self to God. But in deducing the nature of God, Alan's axioms trace the transgression of all the rules of grammar and logic when applied to God. Alan develops demonstrations of the absolute inapplicability of the conclusions and methods of any other science to theology and of any names or predicates to God. In composing a lexicon to codify the radical shifts and multiplicity of meanings of words used in Scripture, Alan creates not a sense of an ordered system but of overwhelming polysemy. In his spiritual quest, Alan casts himself as the knight-theologian fighting for Lady Theology's honor, but he makes very clear that his weapons are ill-suited for the task. He takes up these weapons, the new and fashionable forms of theological discourse, effectively placing scare quotes around the unions of sign and signified, divine and human they propose. Where Boethius's tractates are modest in their pretensions and results, the promises embedded in Alan's forms to join word to thing, soul to God are much grander—axiomatic derivation of God's nature as one, triune and incarnate, a dictionary of all the meanings of terms used in Scripture, but the way in which he delivers on those promises calls those forms and their pretenses into question. Where Boethius's *Consolation* shows the journey from this world to the next, failing only at the end to make the last steps to God, Alan's allegories portray the arrival point of that journey in heaven only to show the otherness of the divine realm and the impossibility of understanding or imagining it. We are with Alan both brought all the way to God and shown the infinite abyss that separates us from God.

Language and the Path Toward God

Pierre Hadot has argued that philosophy went from being a "way of life" in the ancient world to becoming a narrow academic discipline located in the university, and aiming for the most part at the training of other specialists. This transformation occurred, he argues, in the medieval period, as theology took center stage, answering the questions about how one should live and as philosophy was demoted to the role of handmaiden to theology.[3] This is in one sense simply the latest of many criticisms of medieval philosophy dating back the earliest thinkers in the modern period. We need only recall a line of criticism from Hobbes's blistering critique of the obfuscations, technicalities, and distinctions without difference of the scholastics all the way forward to contemporary complaints about the "quagmires of scholasticism." Medieval philosophy is, or at least seems to be, only the study of texts, the repository of puzzles to be solved, and source of a technical language to be explicated. It seems also to be to a large degree the study of language, both in the sense that commentaries on texts are about language, and in the sense that many of the texts written and commented on have language as their topic.

In one sense, the authors explored in this volume are the confirmation of Hadot's and others' complaints about scholasticism (even though they wrote before the true "scholastic period") because they are so focused on the technical problems of language. Abelard and Alan of Lille indeed represent the "culmination" of medieval thought based on the "old logic" and traditional grammatical education bequeathed to the Middle Ages by Boethius.[4] In Alan and Abelard, philosophy turns in on itself, talking in the end about signification rather than the world. Nonetheless, Abelard and Alan are able to turn abstract questions about language into the questions about knowledge of self, reality, and God, the very questions that made philosophy, to use Hadot's language, a spiritual practice. For them as for Boethius, such a practice is not opposed to the study of language but is one that illuminates and is illuminated by the problem of language.

As we have seen, for these thinkers, language, the attempt (and failure) to unite words and things (which, no matter how sophisticated one's theory of language, remains the unachievable goal of language) becomes a metaphor for describing other problems of correspondence and union. The problem of language is woven into and redesigns the fabric of the Christian narrative, the pilgrim's journey toward God, with Christ as mediator, bringing about the union the pilgrim cannot achieve on his own. As signs seek the signified, so the believer desires God; as language attempts to join thought and thing, so God-become-human joins the divine and human. As words never quite capture the reality they attempt to name, so human beings never quite achieve union with the beloved they desire, never quite transform themselves into an object worthy of the love they seek.

The structure of language's striving for things is a repetition of the structure of human life, of the trajectory toward spiritual transformation and toward God. Thus language is a mirror of the human condition of exile and the fragmentation inherent in what it is to be human, that is, to be separated from origin and object of desire.

What has interested me most in these stories and theories, and what I think has been neglected about them, is their complexity and their recognition of their own limits and failures. What is striking about these texts is, first, how different the models of spiritual discipline and the path toward the good they map are, and, second, how clearly they portray the ambivalence, difficulties, and lack of certainty of the travelers along these paths. Boethius gives place to the voices of tragedy and myth, even of worldly ambition and disappointment. Abelard does not just qualify the "happy ending" of Christianity, he postpones any foretaste of it indefinitely, and Alan pushes the conceits of making the journey to God to the point of parody.

They all nonetheless present positive visions of the philosophical (in the broadest sense and as including theology) endeavor here, quests for philosophic understanding and a way of life which embodies it. There is Abelard's discipline of moral and intellectual authenticity, embodied in his ministry to Heloise and her community. There is Boethius's vision of multiple yet integrated perspectives, embodied in his life of many roles and as mediator. There is Alan of Lille's embrace of the new, embodied in the novel forms he takes up even as he pushes them to the point of failure and paradox. For all their "scholasticism" *avant la lettre*—their technical terminology, their careful and myriad distinctions, their reflexive interest in language itself—these thinkers are intensely interested in and their work relevant to existential questions about how to live and how to understand the meaning of that life. The problem they all accept, that it is impossible either to speak truly or to keep silent about God, that they live in a world of words in the absence of things, is not an abstract or merely intellectual puzzle but the highest and deepest concern of human life. It both maps and shows the incompleteness of its trajectory.

NOTES

Introduction: Words in the Absence of Things

1. Augustine, *De doctrina christiana* I. 2. 2.
2. The division of the subjects of inquiry into signs and things originates with Cicero. But as Mazzeo notes, for Augustine "the nature and uses of signs became strictly related to the realities to be sought (discovery) and to their formulation (statement), so that the use of the arts of language is utterly dependent on the structure of reality, a relationship with which no classical rhetorician other than Plato has been concerned." Joseph Anthony Mazzeo, "St. Augustine's Rhetoric of Silence," *Journal of the History of Ideas* 23 (1962): 176. Thus signs are crucial not because they are all that matter but because they are the only path to reality, to things.
3. Peter Brown, *Augustine of Hippo: a Biography* (Berkeley: University of California Press, 1970), p. 264.
4. Augustine, *De doctrina christiana* 1. 2. 2 and 1. 2. 5, CCSL 32. 7–9.
5. See Eileen Sweeney, "Hugh of St. Victor: The Augustinian Tradition of Sacred and Secular Reading Revised," in *Reading and Wisdom: The De doctrina christiana of Augustine in the Middle Ages*, Edward D. English, ed. (Notre Dame, IN: University of Notre Dame Press, 1995), pp. 70–73.
6. This is a view Augustine expresses many times. See for example, *Confessions* 1. 4, CCSL 27. 2–3 and *Ennarrationes in Psalmos* 99. 6, CCSL 39. 1396–97.
7. See Augustine, *Ennarrationes in Psalmos* 99. 6, CCSL 39. 1396–97.
8. It would be impossible even to list the secondary literature on Augustine taking language as central to his work. Here are only a few that have informed my understanding: Marcia L. Colish, *The Mirror of Language: A Study in the Medieval Theory of Knowledge*, rev. ed. (Lincoln: University of Nebraska Press, 1983); Louis Mackey, *Peregrinations of the Word.* (Ann Arbor, MI: University of Michigan Press, 1997); Emmet Flood, "The Narrative Structure of Augustine's *Confessions*: Time's Quest for Eternity," *International Philosophical Quarterly* 28 (1988): 141–49; Margaret W. Ferguson, "Saint Augustine's Region of Unlikeness: The Crossing of Exile and Language," *The Georgia Review* 29 (1975): 843–64; Brian Stock, *Augustine the Reader: Meditation, Self-Knowledge, and the Ethics of Interpretation* (Cambridge, MA: Harvard University Press, 1996). For my reading of Augustine's *De doctrina christiana* as background to Hugh of St. Victor's program of arts study, the *Didascalicon* in the twelfth century, see Sweeney, "Hugh of St. Victor," pp. 61–83.

9. Eugene Vance, "Saint Augustine: Language as Temporality," in *Mervelous Signals: Poetics and Sign Theory in the Middle Ages* (Lincoln: University of Nebraska Press, 1986), p. 34.

10. Cf. Willimien Otten, *From Paradise and Paradigm: A Study of Twelfth-Century Humanism* (Leiden: E.-J. Brill, 2004), pp. 1–8.

11. Cf. Otten, *Paradise and Paradigm*, p. 232, n. 32. Otten sees her own work as returning to twelfth-century works of high culture, in contrast to the project of "new historicism," in order to retrieve what has been lost about these texts in seeing them only as forms overcome by those of high scholasticism.

12. Barbara Newman, *God and the Goddesses: Vision, Poetry and Belief in the Middle Ages* (Philadelphia: University of Pennsylvania Press, 2003) and Otten, *Paradise to Paradigm*. Both works were published after this manuscript was essentially complete; I have nonetheless tried to reflect on and make reference to their work.

13. Newman, *God and the Goddesses*, p. 292.

Chapter 1   Boethius: Translation, Transfer, and Transport

1. The claim that Boethius was not author of all his works, now discredited, was put forth most famously by F. Nitzsch, *Das System des Boethius: und die ihm zugeschriebenen theologischen Schriften: eine kritische Untersuchung* (Berlin: Wiegandt und Grieben, 1860). The argument that Boethius abandoned Christianity at the end of his life is made by A. Momigliano, "Cassiodorus and the Italian Culture of His Time," *Proceedings of the British Academy* 41 (1955): 212. See also Philip Merlan, "Ammonius Hermiae, Zacharias Scholasticus, and Boethius," *Greek, Roman and Byzantine Studies* 9 (1968): 202–203. For medieval views of Boethius's authorship, see Pierre Courcelle, *La Consolation de philosophie dans la tradition littéraire. Antécédents et postérité de Boèce* (Paris: Études Augustiniennes, 1967), pp. 337–43. On these views, see also Henry Chadwick, *Boethius: The Consolations of Music, Logic, Theology, and Philosophy* (Oxford: Clarendon Press, 1981), p. 174.

2. E. T. Silk, "Boethius' Consolation as a Sequel to Augustine's *Dialogues* and *Soliloquia*," *Harvard Theological Review* 32 (1939): 19–39. See also Mark Burrows, "Another Look at the Sources of *De consolatione philosophiae*: Boethius' Echo of Augustine's Doctrine of *Providencia*," *Proceedings of the Patristic, Medieval and Renaissance Conference* 11 (1986): 27–41.

3. R. Carton, "Le christianisme et l'augustinisme de Boèce," in *Mélanges Augustiniens* (Paris: Riviëre, 1931), pp. 243–329.

4. Courcelle, *La Consolation*, pp. 339–42.

5. Wilhelm Weinberger, Introduction in *Ancii Manlii Severini Boethii philosophiae consolationis libri quinque*, CSEL 67 (Vienna: Hölder-Pichler-Tempsky, 1938), p. ix.

6. C. J. de Vogel, "The Problem of Philosophy and Christian faith in Boethius' *Consolatio*," in *Romanitas et Christianitas* (Amsterdam: North-Holland Publishing Co., 1973), p. 367.

7. See above, pp. 38–61 on the *Consolation*, in which I show Boethius's consistent use of the language of vision and perspective throughout the poem to mark the prisoner's progress.

8. Cf. the view of Obertello, who argues that Boethius's works form a unity, leading toward the contemplation of God. See L. Obertello, *Severino Boezio* (Rome: Herder, 1981), pp. 565–781. A similar view is expressed by Edmund Reiss, "The Fall of Boethius and the Fiction of the *Consolatio Philosophiae*," *The Classical Journal* 77 (1981): 46. See also the older studies of E. K. Rand, *Founders of the Middle Ages* (New York: Dover, 1957) and H. M. Barrett, *Boethius: Some Aspects of his Times and Work* (New York: Russell and Russell, 1966).

9. See Chadwick, *Boethius*, p. 125.

10. James Sheil argues that Boethius's logical works are not original but rather simply translations of Greek scholia on Aristotle's logical works. See his "Boethius' Commentaries on Aristotle," *Mediaeval and Renaissance Studies* 4 (1958): 217–44. Though I take it, as other scholars have, that Boethius is making use of other sources rather than developing his commentaries from scratch, I read the logical commentaries as reflecting Boethius's sense of what is most important in the works and commentary tradition. Hence while I do not directly refute Sheil's thesis, I do present evidence that the commentaries cohere with each other and with the rest of the Boethian corpus. On the originality of Boethius's works on the *Topics*, see Eleanore Stump, "Boethius' Work on the *Topics*," *Vivarium* 12, 2 (1974): 77–92. On *Boethius's* other works, see C. J. de Vogel, "Boethiana I," *Vivarium* 9 (1971): 77–93. Though he finds little real originality in Boethius, Jonathan Barnes also rejects Sheil's view of the commentaries. See Jonathan Barnes, "Boethius and the Study of Logic," in *Boethius: His Life, Thought and Work*, Margaret Gibson, ed. (Oxford: Basil Blackwell, 1981), p. 80.

11. Cicero, *De Inventione*, I. 1. 1–3. 4, H. M. Hubbell, ed. and trans., Loeb Classical Library (Cambridge, MA: Harvard University Press, 1949), pp. 2–11.

12. On the background of this question and the relationship of Boethius's view to other Neoplatonic thinkers, see Chadwick, *Boethius*, pp. 108–11.

13. On the influence of Alexander, see Chadwick, *Boethius*, p. 133.

14. Chadwick also notes the combination of Aristotelian and Platonic elements in Boethius's account of abstraction. Chadwick, *Boethius*, p. 133.

15. L. M. de Rijk in "On Boethius' Notion of Being: A Chapter of Boethian Semantics," in *Meaning and Inference in Medieval Philosophy*, Norman Kretzmann, ed. (Boston: Kluwer Academic Publishers, 1988), 16. For de Rijk these remarks signal Boethius's view that words (nouns and verbs specifically) ultimately signify "some immutable and everlasting nature."

16. Brian Stock, *The Implications of Literacy: Written Languages and Models of Interpretation in the Eleventh and Twelfth Centuries* (Princeton: Princeton University Press, 1983), p. 372.

17. Stock, *Implications*, p. 372.

18. Boethius's arguments against relativism follow those of Alexander of Aphrodesias. See Chadwick, *Boethius*, p. 156.

19. The same example reappears in *De trinitate* to support the notion that three different names for the different persons of the Trinity need not imply three different Gods. See *De Trin* 3. 16. 45–46.

20. De Rijk argues that such passages show that, contra Kretztmann, Boethius was not unaware of or uninterested in the distinction between natural and artificial signs. De Rijk, "Boethius' Notion of Being," p. 15. Norman Kretzmann, "Aristotle on Spoken Sound Significant by Convention," in *Ancient Logic and Its Modern Interpretations*, J. Corcoran, ed. (Boston: Kluwer Academic Publishers, 1974), pp. 5, 18–19, n. 5.

21. Cf. de Rijk's reading of this passage, "Boethius' Notion of Being," pp. 9–11.

22. Kappelmacher argues that the project was Porphyry's, stated in a lost work Boethius himself planned to translate and/or comment on. See Alfred Kappelmacher, "Der schriftstellerische Plan des Boethius," in B-FG, pp. 71–81, first published in *Wiener Studien* 46 (1928): 215–25. My own view is that though Boethius might have formed the project influenced by Porphyry, it genuinely became his own. The tractates and the *Consolation* do, as I read them, undertake to show the consistency of Plato and Aristotle.

23. See Burrows, "Another Look," 27–41.

24. Chadwick, *Boethius*, pp. 159–63.

25. In this, Boethius follows some in the Neoplatonic tradition. See Chadwick, *Boethius*, p. 163. For a more detailed look at Boethius's view in relation to those of Proclus and Ammonius, see Luca Obertello, "Proclus, Ammonius and Boethius on Divine Knowledge," *Dionysius* 5 (1981): 127–64.

26. Plato, *Phaedo*, 103d–e.

27. Robert Crouse, "The Ambiguous Stature of Philosophy in Boethius' 'Consolation'," Boston Medieval Philosophy Colloquium Lecture, Boston College, Boston, March 15, 1999. While Schurr, Chadwick, and Bark all argue that the other tractates emerge out of the theological and political controversies of Boethius's day, no such direct connection is as obvious for *De hebdomadibus*. See V. Schurr, *Die Trinitätslehre des Boethius im Lichte der 'Skythischen Kontroversen'* (Paderborn: F. Schöningh, 1935). Bark claims that *De hebdomadibus* was, as it often appears in medieval codices, considered together with *De trinitate* and *Utrum pater* as the "*liber de trinitate*." See William Bark, "Boethius' Fourth Tractate, the So-Called 'De Fide Catholica'," *Harvard Theological Review*, 39 (1946): 59. See also M. Cappuyns, "Boèce," in *Dictionnaire d'histoire et de géographie ecclésiastiques* 9 (1937): col. 371, and H. F. Stewart and E. K. Rand, "Life of Boethius," in Boethius, *The Theological Tractates and The Consolation of Philosophy*, H. F. Stewart, E. K. Rand, and S. J. Tester, trans., Loeb Classical Library (Cambridge, MA: Harvard University Press, 1973), p. xiii.

28. Cf. Giulio D'Onofrio, "Dialectic and Theology: Boethius' 'Opuscula sacra' and Their Early Medieval Readers," *Studi medievali* 27, 1 (1986): 54. D'Onofrio describes Boethius's method as the extension of logical categories to the divine nature.

29. For an account of Boethius's intended audience, see William Bark, "Theodoric vs. Boethius: Vindication and Apology," in B-FG, p. 23, first published in *American Historical Review* 49 (1943–44): 419.

30. On Boethius's likely sources for his different definitions of nature, see Chadwick, *Boethius*, pp. 191–92.

31. This final definition comes from Aristotle, *Physics* 193a 28–31. Nature as that which can act or be acted upon is found in *Phaedrus* 271d; and nature as that which can in some way be and/or be understood comes from the Pythagorean tradition, repeated by Neoplatonic sources. Chadwick, *Boethius*, pp. 191–92.

32. On Boethius's definition of nature and person, see Claudio Micaelli, " 'Natura' et 'persona' nel *Contra Eutychen et Nestorium* di Boezio: Osservazioni su alcuni problemi filosofici e linguistici," *Atti del congresso internazionale di studi Boeziani*, Luca Obertello, ed. (Rome: Herder, 1981), pp. 327–36; Maurice Nédoncelle, "Les variations de Boèce sur la personne," *Revue des sciences religieuses* 29 (1955): 201–38; M. Bergeron, "La structure du concept latin de personne: Comment, chez les latins, 'persona' en est venu à signifier 'relatio'," *Études d'histoire littéraire et doctrinale du XIIIe siècle*, 2nd ser., Publications de l'Institut d'Études Médiévales d'Ottawa, 2 (Paris: J. Vrin, 1932), pp. 121–61.

33. On the way Boethius makes these substitutions and uses them to define person, see Bergeron, "La structure du concept latin," pp. 126–32.

34. On substance predicated of God in this sense, see Nédoncelle, "Les variations de Boèce," pp. 224–27.

35. Stewart and Rand, in Boethius, *The Theological Tractates*, p. 91, note a.

36. This tactic of moving into the second person to directly address the reader is one Boethius also uses in *De hebdomadibus*. See my discussion of *De hebdomadibus* above, pp. 26–33.

37. See Chadwick, *Boethius*, pp. 181–82.

38. Crouse, "Philosophy in Boethius' *Consolation*."

39. Aristotle, *Metaphysics* Z. 6. 1031a28–b23.

40. Cf. Sioban Nash-Marshall, *Participation and the Good: A Study in Boethian Metaphysics* (New York: Herder and Herder, 2000), pp. 69–72.

41. For Proclus as Boethius's source, see Chadwick, *Boethius*, p. 207. See also G. R. Evans, "Boethian and Euclidean Axiomatic Method in the Theology of the Later Twelfth Century," *Archives internationale d'histoire des sciences* 30 (1980): 36–52.

42. The debate about the terms of the tractate go back at least to the ninth century; see "Der Kommentar des Johannes Scotus zu den *Opuscula Sacra* des Boethius," in *Johannes Scotus*, E. K. Rand, ed. (Munich: Quellen und Untersuchungen zur lateinischen Philologie des Mittelalters, 1906), pp. 28–80, cited in Nash-Marshall, *Participation*, p. 230.

43. Cf. Aristotle, *Metaphysics* Z. 4. 1030a1–b13.

44. See L. M. de Rijk, "Boèce logicien et philosophe: Ses positions sémantiques et sa métaphysique de l'être," in *Atti del Congresso internazionale di studi boeziani*, ed. L. Obertello (Rome: Herder, 1981), 151; and de Rijk, "Boethius' Notion of Being," p. 18.

45. See for example, M. D. Roland-Gosselin, *Le "De ente et essentia" de Saint Thomas d'Aquin* (Paris: Bibliothèque Thomiste, 1926), p. 145 and B. Maioli, *Teoria dell'essere e dell'esistente e classificazione delle scienze in M. S. Boezio* (Rome: Bulzoni, 1978), p. 19. For a more complete presentation of these debates, see Nash-Marshall, *Participation*, pp. 232–36.

46. Ralph McInerny, *Boethius and Aquinas* (Washington, DC: Catholic University of America Press, 1990).

47. Pierre Hadot, "La Distinction de l'être et de l'étant dans le 'De hebdomadibus' de Boèce," *Miscellanea Mediaevalia* 2 (1963): 150. Cf. Obertello, *Boezio*, pp. 638–52.

48. Hadot, "La Distinction," 147.

49. Here is axiom 6: "Everything which participates in that which is to be [*eo quod est esse*] so that it might be [*ut sit*] participates in another way in order that it might be something [*aliquid sit*]. And thus that which is [*id quod est*] participates in that which is to be [*eo quod est esse*] so that it might be, but is so that it might participate in another way in anything else whatever [*alio quodlibet*]" (*De Heb.* 42. 41–43).

50. In axiom eight, Boethius does not use the locution *id quod est* but rather *ipsum est* as the counterpart to *esse*, but it seems to come to the same thing because he uses the finite verb form, *est*, implying the determination of *esse* by *forma essendi* from axiom two. Nash-Marshall argues that axiom eight distinguishes between essence and existence; however, she argues that *ipsum est* refers to existence and *esse* in this case means essence rather than existence. Nash-Marshall, *Participation*, p. 261.

51. Nash-Marshall argues quite rightly, I think, that Boethius's position here comes to the view that things depend on the first good both as efficient cause and exemplary cause. That is, to use the language of the debates over Boethius she traces, there is both a real and a logical relationship between the primal good and secondary goods. For her summary and solution, see Nash-Marshall, *Participation*, pp. 121–41, 164–67. Cf. Obertello, "Proclus, Ammonius and Boethius," 163–64, who holds a similar view.

52. Stewart and Rand, in Boethius, *The Theological Tractates*, p. 10, note b.

53. Chadwick notes that the *idem non ipse* is found in Marius Victorinus in an anti-Arian tract. See Chadwick, *Boethius*, p. 216.

54. *De Trin.* IV. 18. 41–20. 43; cf. 18. 30; 18. 37; 20. 47; 20. 61 and 20. 65; note also Boethius's repeated use of the contrast between what we *seem to say* or signify and what is: 18. 15; 18. 21 and 20. 55.

55. Cf. *De Heb.* 48. 130, 134–35, and above, p. 32.

56. Cf. Nédoncelle, "Les variations de Boèce," 237–38 for whom Boethius' concern with terminology and definition in the logical commentaries and tractates is a kind of fall into "verbalism," and a distraction or worse from the metaphysical project taken up in the *Consolation*.

57. For some of these views, see Chadwick, *Boethius*, p. 220, de Vogel, "Philosophy and Christian Faith," pp. 363–64, 368–69 and "Boethiana II," *Vivarium* 10 (1974): 17–26. On the *Consolation*'s Christian language, see Christine Mohrmann, "Some Remarks on the Language of Boethius," B-FG, 302–10, first published in *Latin Script and Letters, A.D. 400–900*, John J. O'Meara and Bernd Naumann, eds. (Leiden: E. J. Brill, 1976), pp. 54–61. For a defense of the *Consolation*, see E. K. Rand, "On the Composition of the 'Consolatio,' " in B-FG, pp. 249–77, first published in *Harvard Studies in Classical Philology* 15 (1904): 1–28. Some recent readings

have argued that the inconsistencies in the *Consolation* are intended. See John Marenbon, *Boethius* (Oxford University Press, 2003), pp. 154–63, Joel Relihan, *Ancient Menippean Satire* (Baltimore: The Johns Hopkins University Press, 1993), pp. 187–94, and Peter Dronke, *Verse with Prose from Petronius to Dante: The Art and Scope of a Mixed Form* (Cambridge, MA: Harvard University Press, 1994), pp. 38–46. For my views of these interpretations, see above, p. 60.

58. Cf. Thomas F. Curley, III, "The *Consolation of Philosophy* as Work of Literature," *American Journal of Philology* (1987): 355.

59. For a different view, see Reiss, "The Fall of Boethius," 43.

60. Donald F. Duclow, "Perspective and Therapy in Boethius' *Consolation of Philosophy*," *Journal of Medicine and Philosophy* 4 (1979): 341.

61. Gruber finds a model for this form in which the author is both comforter and comforted in Seneca. See Joachim Gruber, *Kommentar zu Boethius De consolatione philosophiae* (New York: Walter de Gruyter, 1978), p. 27.

62. On the charges against Boethius and for different assessments of their justification, see Bark, "Theodoric vs. Boethius," 11–32; Philip Rousseau, "The Death of Boethius: The Charge of 'Maleficium,' " *Studi medievali* 20 (1979): 871–889; Thomas Hodgkin, *The Ostro-gothic Kingdom*, in *Italy and Her Invaders*, 2nd ed., (Oxford, 1896), vol. III, p. 493. I find it hard to imagine Boethius, as Rousseau and Hodgkin do, as arrogant and inept at politics, simply because he seems to have had a long and successful career and because his speculative works show a kind of practicality and an ability to bring different perspectives together, resolving conflict by mediation rather than direct confrontation.

63. See Duclow, "Perspective and Therapy," 334–43; see also Wolfgang Schmid, "Philosophisches und medizinisches in der *Consolatio Philosophiae* des Boethius," in *Festschrift Bruno Snell* (Munich: Verlag C. H. Beck, 1956), pp. 113–44; Christine Wolf, "Untersuchungen zum Krankheitsbild in des ersten Buch der *Consolatio Philosophiae* des Boethius," *Rivista di cultura classica e medioevale* 6 (1964): 213–23.

64. Cf. Duclow, "Perspective and Therapy," 337.

65. Although it is awkward in English, I have tried to make both the linguistic relationships of derivation and the logical relationships of contradiction in the passage clear.

66. On this point as the shift from Stoic to Socratic/Platonic argument, see Chadwick, *Boethius*, pp. 231–32 and Fritz Klingner, *De Boethii "Consolatione Philosophiae,"* in *Philologische Untersuchungen* vol. 37 (Berlin: Weidmann, 1921).

67. See Plato's discussion of the unity of virtue in the *Protagoras* 329c–d. Cf. Marenbon, *Boethius*, pp. 106–107, 158. Marenbon either overlooks or does not see these passages as persuasive, arguing that there is a fundamental inconsistency between the account of happiness before and after meter 9.

68. Chadwick finds sources of the poem in Plato's *Timaeus* and Proclus's commentary. See Chadwick, *Boethius*, p. 234. Others have argued against

Proclus as such a strong influence. See Stephen Gersh, *Middle Platonism and Neoplatonism: The Latin Tradition*, (Notre Dame, IN: Notre Dame University Press, 1986), vol. II, p. 701, and Luca Obertello, "Boezio e la cosmogonia platonica," Appendice I, in *Boezio. La Consolazione della Filosofia. Gli opusculi teologici* (Milan, 1979), pp. 407–16. For a reading of the poem as Platonic hymn, see Marenbon, *Boethius*, pp. 152–53.

69. De Vogel argues that in this conclusion, the pagan and Christian elements of the poem join. See de Vogel, "Boethiana II," 7–11.

70. On Boethius's necessary consent to the arguments, see *Consol*. III. pr. 9. 264. 32–3; pr. 10, 278. 65–6, 284. 140; pr. 11, 288. 17–18, 27; pr. 12. 300. 36–37, 304. 76–77. On the character of their conclusions as necessary, see *Consol*. III. pr. 10. 278. 21–22, 38–39; 278, 68; 280. 79; pr. 11. 286. 1.

71. On the possible sources for Boethius's use of Orpheus, see Gruber, *Kommentar zu Boethius*, pp. 315–16.

72. Winthrop Wetherbee, *Platonism and Poetry in the Twelfth Century* (Princeton: Princeton University Press, 1972), p. 78. Cf. Duclow 340.

73. On Boethius's debt to the *Gorgias*, see Klingner, *De Boethii 'Consolatione*, pp. 85 ff., and Courcelle, *La Consolation*, pp. 173–75.

74. Cf. Augustine, *De ordine* 1. 2. 3, CSEL 63. pp. 123–24. Here Augustine uses the analogy between the unity of the universe and the center of a circle, noting that the circle stays one no matter how distant and divided the circumference. However, as Colish notes, Augustine, unlike Boethius, rejects the notion of fate categorically, while Boethius likens it to the circumference of the circle. It is a difference which again illustrates the way in which Boethius tends to work other views into his own in a way Augustine does not. See Marcia L. Colish, *The Stoic Tradition from Antiquity to the Early Middle Ages: Stoicism in Latin Christian Writers through the Sixth Century*, (Leiden: E. J. Brill, 1990), vol. 2, p. 289.

75. Cf. Augustine, *De civitate Dei*, 1. 8–9, CCSL 47. 7–10. Augustine offers similar explanations for apparently unjust or inconsistent fortunes, but he draws from them his moral conclusion that only the incorruptible should be valued. Boethius gives voice to the paradoxes that follow redefining evil and good. But this is not a substantive difference from Augustine who argues, in contrast to the Stoics, that the ultimate goodness of the suffering of the innocent is a mystery rather than a rational conclusion. See Colish, *Stoic Tradition*, vol. 2, p. 155. What Augustine does emphasize more than Boethius is that suffering only makes sense if there is life after death. *De civitate Dei*, 19. 4, CCSL 48. 664–69. For other views which might have served as models for Boethius, see Colish, *Stoic Tradition*, vol. 2, pp. 41–42, 108–14.

76. This comment and the other ways in which Lady Philosophy signals limits in her own understanding make it hard to accept Klingner's thesis that Lady Philosophy represents divine intelligence. Klingner, *De Boethii Consolatione*, p. 166 ff. Courcelle's view that she represents the best that human reason can achieve seems much more plausible. Courcelle, *La Consolation*, pp. 21.

77. See, for example, F. Buffière, *Les mythes d'Homère et la pensée grecque* (Paris: Les Belles Lettres, 1956); Hugo Rahner, *Griechische Mythes in Christlicher Deutung* (Zurich: Rhein Verlag, 1957); Michael Murrin, *The Allegorical*

Epic: Essays in its Rise and Decline (Chicago: University of Chicago Press, 1980) and Erich Kaiser, "Odyssee-Szenen als Topoi," *Museum Helvelticum* 21 (1964): 109–36, 197–224.

78. Seneca, *De constantia sapientis*, in *Moral Essays*, translated by John W. Basore, 48–105. Vol. 1. Loeb Classical Library. Cambridge, MA: Harvard University Press, 1928–35. ii. I, cited in Buffière, *Les mythes*, p. 376 and Seth Lerer, *Boethius and Dialogue: Literary Method in The Consolation of Philosophy* (Princeton: Princeton University Press, 1985), p. 184.

79. Gerard O'Daly, *The Poetry of Boethius* (Chapel Hill, NC: University of North Carolina Press, 1991), p. 222. O'Daly nonetheless argues that Agamemnon is offered as a positive model, while Lerer disagrees. See O'Daly, pp. 222–24, and Lerer, *Boethius and Dialogue*, pp. 191–92.

80. Both Lerer and O'Daly note that this line is an allusion to Seneca's setting of the tragedy. Lerer, *Boethius and Dialogue*, p. 191; O'Daly, *Poetry of Boethius*, p. 222.

81. On Cicero and Lucretius's view of Agamemnon, see O'Daly, *Poetry of Boethius*, p. 224.

82. Wetherbee, *Platonism and Poetry*, p. 79.

83. Cf. Lerer *Boethius and Dialogue*, pp. 185–93.

84. See Lerer, *Boethius and Dialogue*, p. 192 and O'Daly, *Poetry of Boethius*, p. 225.

85. Lerer, *Boethius and Dialogue*, 200. See Seneca, *Hercules Furens*, in *Tragedies*, G. P. Goold, ed., and Frank J. Miller, trans., vol. 1, Loeb Classical Library, (Cambridge, MA: Harvard University Press, 1979), pp. 89–90, cited in Lerer, *Boethius and Dialogue*, p. 200, and Clarence Mendell, *Our Seneca* (New Haven: Yale University Press, 1947), p. 167.

86. See Lerer, *Boethius and Dialogue*, pp. 193–202, O'Daly, *Poetry of Boethius*, pp. 224–34.

87. Wetherbee, *Platonism and Poetry*, p. 82.

88. Colish for example, argues that Hercules is portrayed even by Boethius as "Stoic saint" because of "his willingness to abandon his body and earthly life itself." Colish, *Stoic Tradition*, vol. 2, p. 286.

89. De Vogel argues that this reference to prayer is "unmistakably Christian." See de Vogel, "Boethiana II," pp. 4–17.

90. Chadwick argues that the phrase, "two great truths," refers to "a two source view of truth," one of reason (exemplified by Proclus) and one of Christian faith. This may be true in some larger sense, but the immediate context seems be pointing to the two truths that humans are free and that they are governed by providence. See Chadwick, *Boethius*, pp. 220–21.

91. Thus Boethius seems concerned not only that God's knowledge might impose what is often called a causal necessity (i.e., all events are necessary because part of some unchanging eternal cycle) but also semantical or logical necessity (events are necessary because God knows that they will occur and his knowledge is certain). See W. L. Craig, *The Problem of Divine Foreknowledge from Aristotle to Suarez* (Leiden: E. J. Brill, 1988), pp. 79–98.

92. See Craig, *Divine Foreknowledge*, p. 91, for a similar conclusion. Cf. Marenbon, *Boethius*, pp. 144–45; he argues that Lady Philosophy asserts in the end that

God's knowledge causes and therefore determines all that it knows, contradicting her earlier claim that humans are free.

93. Chadwick, *Boethius*, p. 249; Jaroslav Pelikan, *The Emergence of the Catholic Tradition*, in *The Christian Tradition: A History of the Development of Doctrine*, (Chicago: University of Chicago Press, 1971), vol. 1, p. 44.

94. Pelikan, *The Emergence of the Catholic Tradition*, p. 44.

95. Cf. Relihan, *Ancient Menippean Satire*, pp. 187–94. Relihan argues that Boethius attempts to show the failure of philosophy to deal with his problems.

96. See above notes 67 and 92; Marenbon, *Boethius*, pp. 106, 117, 144–45, 158.

97. Curley's view of the role of poetry in the work, widely subscribed to, is that poetry serves the purpose first of *remedium* and later of *refrigerium*, "a refreshment to restore the mind between bouts of strenuous dialectic." Curley, 358–64. Cf. Dronke, *Verse with Prose*, p. 43; he claims that poetry and allegory portray what cannot be communicated in prose, though he does not say what that might be nor how they do it.

Chapter 2   Abelard: A Twelfth-Century
Hermeneutics of Suspicion

1. See David Knowles, *The Evolution of Medieval Thought*, 2nd edn., D. E. Luscombe and C. N. L. Brooke, eds. (New York: Longman Group Limited, 1988), p. 110; Jean Jolivet, *Arts du langage et théologie chez Abélard* (Paris: J. Vrin, 1969), p. 363; and M. T. Clanchy, *Abelard: A Medieval Life* (Oxford: Blackwell, 1997), p. 334.

2. I do not mean that Abelard anticipates the modern sense of authenticity as creating an original self with values distinct from the surrounding culture. For a precis of authenticity in this sense see Charles Taylor, *The Ethics of Authenticity* (Cambridge: Harvard University Press, 1991).

3. D. E. Luscombe, "Peter Abelard," in *A History of Twelfth-Century Philosophy*, Peter Dronke, ed., (Cambridge: Cambridge University Press, 1988), p. 306.

4. Cf. Willemien Otten, *Paradise and Paradigm: A Study of Twelfth-Century Humanism* (Leiden: E. J. Brill, 2004), pp. 136, 158. Otten also argues for the importance of self-knowledge and its connection to knowledge in general in Abelard. There are two other recent works arguing in different ways that ethics is central to Abelard's thought. See John Marenbon, *The Philosophy of Peter Abelard* (Cambridge: Cambridge University Press, 1997). See my review of Marenbon's book, "Abelard's Progress: From Logic to Ethics," *International Philosophical Quarterly* 40 (2000): 367–76. See also Paul Williams, *The Moral Philosophy of Peter Abelard* (Lanham: University Press of America, 1980).

5. The pendulum of opinion on the authenticity of Abelard's *Historia* has swung back toward authenticity since John Benton's "Fraud, Fiction and Borrowing in the Correspondence of Abelard and Héloïse," in PAPV, pp. 469–512. For a history of the debate before Benton's article, see Peter von Moos, *Mittelalterforschung und Ideologiekritik: Der Gelehrtenstreit um*

Heloise, Kritische Information 15 (Munich: W. Fink, 1974). For the debate since 1972, see John Marenbon, "Authenticity Revisited," in LH, pp. 19–33. For recent defenses of the authenticity of the *Historia* and letters, see Peter Dronke, *Abelard and Heloise in Medieval Testimonies* (Glasgow: University of Glasgow Press, 1976) and D. E. Luscombe, "The Letters of Heloise and Abelard since 'Cluny 1972,' " in PAPWW, pp. 19–39. While I do not take my main task here to be arguing this issue, indirectly my argument, which connects the themes of the *Historia* with Abelard's other work, does constitute a kind of indirect support of its authenticity.

6. Some have argued that this restless search for authenticity characterizes not Abelard but Heloise. Abelard converted to this "ethics of intention" late and at Heloise's urging. See Linda Georgianna, "Any Corner of Heaven: Heloise's Critique of Monasticism," *Mediaeval Studies* 49 (1987): 221–53; Katharina Wilson and Glenda McCleon, "Textual Strategies in the Abelard/Heloise Correspondence," in LH, pp. 121–42, and Clanchy, *Medieval Life*, p. 279. For my views on Heloise's contribution, see above, pp. 118–121. However, I think there is a great deal of evidence of this ethic in Abelard's earlier work, both in the *Historia calamitatum* and in the intellectual spirit in which he takes up problems from universals to the Trinity.

7. Cf. Otten, *Paradise and Paradigm*, p. 135. Abelard, she argues, "opens up new space by confronting rather than ignoring humanity's intrinsic inadequacy."

8. For different views on the nature of theology as practiced at Laon, see Martin Grabmann, *Die Geschichte der scholastischen Methode: nach gedruckten und ungedruckten Quellen*, 2 vols. (Freiburg im Breisgau, 1909–11) vol. 2, pp. 157–68, Joseph de Ghellinck, *Le mouvement théologique de XIIe siècle* (Paris, 1914), pp. 138–48, and Marcia L. Colish, "Another Look at the School of Laon," in AHDLMA, 7–13. See also E. Bertola, "Le Critiche di Abelardo ad Anselmo di Laon e ad Guglielmo di Champeaux," *Rivista della filosofia neoscolastica*, 52 (1960): 495–522, and Jean Châtillon, "Abélard et les écoles," in AST, pp. 146–60. I am not concerned with assessing the facts about the school of Laon or the accuracy of Abelard's portrayal but rather with understanding the way Abelard understands his own work as a reaction to the shortcomings of Anselm.

9. Cf. L.-M. de Rijk, "Peter Abälard (1079–142): Meister und Opfer des Scharfsinns," in PAPWWW, pp. 125–38.

10. See Constant Mews, "On Dating the Works of Peter Abelard," ADHLMA 52 (1985): 73–134; Marenbon, *Peter Abelard*, pp. 40–53; and L. M. de Rijk, "Peter Abelard's Semantics and His Doctrine of Being," *Vivarium* 24, 2 (1986): 103–108. It is widely agreed that the *Glosses on Porphyry* and *Commentary on the Peri hermeneias*, both part of the *Logica ingredientibus*, are earlier (1118–20) than the later glosses on Porphyry (here: *LNPS*) and *De intellectibus* (from the mid-1120s).

11. Brian Stock, *The Implications of Literacy: Written Language and Models of Interpretation in the Eleventh and Twelfth Centuries* (Princeton: Princeton University Press, 1983), p. 392.

12. I translate *intellectus* as "understanding" rather than "idea," as Tweedale does; "idea" gives the impression that *intellectus* is a product rather than act of the understanding. See Martin Tweedale, *Abailard on Universals* (Amsterdam: North Holland Publishing Co., 1976), pp. 169–71. See also L. M. de Rijk's objection to Tweedale's translation in "Martin M. Tweedale on Abailard: Some Criticisms of a Fascinating Venture," *Vivarium* 23, 2 (1985): 90.

13. Cf. Tweedale, *Abailard*, pp. 185–88 and Marenbon, *Peter Abelard*, pp. 194–95. Since in an important way, divine ideas seem to have no role to play in our knowing process, commentators like Tweedale and Marenbon have a tendency to ignore Abelard's adherence to the view that there are divine ideas.

14. Marenbon reads Abelard more optimistically on the possibility of knowing the true natures of nonabstract things. Although he quotes the passage I have just cited, he does not read it as qualifying the claim that we know the natures of sensible forms for Abelard. See Marenbon, *Peter Abelard*, pp. 194–95.

15. Constant J. Mews, "Aspects of the Evolution of Peter Abaelard's Thought on Signification and Predication," in GPC, p. 20.

16. See L.M. de Rijk, "The Semantical Impact of Abailard's Solution of the Problem of Universals," in PAPWWW, pp. 148–49.

17. Abelard mentions Plato as the source of this view but he mentions no particular Platonic text, nor does Geyer's critical apparatus. Abelard did not know any Platonic dialogues directly other than the *Timaeus*.

18. Klaus Jacobi, "Abelard and Frege: The Semantics of Words and Propositions," in *Atti del Convengo internazionale di storia della logica, San Gimignano, 4–8 dicembre 1982*, V. M. Abrusci, E. Casari and M. Mugnai, eds. (Bologna: CLUEB, 1983), pp. 92–93.

19. De Rijk, "The Semantical Impact," p. 144.

20. Cf. Stock, *Implications of Literacy*, p. 381.

21. Stock, *Implications of Literacy*, p. 381.

22. Klaus Jacobi, "Peter's Abelard's Investigations into the Meaning and Functions of the Speech Sign 'Est,' " in *The Logic of Being: Historical Studies*, S. Knuuttila and J. Hintikka, eds. (Boston: D Reidel, 1986), p. 154.

23. Jacobi, "Abelard and Frege," 89–90. Cf. Jacobi, "Peter Abelard's Investigations," p. 171, and Mews, "Aspects of the Evolution," p. 16. Jacobi uses these adjectives to contrast with Norman Kretzmann's assessment of Abelard in "The Culmination of the Old Logic in Peter Abelard," in *Renaissance and Renewal in the Twelfth Century*, R. L. Benson and G. Constable, eds. (Cambridge: Harvard University Press, 1982), pp. 488–501.

24. On Abelard's theory of *dicta*, see L.-M. de Rijk, "La Signification de la proposition (*dictum propositionis*) chez Abélard," PAPV, pp. 547–55 and de Rijk, "Peter Abelard's Semantics," 99–123.

25. Abelard further demonstrates his willingness to look beneath the surface rejecting an elegantly unified theory of analysis of propositions on the basis of an important but overlooked body of exceptions—those with impersonal verbs. These propositions cannot be fitted into the subject—predicate straight jacket. Klaus Jacobi, "Unpersönliche Aussagen in Abaelards Kommentar zur *Peri*

Hermeneias," in *Mediaeval Semantics and Metaphysics,* E.-P. Bos, ed. (Nijmegen: Ingenium Publishers, 1985), pp. 1–63; cf. Tweedale, *Abailard,* pp. 245–54.

26. Jacobi, "Peter Abelard's Investigations," pp. 154–55.

27. Martin Tweedale, "Logic: From the Late Eleventh Century to the Time of Abelard," in *A History of Twelfth–Century Western Philosophy,* Peter Dronke, ed. (Cambridge: Cambridge University Press, 1988), p. 220.

28. Tweedale, "Logic," 221. But contra Tweedale, see de Rijk, "The Semantical Impact," and "Martin M. Tweedale on Abailard."

29. Jean Jolivet, "Non-réalisme et platonisme chez Abélard: Essai d'interprétation," in AST, pp. 190–91 and passim. Jolivet argues that Abelard's logical analysis tends toward Platonism when the concern is semantic, and tends away from realism as it considers syntax. See also Jolivet, *Arts du langage,* p. 354.

30. Jolivet, "Non-réalisme," p. 188.

31. The language of war and battle in Abelard's writing has often been noted, but most commentators have not seen it as affecting the content of Abelard's thought. See, however, Andrew Taylor, "A Second Ajax: Peter Abelard and the Violence of Dialectic," in *The Tongue of the Fathers: Gender and Ideology in Twelfth-Century Latin,* David Townsend and Andrew Taylor, eds. (Philadelphia: University of Pennsylvania Press, 1998), pp. 15–31.

32. See the discussion by Constant Mews, "The Development of the *Theologia* of Peter Abelard," in PAPWWW, pp. 183–98. See also E. M. Buytaert, "Abelard's Trinitarian Doctrine," in PA, pp. 127–52.

33. Abelard quotes II Tim. 3, 1–3, I Cor. 10–11, II Peter 3, 3, I John 3, 18–19, Jude 17–9, 22, I Peter 3, 15–16, and Col. 4, 6. See *TSch* II. 426.

34. On the degree of originality of the form of the *Sic et non,* see E. Bertola, "I precedenti storici del metodo del *Sic et non* di Abelardo," *Rivista de filosofia neo-scolastica* 53 (1961): 258–79; Jolivet, *Arts du langage,* pp. 238–50. On Abelard's knowledge of the Fathers from earlier collections see J.G. Sikes, *Peter Abailard* (London: Cambridge University Press, 1932), p. 77. On these collections in general see de Ghellinck, *Le mouvement théologique,* chap. 1, and Jean Leclercq, *The Love of Learning and the Desire for God,* 3rd ed., Catharine Mishari, trans. (New York: Fordham University Press, 1982), pp. 182–84. See also Eileen Sweeney, "Rewriting the Narrative of Scripture: 12th Century Debates Over Reason and Theological Form," *Medieval Philosophy and Theology* 3 (1993): 1–34.

35. Beryl Smalley, "*Prima Clavis Sapientiae*: Augustine and Abelard," in *Studies in Medieval Thought and Learning From Abelard to Wyclif* (London: Hambledon, 1981), pp. 1–8. See also Marcia Colish, "Systematic Theology and Theological Renewal in the Twelfth Century," *Journal of Medieval and Renaissance Studies,* 18:2 (1988): 142–43.

36. Augustine, *De doctrina christiana,* 3. 27. 38, CCSL 32. 99–100.

37. Among others, Abelard quotes the following as objections to the study of poetry: Jerome, *Epistula* 70, 2, CSEL 54. 701; *Epistula* 21, 13, CSEL 54. 122, 123; Boethius, *Consol.* I. pr. 1. 134. 26–44; Ephesians 5: 3–4; Augustine is the source for Abelard's account of Plato's censorship of the poets: *De civitate Dei* 2. 14, CCSL 47. 45–46.

38. Augustine, *De doctrina christiana*, 4. 10. 24, CCSL 32. 132–33; 4. 11. 26, CCSL 32. 134–35.
39. In the *Dialectica* Abelard strongly objects to an allegorical reading of Plato. The dating of the *Dialectica* is a matter of some debate. The older view is that it is among the last of his works, later than this version of the theology. Mews argues that the *Dialectica* is earlier (1117–20). Mews, "On Dating the Works of Peter Abelard," 78–89. Marenbon also makes the argument that the *Dialectica* and its view of the World-Soul is early, superseded by the more mature allegorical reading of the same doctrine in the theologies. See Marenbon, *Peter Abelard*, pp. 40–43.
40. Abelard's responses to separate objections about the Trinity do coalesce around the distinction between predicates which pertain to persons and those which pertain to essence. In the *Theologia 'scholarium,'* Abelard's responses are further focused on the basic themes of divine simplicity, modes of identity and difference, definition of person and relations between the persons. Nonetheless, his answers are not systematically framed by these distinctions or themes.
41. E. M. Buytaert, "Abelard's Trinitarian Doctrine," in PA, pp. 129.
42. On the possible sources for Abelard's bronze seal analogy see Constant J. Mews, "Introduction" in *Petri Abaelardi Opera theologica*, CCCM, vol. 11, pp. 207–9.
43. Marenbon, *Peter Abelard*, pp. 233–34, citing Abelard, *TChr* 73. 33–44.
44. Abelard does not quite accept this view, which he takes to be Plato's, in the *TChr* but supports it in the *TSch*. Cf. *TSch*, 362. 509–363. 511.
45. Marenbon, *Peter Abelard*, p. 249.
46. J. Cottiaux, "La conception de la théologie chez Abélard," *Revue d'histoire ecclésiastique* 28 (1932): 821.
47. Cottiaux, "La Conception," p. 821.
48. Cottiaux, "La Conception," p. 821.
49. Cottiaux, "La Conception," p. 819.
50. Augustine, *De civitate Dei*, 8. 3, CCSL 47. 218–19.
51. Augustine, *De magistro* 11. 38, CSEL 29. 157.
52. Cf. *Ep.* 7. 274–76 and *Eth.* 12. 29–31. Abelard recommends some more moderate practices in the rule (*Ep.* 7) and in the *Ethics* he notes the inevitability and nonsinful character of sensual desire. See above, pp. 121–22 for my discussion of these passages. In neither case is moderation the aim per se.
53. The tension is between this claim and Abelard's earlier claims about the implicit Christianity of pagan philosophers in their way of life and belief in God the creator. Abelard implicitly addresses it by noting the failure of philosophers, even given their knowledge of God, to give up their pride and to resist despair. See Otten, *Paradise and Paradigm*, pp. 171–73. In this way, Abelard's view comes close to Augustine's when he describes the consequences of finding the Word but not the Word made flesh in the Platonists. Augustine, *Confessions* 8. 9.
54. Cf. Luke 19: 12–15 and Matthew 26: 14–15.

55. Clanchy, *Medieval Life*, p. 272. Cf. Taylor, "Second Ajax," p. 14. Marenbon too takes Abelard despite his disclaimers to assume "a common measure between God's goodness and that of other things." Marenbon, *Peter Abelard*, p. 218. Otten on the one hand approves Marenbon's view yet concludes that Abelard knew that his new syllogistic form of theology would "never encapsulate divine splendor itself." Otten, *Paradise and Paradigm*, p. 157.

56. Clanchy, *Medieval Life*, p. 269.

57. Cottiaux, "La Conception," pp. 537–38.

58. Jolivet, *Arts du langage*, p. 360. My translation.

59. Jolivet, *Arts du langage*, p. 273, n. 157; 346. My translation. Cf. Taylor, "Second Ajax," pp. 26–27. Taylor argues, however, that this is the construction of "masculine technocratic idiolect" allowing Abelard to achieve academic mastery by excluding those who lack the technique.

60. Lorenz Weinrich, "Peter Abelard as Musician," *Musical Quarterly* 55 (1969): 295–312. For a careful analysis of how often and how many of Abelard's hymns were used at the Paraclete, see Chrysogonus Waddell, "Introduction and Commentary," in *Hymn Collections from the Paraclete*, vol. I (Trappist, KY: Cisterican Liturgy Series, no. 8, 1989), pp. 54–85.

61. For some of these autobiographical readings, see G. Vecchi, *Pietro Abelardo, I 'Planctus.'* (Modena: Societa Tipografica Modenese,1951), p. 14, F. Laurenzi, *Le poesie ritmiche de Pietro Abelardo* (Rome: Pustet, 1911), p. 29; Wolfram von den Steinen, "Die Planctus Abaelards-Jephthas Tochter," *Mittellateinisches Jahrbuch*, 4 (1967): 128. Peter Dronke expresses sensible skepticism about these readings in "Peter Abelard: *Planctus* and Satire," in *Poetic Individuality in the Middle Ages: New Departures in Poetry 1000–1150* (Oxford: Clarendon Press, 1970), pp. 116–18.

62. Peter Dronke, "*Planctus* and Satire," pp. 128–33.

63. For a listing of manuscripts of laments, their themes and authors showing these tendencies, see also Janthia Yearly, *The Medieval Latin Lament* (PhD. Diss., York, 1983), Tables 1, 2, 3A and 3B. Some of the same material is also available in Janthia Yearly, "A Bibliography of *planctus*," *Journal of the Plainsong and Medieval Music Society* 4 (1981): 12–52, and John Stevens, *Words and Music in the Middle Ages: Song, Narrative, Dance, and Drama, 1050–1350* (Cambridge: Cambridge University Press, 1986), p. 119.

64. Yearly, *Medieval Latin Lament*, pp. 76, 78.

65. Yearly, *Medieval Latin Lament*, p. 77.

66. Richard of St. Victor, *The Twelve Patriarchs; The Mystical Ark; Book Three of the Trinity*, Grover A. Zinn, trans. (New York: Paulist Press, 1979).

67. On earlier allegorical readings of Dinah's story, see Lucille Claire Thibodeau, *The Relation of Peter Abelard's "Planctus Dinae" to Biblical Sources and Exegetic Tradition: A Historical and Textual Study* (PhD diss., Harvard University, 1990). For Carolingian and twelfth-century interpretations, see John R. Clark, "The Traditional Figure of Dina and Abelard's First Planctus," *Proceedings of the Patristic, Medieval and Renaissance Conference*, 7 (1982): 117–28.

68. See Thibodeau, *The Relation of "Planctus Dinae,"* pp. 64–75.

69. See Thibodeau, *The Relation of "Planctus Dinae,"* p. 106. According to Thibodeau, for Jerome, Hippolytus, Ambrose, and Rufinus the brothers prefigure the scribes and pharisees.

70. See Thibodeau, *The Relation of "Planctus Dinae,"* pp. 134–35. According to Thibodeau this is the view of Marbod of Rennes.

71. Dronke, *"Planctus* and Satire," 114–15.

72. Cf. Thibodeau, *The Relation of "Plantus Dinae,"* pp. 227–28. For Thibodeau, there is a clear development in Dinah's changing perspective from a more to a less self-involved one.

73. Philo allegorizes Dinah as "Justice" or "Judgement." See Philo, *The Migration of Abraham,* in *The Works of Philo,* C. D. Yonge, trans. (Peabody, MA: Hendrickson Press, 1993), p. 275. For an account of how this view is reflected in Abelard's *Ethics,* see above, pp. 114–17.

74. Philo, *The Migration of Abraham,* p. 275.

75. Philo, *On the Change of Names,* in *The Works of Philo,* C. D. Yonge, trans. (Peabody, MA: Hendrickson Press, 1993), pp. 347–48.

76. Ambrose, *Jacob and the Happy Life (De Iacob et vita beata),* in *Seven Exegetical Works,* Michael McHugh, trans. (Washington, DC: Catholic University of America Press, 1971).

77. Ambrose, *Jacob,* pp. 163, 165.

78. Ambrose, *Jacob,* p. 167.

79. Ambrose, *Jacob,* p. 168.

80. Ambrose, *Joseph (De Ioseph),* in *Seven Exegetical Works,* Michael McHugh, trans. (Washington, DC: Catholic University of America Press, 1971), p. 200.

81. On the significance of Abelard's choice of Jacob over Rachel see Juanita Feros Ruys, *"Quae maternae immemor naturae:* The Rhetorical Struggle over the Meanings of Motherhood in the Writings of Heloise and Abelard," in LH, pp. 332–33.

82. Margaret Alexiou and Peter Dronke, "The Lament of Jephtha's Daughter: Themes, Traditions, Originality," *Studi medievali* 12 (1971): 851.

83. Cf. Marenbon's somewhat different interpretation of this lament, Marenbon, *Peter Abelard,* pp. 319–20.

84. In a parallel way, Abelard tells Heloise she will lose him if she does not give up her love for him since he will achieve salvation without her. See *Ep.* 4. 87–88 and my discussion above, p. 118.

85. For my discussion of this aspect of Abelard's *Ethics,* see above, pp. 115–16.

86. Cf. Ruys, *"Quae maternae immemor naturae,"* 334–36.

87. Dronke, *"Planctus* and Satire," p. 131; cf. Gregory the Great, *Moralia,* 7. 28, CCSL 143. 361–62.

88. Dronke, *"Planctus* and Satire," p. 132.

89. *Ep.* 4. 881–87, *Ep.* 6. 268–70. See my discussion of these passages above, pp. 118–19. Mary McLaughlin makes the most sustained argument for Abelard's feminism in "Peter Abelard and the Dignity of Women: Twelfth-Century 'Feminism' in Theory and Practice," in PAPV, 287–334. Dronke argues that Abelard is in this poem satirizing misogyny to one of its

NOTES   201

proponents, Heloise, laying out the case for it in such an extreme way as
to show it to be false. See Dronke, "*Planctus* and Satire," pp. 136–42.
More recent work focused on defending Heloise and/or showing her
feminism has indirectly accused Abelard of sexism. See Barbara Newman,
"Authority, Authenticity, and the Repression of Heloise," *Journal of
Medieval and Renaissance Studies* 22 (1992): 111–46, and Linda
Georgianna, " 'In Any Corner of Heaven': Heloise's Critique of
Monastic Life," in LH, pp. 187–216. See also Catherine Brown,
"*Muliebriter*: Doing Gender in the Letters of Heloise," in *Gender and Text
in the Later Middle Ages*, Jane Chance, ed. (Gainesville, FL: University
Press of Florida, 1996), pp. 25–51. Lastly, there are a number of recent
articles arguing for the "maleness" of Abelard's methods and self-defini-
tion. Besides Andrew Taylor's article, "A Second Ajax" (mentioned
above, p. 199, n. 59), see also Martin Irvine, "Abelard and (Re)writing
the Male Body: Castration, Identity, and Remasculinization," and
Bonnie Wheeler, "Origenary Fantasies: Abelard's Castration and
Confession," in *Becoming Male in the Middle Ages,* Jeffrey Jerome Cohen
and Bonnie Wheeler, eds. (New York: Garland Publishing, 1997),
pp. 87–106, 107–128.
90. Peggy McCracken, "The Curse of Eve: Female Bodies and Christian
Bodies in Heloise's Third Letter," in LH, p. 220.
91. McLaughlin, "Abelard and the Dignity of Women," 296–97, 306–308.
Cf. Abelard, *Exp Hex*, PL 178. 760B–776D.
92. On the tale and its history, see George Sarton, "Aristotle and Phyllis," *Isis*,
14 (1930): 8–19. See also Émile Mâle, *Religious Art in France, the Thirteenth
Century: A Study of Medieval Iconography and its Sources* (Princeton: Princeton
University Press, 1984), pp. 330–32.
93. Sarton, "Aristotle and Phyllis," pp. 11, 19.
94. Dronke, "Planctus and Satire," p. 131.
95. Yearly lists one lament of David for Absalom, dating from the tenth
century. Yearly, "Bibliography of *planctus*," p. 26.
96. Annelies Wouters, "Une larme pour Abner: Une lamentation de l'Ancien
Testament remaniée par Pierre Abélard," in *Pierre Abélard: Colloque
International de Nantes*, Jean Jolivet and Henri Habrias, eds. (Rennes:
Presses Universitaires Rennes, 2003), p. 298.
97. Wouters, "Une larme pour Abner," p. 298.
98. Wouters, "Une larme pour Abner," pp. 295–303.
99. Wouters, "Une larme pour Abner," p. 302. Cf. II Samuel 3: 39.
100. Yearly lists a fairly large number of manuscripts of laments of David for
Jonathan. There are so many manuscripts because this lament was a
responsory used regularly in the liturgy. Some of the manuscripts seem to
predate Abelard's development of the theme. See Yearly, "Bibliography of
planctus," pp. 17, 20, 22, 25, 27.
101. The phrase "aesthetics of irresolution" is Thomas Reed's in *Middle
English Debate Poetry and the Aesthetics of Irresolution* (Columbia, MO:
University of Missouri Press, 1990), p. 27. It is cited by Phyllis R. Brown and

John C. Pieffer II in "Heloise, Dialectic, and the *Heroides*," in LH, p. 157. Brown and Peiffer suggest that one model for Abelard and Heloise's letters (though not the laments) is Ovid's *Heroides*. The *Heroides*, like the laments, imagines alternate views of well-known stories from other points of view than the canonical versions. On the Heroides as a part of twelfth-century study of the trivium, see Birger Munk Olsen, *I Classici nel canone scolastico altomedievale* (Spoleto: Centro italiano di studi sull'alto Medioevo, 1991), p. 120, and James H. McGregor, "Ovid at School: From the Ninth to the Fifteenth Century," *Classical Folia* 32 (1978): 29.

102. Dronke argues that the laments are neither theological nor typological. See Dronke, "*Planctus* and Satire," p. 131.

103. For my discussion of providence in the *Theologia "scholarium,"* see above, p. 89.

104. Augustine, *De doctrina christiana*, 3. 10. 15, CCSL 32. 87. Cf. David Luscombe, "Peter Abelard and Twelfth-Century Ethics," in *Abelard's Ethics*, D. Luscombe, ed. and trans., (Oxford: Clarendon Press, 1971), p. xxxiv. See also J. Rohmer, "La finalité morale chez les théologiens de saint Augustin à Duns Scot," *Études de philosophie médiévale* 27 (1939): 31–49.

105. Cf. Jolivet's description of Abelard's ethics as the attempt to "define sin in itself, independent of everything which could be a psychological reality or positive act." Jolivet, *Arts du langage*, p. 356. My translation.

106. On Abelard's notion of the will, see also Maurice de Gandillac, "Intention et loi dans l'Éthique d'Abèlard," in PAPV, pp. 588–89. Cf. Augustine's discussion of the same example in *De libero arbitrio* 1. 4, CSEL 74. 9–11. Augustine, after first seeming to absolve the servant, condemns his act as motivated by the desire for temporal over eternal things.

107. Clanchy notes that one of the seven charges against Abelard at Sens concerning his ethics is that he taught that "neither action nor will nor desire nor the pleasure which drives it, is a sin; nor should we wish to extinguish it [i.e., desire]." Critics took this to mean that sin should not be extinguished. Clanchy points out that Abelard is simply expressing the moderate view that the desires to eat and drink are necessary to life and should not be extinguished. See Clanchy, *Medieval Life*, p. 281. But Abelard is also saying something stronger, though not what his critics attributed to him. He is claiming that part of the reason desires should not be extinguished is so that one has something to fight against in order to be virtuous. This is also noted by Pascale Bourgain in "Héloïse," in AST, p. 234.

108. On Abelard's view of martyrdom and the case of Jephtha's daughter, see above, pp. 105–6.

109. On the obligation to confess, see D. E. Luscombe, *Eth.* 98–99, n. 2. See also P. Anciaux, *La théologie du sacrement de pénitence au XIIe siècle* (Louvain: Nauwelaerts, 1949), pp. 176–82.

110. The debate over the authenticity of Heloise's letters has raged longer and with more passion than the debate over Abelard's letters. See John Benton, "A Reconsideration of the Authenticity of the Correspondence

of Abelard and Heloise," in PAPWWW, pp. 41–52," J. T. Muckle in his introduction to "The Personal Letters Between Abelard and Heloise," *Mediaeval Studies* 15 (1953): 59, 67, D. W. Robertson, *Abelard and Heloise* (New York: Dial Press, 1972), p. 121, and Chrysogonus Waddell in *The Paraclete Statutes Institutiones Nostrae: Introduction, Edition and Commentary* (Trappist, KY: Gethsemani Abbey, 1987), p. 53. All three negate any real contribution of Heloise to the letters written in her name. For defenses of Heloise and her authorship see Peter Dronke, "Medieval Testimonies," "Heloise's *Problemata* and *Letters*: Some Questions of Form and Content," in PAPWWW, pp. 53–73, and "Heloise," in *Women Writers of the Middle Ages: A Critical Study of Texts from Perpetua (d. 203) to Marguerite Porete (d. 1310)* (New York: Cambridge University Press, 1984), pp. 107–39. See also Barbara Newman, "Authority, Authenticity and the Repression of Heloise," *Journal of Medieval and Renaissance Studies* 22: 2 (1992): 121–57; Bourgain, "Héloïse," 211–37, Jacques Monfrin, "Le problème de l'authenticité de la correspondance d'Abélard et d'Héloïse," in PAPV, 409–23, and Peter von Moos, "Le silence d'Héloïse et les idéologies modems," in PAPV, pp. 425–68.

111. Cf. Brown, *"Muliebriter,"* pp. 36–37.
112. Brown, *"Muliebriter,"* p. 38.
113. Georgianna, " 'Any Corner of Heaven,' " p. 251.
114. Morgan Powell, "Listening to Heloise at the Paraclete: Of Scholarly Diversion and a Woman's 'Conversion,' " in LH, p. 268.
115. Etienne Gilson, *Heloise and Abelard*, L. K. Shook, trans. (Chicago: Henry Regenery, 1951), p. 104. Dronke makes Heloise's nonconversion an argument for the letters' authenticity. A forgery designed, as some have argued, to create a founding document for the Pareclete, would work to show the founders in a favorable light. See Peter Dronke, "Héloïse and Marianne: Some Reconsiderations," *Romanische Forschungen* 72 (1960): 223–56, and Dronke, "Heloise," p. 129. For other views see von Moos, "Le Silence," 456–58. Cf. Bourgain, "Heloise," pp. 229–333.
116. Cf. Georgianna, " 'Any Corner of Heaven,' " p. 248.
117. This view is in many ways shared by Eileen Kearney. See Eileen Kearney, "*Scientia* and *Sapientia*: Reading Sacred Scripture at the Paraclete," in *From Cloister to Classroom: Monastic and Scholastic Approaches to Truth*, E. Rozanne Elder, ed. (Kalamazoo: Cistercian Publications, 1986), pp. 111–29. Brown and Peiffer criticize the view that the rule represents a positive conclusion to Abelard and Heloise's relationship and spiritual struggles, noting, as others have, that Heloise does not seem to have used the rule Abelard composed that is supposed to ground this joint enterprise, and that in any case much of Heloise's building of her community occurred before Abelard wrote the *Historia* or subsequent letters. They conclude that it is Abelard, not Heloise, as most have assumed, for whom we have no evidence of conversion. See Phyllis R. Brown and John C. Peiffer II, "Heloise, Dialectic and the *Heroides*," in LH, pp. 151–52. For a more positive account of the later correspondence see Brian Patrick McGuire, "Heloise

and the Consolation of Friendship," in LH, pp. 303–21. See also Michael
Calabrese, "Ovid and the Female Voice in the *De amore* and the *Letters* of
Abelard and Heloise," *Modern Philology* 95 (1997): 26.

118. Rom. 14: 17, 20–21.

119. Cf. Georgianna, "Any Corner of Heaven,' " 251–52, and Wilson and
McCleod, "Textual Strategies," pp. 124–25.

120. Augustine, *Epistulae*, 78, 9, CSEL 34. 344.

121. Marenbon, *Peter Abelard*, pp. 310–13.

122. Here Abelard echoes the language Heloise used earlier in the correspondence (*Ep.* 3. 82) that she would be satisfied in "whatever corner of
heaven" God placed her; Georgianna makes this phrase the title of her
article on Heloise, as epitomizing the ethic Georgianna attributes to
Heloise but denies characterizes Abelard.

123. Cf. Augustine, *De doctrina christiana*, 3. 10. 15–12. 19, CCSL 32. 87–90.

124. Augustine, *De baptismo*, 3, 5, CSEL 51. 203.

125. Cf. McLaughlin, "Peter Abelard and the Dignity of Women," p. 319.

126. Origen, *Homilia XII in Genesim*, PG 12, 229. See Gen. 24: 15–33.

127. Kearney, "*Scientia* and *Sapientia*,' " pp. 115–19.

128. M. T. Clanchy, "Abelard's Mockery of St. Anselm," *Journal of Ecclesiastical
History* 41, 1 (1990): 1–23.

129. Charles Burnett has published an edition, analysis, and translation of the
work discussing its status as fragmentary or complete. See Charles Burnett,
"Peter Abelard 'Soliloquium,' " *Studi medievali* 25 (1984): 857–94.

130. Charles F. Burnett, " 'Confessio fidei ad Heloisam'—Abelard's Last Letter
to Heloise?" *Mittellateinisches Jahrbuch* 21 (1986): 149.

131. "De-reification" is Jolivet's term. See Jolivet, *Arts du langage*, pp. 351–52.

Chapter 3   Alan of Lille: Language and its
Peregrinations to and from Divine Unity

1. For one such view, see Gillian R. Evans, *Alan of Lille: The Frontiers of
Theology in the Later Twelfth Century* (Cambridge: Cambridge University
Press, 1983), pp. 166–71.

2. See M.-D. Chenu, "Un essai de méthode théologique au XIIᵉ siècle,"
Revue des sciences philosophiques et théologiques 25 (1935): 258–67, and
M.-D. Chenu, "The Symbolist Mentality," in *Nature, Man, and Society in
the Twelfth Century*, Jerome Taylor and Lester Little, trans. (Chicago:
University of Chicago, 1968), pp. 99, 100, and passim.

3. See the assessment of Richard H. and Mary A. Rouse, "*Statim invenire*:
Schools, Preachers, and New Attitudes to the Page," in *Renaissance and
Renewal in the Twelfth Century*, Robert L. Benson and Giles Constable, eds.
(Cambridge, MA: Harvard University Press, 1982), pp. 201–25.

4. Evans also notes Alan's embrace of the "new" and his identification of
theology as the discipline of the new. Evans, *Alan of Lille*, p. 52.

5. See Kent Kraft, "Modernism in the Twelfth Century," *Comparative Literature Studies* (1981): 287–95. For an opposing view, see Ernst Robert Curtius, *European Literature and the Latin Middle Ages*, Willard Trask, trans. (New York: Harper and Row, 1953), p. 119, and James Sheridan, "Introduction," in *Anticlaudianus, or the Good and Perfect Man*, James Sheridan, trans. (Toronto: Pontifical Institute of Mediaeval Studies, 1973), p. 40.

6. Gilbert of Poitiers, *Expositio in Boecii librum primum de trinitate*, in *The Commentaries on Boethius by Gilbert of Poitiers*, Nikolaus M. Häring, ed. (Toronto: Pontifical Institute of Mediaeval Studies, 1966), pp. 48, 55. Cited in Evans, *Alan of Lille*, p. 52.

7. Evans, *Alan of Lille*, pp. 52–53.

8. M. T. D'Alverny, *Textes inédits d'Alain de Lille* (Paris: J. Vrin, 1965), p. 67.

9. I do not want to reduce Alan's work to polemics against particular contemporaries because I think his vision of the dangers for theologians and humanists is broader than that. Nonetheless, it is helpful to see Alan's allegories as a reply to Bernard Sylvestris' *Cosmographia*, his theological dictionary as an alternative to Peter the Chanter's *Distinctiones Abel* and his account of theological language in the *Summa quoniam homines* and *Regulae* as countering the tendencies of Prepositinus and Gilbert of Poitiers. In my discussion of these works of Alan I try to make these connections.

10. Cf. Gilbert of Poitiers, *Expositio in Boecii librum de bonorum ebdomade*, in *The Commentaries on Boethius by Gilbert of Poitiers*, Nikolaus Häring, ed. (Toronto: Pontifical Institute of Mediaeval Studies, 1966), Prol. 9–13; 1, 12; 185–86, 189–90. Gilbert's introduction to his commentary has many of the same characteristics, but Alan emphasizes more the hiddenness and difficulty of the discipline of theology.

11. Jean Jolivet, "Remarques sur les '*Regulae theologicae*' d'Alain de Lille," in ALGCJG, p. 90.

12. For a comparison of Alan's *Regulae* with Boethius and Euclid see Gillian R. Evans, "Boethian and Euclidean Axiomatic Method," *Archives internationales d'histoire des sciences* 30 (1980): 36–52. Another possible influence is Proclus. Alan was likely one of the early western readers of the *Liber de causis* based on Proclus' *Elements of Theology*. See Evans, *Alan of Lille*, p. 65.

13. Boethius, *De Trin.*, I. 4. 18, 26–31.

14. Gilbert, *Expositio in de trinitate*, pp. 122–24.

15. Gilbert of Poitiers, *Expositio in de trinitate*. 116–17. Cf. Klaus Jacobi, "Sprache und Wirklichkeit: Theoriebildung über Sprache im frühen 12. Jahrhundert," in *Sprachtheorien in Spätantike und Mittelalter,* Sten Ebbeson, ed., (Tübingen: Gunter Narr Verlag, 1995), pp. 97–98 and Marcia L. Colish, *Peter Lombard*, (Leiden: E. J. Brill, 1994), vol. 1, pp. 131–36. Colish argues that Gilbert contradicts himself in extending this rule to God notwithstanding the fact that the metaphysical distinction on which it is based, does not exist in God.

16. Prepositinus, *De nominibus divinis: regule*, in Giuseppe Angelini, *L'Ortodossia e la grammatica: Analisi di struttura e deduzione storica della teologia trinitaria di Prepositino* (Rome: Università Gregoriana, 1972), pp. 248–49.

17. Irène Rosier, "*Res significata et modus significandi*: Les implications d'une distinction médiévale," in *Sprachtheorien in Spätantike und Mittelalter*, Sten Ebbeson, ed., (Tübingen: Gunter Narr Verlag, 1995), p. 143.

18. Rosier, "*Res significata*," pp. 142–43.

19. Alan does exclude names designating privation, submissiveness, and violence more categorically (*Reg.* 33).

20. Peter Helias, *Summa* (Arsenal 711 fol. 18va) cited and translated by Hunt, in R. W. Hunt, "Studies on Priscian in the 11th and 12th Centuries I," in *Collected Papers on the History of Grammar in the Middle Ages*, G. L. Bursill-Hill, ed. (Amsterdam: John Benjamins B.V., 1980), p. 27. My emphasis.

21. Boethius, *Comm. PH* I. 3. 67. 7–10.

22. Evans, *Alan of Lille*, pp. 79–80.

23. Gilbert, *Expositio in de Trinitate*, 1. Prol. 3; 3. 1; 4. 22, 28 and 104; 5. 20; 2. Prol. 1; 1. 2.

24. Sten Ebbesen, "Introduction," in *Sprachtheorien in Spätantike und Mittelalter*, Sten Ebbeson, ed., (Tübingen: Gunter Narr Verlag, 1995), pp. xiv–xv.

25. Kenneth Burke, *A Rhetoric of Motives* (Berkeley: University of California Press, 1969), pp. 114–27, 137–42, 174–80, 301–13.

26. For a discussion of the entry in Alan's theological dictionary for *abyssus*, see above, p. 151.

27. The example comes from Boethius's *De differentiis topiciis*, PL 64, 1193C–94A.

28. Prepositinus, *De nominibus divinis*, pp. 245–46.

29. This is the epigram to Kenneth Burke's *A Grammar of Motives* (New York: Prentice-Hall, 1945), one which Alan could accept for this work as well.

30. Jean Châtillon is an exception. He sees a tension between Alan's desire to make theology a science analogous to the other sciences and the "radical equivocity" of Alan's theory of theological language, only resolved at the end of Alan's life, when he retreated into the silence of the abbey of Cîteaux, having given up all teaching, writing, and preaching. See Jean Châtillon, "La méthode théologique d'Alain de Lille," ALGCJG, pp. 47–60.

31. On the difference between Alan and the *nominales*, see M. D. Chenu, "Grammaire et théologie au XIIe et XIIIe siècle," ADHDLMA 10 (1935): 5–28.

32. Jan Ziolkowski, *Alan of Lille's Grammar of Sex: The Meaning of Grammar to a Twelfth-Century Intellectual* (Cambridge, MA: Harvard University Press, 1985), pp. 125–26. See also Gillian R. Evans, *Old Arts and New Theology: The Beginnings of Theology as an Academic Discipline* (Oxford: Oxford University Press, 1980), pp. 117–19.

33. Evans, *Alan of Lille*, pp. 166–71.

34. Rouse and Rouse, "*Statim invenire*: Schools, Preachers, and New Attitudes to the Page," in *Renaissance and Renewal in the Twelfth Century*, Robert L. Benson and Giles Constable, eds. (Cambridge, MA: Harvard University Press, 1982), pp. 212–18. On distinction collections in general, see André Wilmart, "Notes sur les plus anciens recueils de distinctions bibliques," in

Mémorial Lagrange. Cinquantenaire de l'École biblique et archéologique française de Jérusalem (Paris: J. Gabalda, 1940), pp. 339–99, and Beryl Smalley, *The Study of the Bible in the Middle Ages*, 2nd ed. (Oxford: Blackwell, 1952), pp. 245–49.

35. Rouse and Rouse, "Statim invenire," pp. 212–13.

36. For Priscian's definitions, see Priscian, *Institutiones grammaticae*, 2. 4. 18, in *Grammatici latini*, Heinrich Kiel, ed., vol. 4 (Leipzig: B. G. Teubner 1864, repr., Hildesheim: George Olms Verlag, 1961).

37. On adjectives, Alan has theology contradict the view of dialectic rather than grammar; in grammar, adjectives are undifferentiated from nouns. Cf. Evans, *Alan of Lille*, p. 36.

38. Cf. Alan's discussion of the verb in the *Reg.* 38 and my discussion of this passage, above, p. 136.

39. Evans conjectures that the immateriality of the subject may be a reference to transubstantiation. Evans, *Alan of Lille*, p. 37. Cf. Alan of Lille, *De fide catholica. Contra haereticos, Valdenses, Judaeos et paganos* PL 210, 360B. Though Evans does not note it, Alan uses the same terms in the *Regulae* to explain the Eucharist. *Reg.* 107, 211–12. However, it can be read as having a more general application. See *Reg.* 13.

40. Alan of Lille, "De incarnatione Christi," PL 210. 578–79.

41. See Luisa Valente, "Langage et théologie pendant la seconde moitié du XIIe siècle," in *Sprachtheorien in Spätantike und Mittelalter*, Sten Ebbesen, ed. (Tübingen: Gunter Narr Verlag, 1995), pp. 39–44.

42. Evans, *Alan of Lille*, p. 34.

43. Cf. Boethius, *EN* I. 77–81 and above, p. 23.

44. Gilbert of Poitiers, *Expositio in Boethii librum contra Euticen et Nestorium*, in *The Commentaries on Boethius by Gilbert of Poitiers*, Nikolaus M. Häring, ed. (Toronto: Pontifical Institute of Mediaeval Studies, 1966), pp. 242–64.

45. See Maurice de Gandillac, "La nature chez Alain de Lille," ALGCJG, pp. 61–75, and Barbara Newman, *God and the Goddesses: Vision, Poetry and Belief in the Middle Ages* (Philadelphia: University of Pennsylvania Press, 2003), p. 71.

46. Rouse and Rouse, "Statim Invenire," p. 210.

47. See Rouse and Rouse, "Statim Invenire," pp. 213–15, and Gillian R. Evans, *Alan of Lille*, pp. 28–29, for some examples from the collection by Peter the Chanter. For more on the *distinctiones* form see also Richard and Mary Rouse, "Biblical Distinctions in the Thirteenth Century," AHDLMA 41 (1974): 27–37.

48. Louis Mackey, *Peregrinations of the Word* (Ann Arbor: University of Michigan Press, 1997), pp. 121–24.

49. Chenu, "Symbolist Mentality," p. 132.

50. See Newman, *God and the Goddesses*, pp. 294–304 and above, pp. 4–5.

51. Rouse and Rouse, "Statim Invenire," p. 216. According to Evans, Peter the Chanter's *Summa Abel* may be a bit earlier than Alan's dictionary, but both were early examples of the genre. Gillian R. Evans, "The Place of Peter the Chanter's *De tropis loquendi*," *Analecta Cisterciensia* 39 (1983): 245.

52. D'Alverny, *Textes inédits*, p. 71.

53. See Evans' comparison of Alan and Peter the Chanter in Evans, *Alan of Lille*, pp. 25–33. For more on Peter the Chanter's dictionary, the *Distinctiones Abel*, see Luisa Valente, *Phantasia contrarietatis: Contradizzioni scritturali, discorso teologico et arti del linguaggio nel "De tropis loquendi" di Pietro Cantore (d. 1197)* (Florence, Olschki, 1997) and Stephen A. Barney, "Visible Allegory: the *Distinctiones Abel* of Peter the Chanter," in *Allegory, Myth, and Symbol*, Morton W. Bloomfield, ed. (Cambridge, MA: Harvard University Press, 1981), pp. 87–108.

54. Evans, "Place of Peter the Chanter," 246.

55. Augustine, *De doctrina christiana* 3. 27. 38, CCSL 32. 99–100.

56. The same Augustinian principle informs Alan's allegories in a different way. See above, p. 173.

57. See Richard Hamilton Green, "Alan of Lille's *De planctu naturae*," *Speculum* 31 (1956): 649–74; for his review of other critics, see 649–50, nn. 1–4. See also J. Huizinga, *Über die Verknüpfung des Poetischen mit dem Theologischen bei Alanus de Insulis* (Amsterdam: 1932), especially Noord-Hollandsche uitgevers maatschappij, pp. 54–82, 91–92; Guy Raynaud de Lage, *Alain de Lille: poète du XIIe siècle* (Montréal: Institut d'Études Médiévales, 1951), especially pp. 73–74 on nature and morality; C. S. Lewis, *The Allegory of Love* (Oxford: Oxford University Press, 1936), pp. 98–109. See also Wetherbee, *Platonism and Poetry*, pp. 187–219 and George Economou, *The Goddess Natura in Medieval Literature* (Cambridge, MA: Harvard University Press, 1972), pp. 100–102.

58. Ziolkowski, *Grammar of Sex*, pp. 74, 95–107, 139. Cf. Maureen Quilligan, "Allegory, Allegoresis, and the Deallegorization of Language: The *Roman de la rose*, the *De planctu naturae*, and the *Parlement of Foules*," in *Allegory, Myth, and Symbol*, Morton W. Bloomfield, ed. (Cambridge, MA: Harvard University Press, 1981), p. 185, and James Simpson, *Sciences and the Self in Medieval Poetry*: Alan of Lille's *Anticlaudianus* and John Gower's *confessio amantis* (Cambridge: Cambridge University Press, 1995), pp. 45, 67, 133.

59. On this view of allegory in general, see J. Hillis Miller, "The Two Allegories," in *Allegory, Myth, and Symbol*, pp. 355–70; Stephen J. Greenblatt, Introduction, in *Allegory and Representation*, Stephen J. Greenblatt, ed. (Baltimore, 1981), pp. vii–xiii; and Paul de Man, *Allegories of Reading: Figural Language in Rousseau, Nietzsche, Rilke, and Proust* (New Haven: Yale University Press, 1979). For this model applied to medieval allegory, though not to Alan, see Laurie A. Finke, "Truth's Treasure: Allegory and Meaning in *Piers Plowman*," in *Medieval Texts and Contemporary Readers*, Laurie A. Finke and Martin B. Shichtman, eds. (Ithaca: Cornell University Press, 1987), pp. 51–68.

60. Alexandre Leupin, *Barbarolexis: Medieval Writing and Sexuality* (Cambridge: Harvard University Press, 1989), pp. 6–16, 72; Mark D. Jordan, *The Invention of Sodomy in Christian Theology* (Chicago: University of Chicago Press, 1997), p. 87; Susan Schibanoff, "Sodomy's Mark," in *Queering the Middle Ages*, Glenn Burger and Steve F. Kruger, eds. (Minneapolis: University of Minnesota Press, 2001), p. 29; Larry Scanlon, "Unspeakable Pleasures: Alain de Lille, Sexual Regulation and the Priesthood of Genius," *Romantic Review* 86

(1995): 219, 226. For accounts of Alan's condemnations of sodomy as successful, see Gerald Herman, "The 'Sin against Nature' and Its Echoes in Medieval French Literature," *Annuale Mediaevale* 17 (1976): 76–77, and Elizabeth B. Keiser, *Courtly Desire and Medieval Homophobia: The Legitimation of Sexual Pleasure in "Cleanness" and Its Contexts* (New Haven: Yale University Press, 1997), pp. 71–92.

61. Jordan, *Invention of Sodomy*, pp. 89–91.

62. Cf. Jon Whitman's description of allegory in *Allegory: The Dynamics of an Ancient and Medieval Technique* (Cambridge, MA: Harvard University Press, 1987), p. 262.

63. Bernard Silvestris, *Cosmographia*, in *The Cosmographia of Bernardus Silvestris*, Winthrop Wetherbee, trans. (New York: Columbia University Press, 1973). For Silva's praise of Nature's successful ordering and refining of her coarseness, see *Cosmographia, Microcosmos*, 2, 93–94. For a sense of some of the darker elements of Bernard's poem, see Wetherbee's introduction to his translation, pp. 4–5 and Newman, *God and the Goddesses*, p. 62.

64. Ziolkowski, *Grammar of Sex*, pp. 16–17. See Donatus, *Ars grammatica in Grammatici latini*, ed. Heinrich Keil, vol. 4 (Leipzig: B. G. Teubner, 1857–80, repr. Hildeheim: George Olms Verlag, 1961), p. 399.

65. Cf. Scanlon, "Unspeakable Pleasures," 221–22, and Schibanoff, "Sodomy's Mark," pp. 33–35.

66. See Green, "Alan of Lille's *De planctu*," 649–74, Huizinga, *Über die Verknüpfung*, pp. 54–82, 91–92, Raynaud de Lage, *Alain de Lille*, pp. 43–44, 95–96, 105, 114, Lewis, *The Allegory of Love*, pp. 105, 106, 108. See also Winthrop Wetherbee, "The Function of Poetry in the 'De planctu naturae' of Alain of Lille," *Traditio* 25 (1969): 108. See also above, pp. 172–3 for more negative evaluations of Alan's poetry.

67. Ziolkowski, *Grammar of Sex*, p. 47.

68. But see Newman, *God and the Goddesses*, pp. 67, 70, 72 and Jordan, *Invention of Sodomy*, p. 68. Newman argues, as I do, that Alan's contradiction of his own rules is self-conscious.

69. An anonymous poem dating from around the same time as *De planctu*, the *Altercatio Ganimedis et Helene*, takes up the same theme using the same grammatical metaphor. In this poem, Ganymede, who wants to be subject rather than predicate making love with Helen, defends his passive position by an appeal to grammar which requires the joining of masculine to masculine. See Ziolkowski, *Grammar of Sex*, pp. 69–70 and Newman, *God and the Goddesses*, pp. 91–93.

70. Maureen Quilligan, "Words and Sex: The Language of Allegory in the *De planctu naturae, the Roman de la Rose,* and Book III of *The Faerie Queene*," *Allegorica* 2 (1977): 197; Green, "Alan of Lille's *De planctu*," 656–59. See also Chenu, "Symbolist Mentality," p. 99.

71. Cf. Wetherbee, *Platonism and Poetry*, pp. 194–95.

72. Cf. Scanlon, "Unspeakable Pleasures," pp. 224–25.

73. For Bernard Silvestris' portrayal of Nature's partnership with "Noys," divine providence, see *Cosmographia, Megacosmos*, 2, 69–70. Further,

Bernard has the heavenly Urania who proclaims to Nature, "Go then, Nature, I follow; for no error can befall, if the way is determined by your guidance." *Cosmographia, Microcosmos,* 4, 98.

74. See Linda E. Marshall, "The Identity of the 'New Man' in the 'Anticlaudianus' of Alan of Lille," *Viator* 10 (1979): 90, and Newman, *God and the Goddesses,* pp. 79, 87.

75. For discussions of the identity of the new man, see Marshall, "The Identity of the 'New Man,' pp. 77–94," Evans, *Alan of Lille,* p. 170, and Newman, *God and the Goddesses,* pp. 82–86.

76. I have adjusted Sheridan's translation. Prudence also "wavers" at the outset of the poem when pressed to lead the delegation to heaven. But this is partly because she has been asked to take up an office she knows to be beyond her natural powers, and partly it is simply typical of Alan's portrayal of all the virtues as a hard won equilibrium between opposing inclinations. See above, pp. 169–70. See *AC* 2. 72; 163–65 and 2. 79; 310–11. However, in the opening scene she resolves her ambivalence and takes a firm stand; in heaven, by contrast, she is eventually carried by Faith, administered a heavenly drink, and handed a mirror to mediate her sight. See *AC,* 6. 156–60; 1–140. Sheridan notes that the first use of such a mirror was to shield Perseus from the face of Medusa, surely suggestive of the connection between the two extremes falling outside of nature which I contend Alan is constructing. Cf. Richard Hamilton Green, "Alan of Lille's *Anticlaudianus:* Ascensus Mentis in Deum," *Annuale Mediaevale* 8 (1967): 13–16, for a view of Prudence as less abruptly and less completely transformed in heaven.

77. Cf. Bernard Sylvestris' portrayal of the encounter of Nature with heaven. She is somewhat dazzled and blinking but is described as "worthy to be received" there. *Cosmographia, Microcosmos,* 3, 96–97.

78. Cf. Marshall, "The Identity of the 'New Man,' " 92–93. I differ with Marshall not on whether there is a shift in language and the mode of representation in theology but on whether for Alan theology can *succeed* in representing the miraculous.

79. See above, p. 160.

80. Cf. *DP* 8. 141; 143–45.

81. Ziolkowski, *Grammar of Sex,* p. 133.

82. Boethius, *Consol.* IV. pr. 6. 356–71.

83. Cf. *Reg.* 8–9, 22, 133, 139.

84. I have adjusted Sheridan's translation.

85. I have adjusted Sheridan's translation.

86. Cf. Bernard Silvestris, *Cosmographia, Microsmos,* 1–2, 91–94.

87. See Sheridan's comment about the verb *"federo"* in his translation, *AC,* 174, n. 9. For other possible meanings, see J. Ch. Payen, "L'utopie du contrat social dans l'*Anticlaudianus,*" in ALGCJG, pp. 125–27.

88. Cf. Bernard Silvestris, *Cosmographia, Microcosmos,* 14, 126–27. While Bernard portrays the creation of the universe in mostly positive terms, his account of the creation of human being is darker and more ambivalent. Cf. Newman, *God and the Goddesses,* pp. 62–63.

89. See, for example, Simpson, *Sciences and the Self*, pp. 42–56, 275–79 and passim. Cf. Alan of Lille, *De virtutibus et de vitiis et de donis Spiritus Sancti*, Odon Lottin, ed., *Mediaeval Studies*, 12 (1950): 22–23. Philippe Delhaye, "La vertu et les vertus dans les oeuvres d'Alain de Lille," *Cahiers de civilisation médiévale* 6 (1963): 13–25, especially 13–14, 22. For some Augustinians of the period, Delhaye notes, the human virtues are without value and seen as sinful. For Delhaye, Alan avoids the Augustinian extreme, as well as the extreme of Alcuin, who nearly forgets charity in his enthusiasm for the classical or human virtues. In my view, Alan's use of the human virtues fits the model of his use of other new material available in the arts; he takes up the classical virtues enthusiastically but significantly undercuts their value, especially when compared with what is available in theology.

90. The dual possibility of a brutishness and apotheosis is also described in the *Summa* and *Regulae*. See, for example, *SQH* 1. 121–22, and *Reg* 99, 204–5.

91. Newman distinguishes between the natural and cultural in Alan, but what is striking about Alan is how symmetrical they are. See Newman, *God and the Goddesses*, p. 54.

92. See Economou, *The Goddess Natura*, pp. 86, 91 on how Alan shifts the traditional presentation of Venus.

93. On these passages, compare Huizinga, *Über die Verknüpfung*, pp. 63–65, and Marshall, "The Identity of the 'New Man,' " p. 92.

94. Cf. Gandillac, "La nature chez Alain de Lille," pp. 61–75. For a view of nature in Alan closer to mine, see Willemien Otten, "Nature and Scripture: Demise of a Medieval Analogy," *Harvard Theological Review* 88: 2 (1995): 277–83.

95. Cf. Scanlon, "Unspeakable Pleasures," 236–42, and Schibanoff, "Sodomy's Mark," pp. 36–37. Both Scanlon and Schibanoff argue that Genius' excommunication of sinners is meant to be a real resolution to his inability to correct nature's mistake by writing. For Scanlon, the act of excommunication gives the kind of pleasure it outlaws. In my view, there is a kind of illicit pleasure in Alan's work but it seems to me that it is not in the act of prohibition but in the excessive descriptions of vice and theology.

96. Simpson sees a tension between the theological vision of Books 1–6 and the creation and victory of the "new man" and resolves it by arguing that the creation and victory of the new man occurs *before* the journey of Prudence to heaven for a soul. Simpson, *Sciences and the Self*, pp. 66–91.

97. Quilligan, "Allegory, Allegoresis," p. 174.

98. Lewis, *The Allegory of Love*, p. 106.

99. Sheridan, "Introduction," *AC*, 36–37; Sheridan, "Introduction," *DP* 33.

100. Green, "Alan of Lille's *Anticlaudianus*," p. 3.

101. Green, "Alan of Lille's *Anticlaudianus*," pp. 5–7.

102. Augustine, *De doctrina christiana* 1. 2. 2, CCSL 32. 7.

103. Augustine, *De doctrina christiana* 3. 5. 9, CCSL 32. 82–83; 3. 6. 10–17.11, CCSL 32. 83–84; 3. 8. 12, CCSL 32, 85. See also Eileen C. Sweeney, "Hugh of St. Victor: The Augustinian Tradition of Sacred and Secular

Reading Revised," in *Reading and Wisdom: The De doctrina christiana of Augustine in the Middle Ages*, Edward D. English, ed. (Notre Dame: University of Notre Dame Press, 1995), p. 71.

104. Quilligan, "Allegory, Allegoresis," p. 185.

105. See Peter Dronke's account of this definition in *Fabula: Explorations into the Uses of Myth in Medieval Platonism* (Leiden: E. J. Brill, 1974), p. 146.

Conclusion: Language and the *Ascensus Mentis ad Deum*

1. Umberto Eco, *The Search for the Perfect Language*, James Fentress, trans. (Cambridge, MA: Blackwell, 1995).

2. Thomas Aquinas, *Summa theologiae* II–II, q. 180, a. 6, obj. 2 and 3. Cf. Pseudo-Dionysius, *De divinibus nominibus*, sec. 8, PG 3, 704; Richard of St. Victor, *Benjamin minor sive De gratia contemplationis* 1. 5, PL 196, 68.

3. Pierre Hadot, *Philosophy as a Way of Life*, Arnold I. Davidson, ed., Michael Chase, trans. (Maldon, MA: Blackwell, 1995), pp. 269–71.

4. Norman Kretzmann, "The Culmination of the Old Logic in Peter Abelard," in *Renaissance and Renewal in the Twelfth Century*, R. L. Benson and G. Constable, eds. (Cambridge, MA: Harvard University Press, 1982). "Old logic" refers to that based on the parts of Aristotle's Organon available before the thirteenth century: *Categories*, *Peri hermeneias*, and *Prior Analytics*.

BIBLIOGRAPHY

Abelard, Peter. "Confessio fidei ad Heloisam," in Charles F. Burnett, " 'Confessio fidei ad Heloisam'—Abelard's Last Letter to Heloise?" *Mittellateinisches Jahrbuch* 21 (1986): 147–55.

————. *Ethica sive Scito teipsum*. In *Peter Abelard's "Ethics,"* edited by D. Luscombe Oxford: Clarendon Press, 1971.

————. "Abelard's Rule for Religious Women." Edited by T. McLaughlin, *Mediaeval Studies* 18 (1956): 241–92.

————. *Expositio in hexaemeron*, PL 178, 729–841.

————. *Glossae super Porphyrium*, in *Peter Abaelards philosophische Schriften*, edited by B. Geyer. Beiträge zur Geschichte der Philosophie des Mittelalters, vol. 21, heft 1. Münster: Aschendorff, 1919.

————. *Glossae super Peri ermenias*, in *Peter Abaelards philosophische Schriften*, edited by B. Geyer. Beiträge zur Geschichte der Philosophie des Mittelalters, vol. 21, heft 3. Münster: Aschendorff, 1927.

————. *Historia calamitatum*. Edited by J. Monfrin. Paris: J. Vrin, 1962.

————. *Hymnarius paraclitensis*. Edited by Josef Szövérffy. Boston: Beacon Press, 1975.

————. *Logica nostrorum petitioni sociorum*, in *Peter Abaelards philosophische Schriften*, edited by B. Geyer. Beiträge zur Geschichte der Philosophie des Mittelalters, vol. 21, heft 4. Münster: Aschendorff, 1933.

————. *Petri Abaelardi opera theologica*. Edited by E. Buytaert and C. Mews. CCCM, vols. 11–13, Turnhout: Brepols, 1969–87.

————. *Petri Abaelardi Planctus*, edited by Wilhelm Meyer. Erlangen: Junge & Sohn, 1890.

————. "Planctus virginum Israel super filia Jephthe Galadite," edited by Wolfram von den Steinen in "Die Planctus Abaelards—Jephthas Tochter," *Mittellateinisches Jahrbuch*, 4 (1967): 142–44.

————. "Planctus Israel super Sanson," edited and translated by Peter Dronke in Peter Dronke, "*Planctus* and Satire," in *Poetic Individuality in the Middle Ages*. Oxford: Clarendon Press, 1970, pp. 121–23.

————. "Planctus David super Saul et Jonathan," edited and translated by John Stevens in John Stevens, *Words and Music in the Middle Ages: Song, Narrative, Dance, and Drama, 1050–1350*. Cambridge: Cambridge University Press, 1986, pp. 125–26.

————. *Sic et non*. Edited by B. Boyer and R. McKeon. Chicago: University of Chicago Press, 1977.

Abelard, Peter. *Soliloquium*, in "Peter Abelard 'Soliloquium'. A critical edition," edited by C. Burnett. *Studi Medievali* 25, 2 (1984): 857–94.

Abelard and Heloise. "The Letter of Heloise on Religious Life and Abelard's First Reply, edited by J. T. Muckle. *Mediaeval Studies* 17 (1955): 240–81.

Abelard and Heloise. "The Personal Letters between Abelard and Heloise," edited by J. T. Muckle. *Mediaeval Studies* 15 (1953): 47–94.

Abélard en son temps. Acts du Colloque international organisé à l'occasion du 9e centenaire de la naissance de Pierre Abélard (May 14–19, 1979). Paris: Les Belles Lettres, 1981.

Alain de Lille, Gautier de Châtillon, Jakemart Giélée, et leur temps, edited by H. Roussel and F. Suard. Lille: Centre d'Études Mediévales et Dialectales de l'Université de Lille III, 1980.

Alan of Lille. *Anticlaudianus.* Edited by R. Bossuat. Paris: J. Vrin, 1955).

——. *Anticlaudianus, or the Good and Perfect Man.* Translated by James J. Sheridan. Toronto: Pontifical Institute of Mediaeval Studies, 1973.

——. *De fide catholica. Contra haereticos, Valdenses, Judaeos et paganos.* PL 210, 305–430.

——. "De incarnatione Christi," PL 210, 578–79.

——. *Liber in distinctionibus dictionum theologicalium,* PL 210, 685–1012.

——. *De planctu naturae.* Edited by N. M. Häring. *Studi Medievali* 19 (1978): 797–879.

——. *Plaint of Nature.* Translated by James J. Sheridan. Toronto, Pontifical Institute of Mediaeval Studies, 1980.

——. *Regulae caelestis iuris.* Edited by N. M. Häring. AHDLMA 48 (1981): 97–226.

——. *Summa quoniam homines.* Edited by P. Glorieux. "La Somme *Quoniam Homines*," AHDLMA 20 (1954): 113–64.

Alexiou, Margaret, and Peter Dronke. "The Lament of Jephtha's Daughter: Themes, Traditions, Originality." *Studi medievali* 12.2 (1971): 819–63.

Alford, John A. "The Grammatical Metaphor: A Survey of Its Use in the Middle Ages." *Speculum* 57 (1982): 728–60.

Alverny, Marie Thérèse d'. *Textes inédits d'Alain de Lille.* Paris: J. Vrin, 1965.

Ambrose. *Seven Exegetical Works.* Translated by Michael P. McHugh. Washington, DC: The Catholic University of America Press, 1972.

Anciaux, P. *La théologie du sacrement de pénitence au XIIe siècle.* Louvain: Nauwelaerts, 1949.

Angelini, Giuseppe. *L'Ortodossia e la grammatica: Analisi di struttura e deduzione storica della teologia trinitaria di Prepositino.* Rome: Università Gregoriana, 1972.

Armstrong, A. H. *The Cambridge History of Later Greek and Early Medieval Philosophy.* Cambridge: Cambridge University Press, 1967.

Augustine. *De civitate Dei.* CCSL 47, 1–314.

——. *De baptismo.* CSEL 51, 145–375.

——. *De doctrina christiana.* CCSL 32, 1–167.

——. *Ennarrationes in Psalmos.* CCSL 38–40.

——. *Epistulae.* CSEL 34.

——. *De libero arbitrio.* CSEL 74, 3–154.

——. *De magistro.* CSEL 29, 157–203.

——. *De ordine.* CSEL 63, 121–85.

Bark, William. "Boethius' Fourth Tractate, the So-Called 'De Fide Catholica.' " *Harvard Theological Review* 39 (1946): 55–69.

———. "Theodoric vs. Boethius: Vindication and Apology." In B-FG, pp. 11–32. First published in *American Historical Review* 49 (1943–44): 410–26.

Barnard, Leslie W. "To Allegorize or not to Allegorize?" *Studia Theologica* 36 (1982): 1–10.

Barnes, Jonathan. "Boethius and the Study of Logic." In *Boethius: His Life, Thought, and Influence*, edited by Margaret Gibson, pp. 73–89. Oxford: Basil Blackwell, 1981.

Barney, Stephen A. "Visible Allegory: the *Distinctiones Abel* of Peter the Chanter," in *Allegory, Myth, and Symbol*, edited by Morton W. Bloomfield, pp. 87–108. Cambridge, MA: Harvard University Press, 1981.

Barrett, H. M. *Boethius: Some Aspects of his Times and Work.* New York: Russell and Russell, 1966.

Bennett, Beth S. "The Rhetoric of Martianus Capella and Anselm de Besate in the Tradition of Menippean Satire." *Philosophy and Rhetoric* 22, 2 (1991): 128–42.

Benton, John. "A Reconsideration of the Authenticity of the Correspondence of Abelard and Heloise." In PAPWW, pp. 41–52.

———. "Fraud, Fiction and Borrowing in the Correspondence of Abelard and Héloïse." In PAPV, pp. 469–512.

Bergeron, M. "La structure du concept latin de personne: Comment, chez les latins, 'persona' en est venu à signifier 'relatio,' " *Études d'histoire littéraire et doctrinale du XIIIe siècle*, 2nd ser., Publications de l'Institut d'Études Médiévales d'Ottawa, 2. Paris: J. Vrin, 1932, pp. 121–61.

Bernard Silvestris, *Cosmographia*, in *The Cosmographia of Bernardus Silvestris*, translated by Winthrop Wetherbee, New York: Columbia University Press, 1973.

Bertola, E. "I precedenti storici del metodo del *Sic et non* di Abelardo." *Rivista di filosofia neo-scolastica* 53 (1961): 258–79.

———. "Le critiche di Abelardo ad Anselmo di Laon e ad Guglielmo di Champeaux." *Rivista della filosofia neo-scolastica* 52 (1960): 495–522.

Biard, Joël. "Sémantique et ontologie dans *l'Ars meliduna.*" In GPC, pp. 121–44.

Boethius. *Commentaria in Porphyrium.* PL 64, 71–158.

———. *Commentarium in librum Peri hermeneias.* Edited by K. Meiser. 2 vols. Leipzig: Teubner, 1880; rpt. NY-London, 1987.

———. De differentiis topiciis, PL 64, 1173–1218.

———. *The Theological Tractates and the Consolation of Philosophy.* Translated by H. F. Stewart, E. K. Rand, and S. J. Tester. Loeb Classical Library, vol. 74. Cambridge, MA: Harvard University Press, 1973.

———. Edited by Manfred Fuhrmann and Joachim Gruber. Darmstadt: Wissenschaftliche Buchgesellschaft, 1984.

Bos, Egbert Peter. "La théorie de la signification de la 'uox significatiua ad placitum' dans les *Introductiones montanae maiores.*" In GPC, pp. 73–90.

Bourgain, Pascale. "Héloïse." In AST, pp. 211–37.

Braakhuis, Henricus Antonius Giovanni. "Signification, Appellation and Predication in the *Ars meliduna.*" In GPC, pp. 107–20.

Brown, Catherine. "Muliebriter: Doing Gender in the Letters of Heloise." In *Gender and Text in the Later Middle Ages*, edited by Jane Chance, pp. 25–51. Gainsville, FL: University Press of Florida, 1996.

Brown, Peter. *Augustine of Hippo: a Biography*. Berkeley: University of California Press, 1970.

Brown, Phyllis R. and John C. Peiffer II. "Heloise, Dialectic, and the *Heroides*." In LH, pp. 143–160.

Buffière, F. *Les mythes d'Homère et la pensée grecque*. Paris: Les Belles Lettres,1956.

Burke, Kenneth. *A Grammar of Motives*. New York: Prentice-Hall, 1945.

———. *The Rhetoric of Motives*. Berkeley: University of California Press, 1969.

———. *The Rhetoric of Religion: Studies in Logology*. Berkeley: University of California Press, 1970.

Burnett, Charles. "*Confessio fidei ad Heloisam*: Abelard's Last Letter to Heloise? A Discussion and Critical Edition of the Latin and Medieval French Versions." *Mittellateinisches Jahrbuch* 21 (1986): 147–55.

Burrows, Mark. "Another Look at the Sources of *De consolatione philosophiae*: Boethius' Echo of Augustine's Doctrine of *Providencia*." *Proceedings of the Patristic, Medieval and Renaissance Conference* 11 (1986): 27–41.

Buytaert, E. M. "Abelard's Trinitarian Doctrine." In PA, pp. 127–52.

Calabrese, Michael. "Ovid and the Female Voice in the *De amore* and the *Letters* of Abelard and Heloise." *Modern Philology* 95 (1997): 1–26.

Caplan, Harry. *Of Eloquence: Studies in Ancient and Mediaeval Rhetoric*. Edited by Anne King and Helen North. Ithaca: Cornell University Press, 1970.

Cappuyns, M. "Boèce." In *Dictionnaire d'histoire et de gèographie ecclésiastiques*, edited by Alfred Baudrillart, pp. 348–80. Vol. 9. Paris: Letouzey et Ané, 1937.

Carton, R. "Le christianisme et l'augustinisme de Boèce." In *Mélanges Augustinniens*, pp. 243–329. Paris: Riviëre, 1931.

Chadwick, Henry. *Boethius: The Consolations of Music, Logic, Theology, and Philosophy*. Oxford: Clarendon Press, 1981.

Châtillon, Jean. "Abélard et les écoles." In AST, pp. 133–60.

———. "La méthode théologique d'Alain de Lille." In ALGCJG, pp. 47–60.

Chenu, M.-D. "Grammaire et théologie aux XIIe et XIIIe siècles." AHDLMA 10 (1935): 5–28.

———. *La théologie au douzième siècle*. 3rd ed. Paris: J. Vrin, 1976.

———. "The Symbolist Mentality." In *Nature, Man, and Society in the Twelfth Century: Essays on New Theological Perspectives in the Latin West*, edited and translated by Jerome Taylor and Lester Little, pp. 99–145. Chicago: University of Chicago Press, 1968.

———. "Un essai de méthode théologique au XIIe siècle." *Revue des sciences philosophiques et théologiques* 25 (1935): 258–67.

Cicero. *De inventione*. Translated and edited by H. M. Hubbell. Loeb Classical Library, vol. 18. Cambridge, MA: Harvard University Press, 1949.

Clanchy, M. T. *Abelard: A Medieval Life*. Oxford: Blackwell, 1997.

———. "Abelard's Mockery of St. Anselm." *Journal of Ecclesiastical History* 41, 1 (1990): 1–23.

Clark, John R. "The Traditional Figure of Dinah and Abelard's First *Planctus*." *Proceedings of the Patristic, Medieval and Renaissance Conference* 7 (1982): 117–28.

Colish, Marcia L. "Another Look at the School of Laon." AHDLMA 53 (1986): 7–22.

———. "Gilbert, the Early Porretans, and Peter Lombard: Semantics and Theology." In GPC, pp. 229–50.

———. *The Mirror of Language: A Study in the Medieval Theory of Knowledge*. rev. ed. Lincoln: University of Nebraska Press, 1983.

———. *Peter Lombard*. 2 vols. Leiden: E. J. Brill, 1994.

———. *The Stoic Tradition from Antiquity to the Early Middle Ages: Stoicism in Latin Christian Writers through the Sixth Century*. 2 vols. Leiden: E. J. Brill, 1990. (see Ch. 1, n. 74, p. 192).

———. "Systematic Theology and Theological Renewal in the Twelfth Century." *Journal of Medieval and Renaissance Studies* 18, 2 (Fall 1988): 135–56.

Collins, James. "Progress and Problems in the Reassessment of Boethius." *The Modern Schoolman* 23 (1945): 1–23.

Cottiaux, J. "La conception de la théologie chez Abélard." *Revue d'histoire ecclésiastique* 28 (1932): 247–95, 533–51, 788–828.

Courcelle, Pierre. *La consolation de philosophie dans la tradition littéraire. Antécédents et postérité de Boèce*. Paris: Études Augustiniennes, 1967.

Craig, W. L. *The Problem of Divine Foreknowledge and Future Contingents from Aristotle to Suarez*. Leiden: E. J. Brill, 1988.

Crouse, Robert. "The Ambiguous Stature of Philosophy in Boethius' *Consolation*." Boston Medieval Philosophy Colloquium Lecture. Boston College, Boston. March 15, 1999.

Curley, Thomas F., III. "The *Consolation of Philosophy* as a Work of Literature." *American Journal of Philology* 108 (1987): 345–67.

Curtius, Ernst Robert. *European Literature and the Latin Middle Ages*. Translated by Willard R. Trask. Bollingen Series XXXVI. New York: Harper and Row, 1953.

Delhaye, Philippe. "La vertu et les vertus dans les œuvres d'Alain de Lille." *Cahiers de civilisation médiévale* 6 (1963): 13–25.

———. "Le dossier anti-matrimonial de l'*Adversus Jovinianum* et son influence sur quelques ècrits latins du XIIe siècle." *Mediaeval Studies* 13 (1951): 65–86.

De Man, Paul. *Allegories of Reading: Figural Language in Rousseau, Nietzsche, Rilke, and Proust*. New Haven: Yale University Press, 1979.

Desmond, Marilynn. "Subjectivity and Sexual Violence in Heloise's Letters." In *The Tongue of the Fathers: Gender and Ideology in Twelfth-Century Latin*, edited by David Townsend and Andrew Taylor, pp. 35–54. Philadelphia: University of Pennsylvania Press, 1998.

Donatus. *Ars grammatica*. In *Grammatici latini*, edited by Heinrich Keil. Vol. 4. Leipzig: B. G. Teubner, 1857–1880.

D'Onofrio, Giulio. "Dialectic and Theology: Boethius' 'Opuscula sacra' and Their Early Medieval Readers." *Studi Medievali* 27, 1 (1986): 45–67.

Dronke, Peter. *Abelard and Heloise in Medieval Testimonies*. Glasgow University of Glasgow Press, 1976.

Dronke, Peter. *Fabula: Explorations into the Uses of Myth in Medieval Platonism.* Leiden: E. J. Brill, 1974.

———. "Heloise." In *Women Writers of the Middle Ages: A Critical Study of Texts from Perpetua (d. 203) to Marguerite Porete (d. 1310),* edited by Peter Dronke, pp. 107–43. New York: Cambridge University Press, 1984.

———. "Héloïse and Marianne: Some Reconsiderations." *Romanische Forschungen* 72 (1960): 223–256.

Dronke, Peter. "Heloise's *Problemata* and *Letters*: Some Questions of Form and Content." In PAPWW, pp. 53–73.

———. *Poetic Individuality in the Middle Ages: New Departures in Poetry 1000–1150.* Oxford: Clarendon Press, 1970.

———. *Verse with Prose from Petronius to Dante: The Art and Scope of a Mixed Form.* Cambridge, MA: Harvard University Press, 1994.

Duclow, Donald F. "Perspective and Therapy in Boethius's *Consolation of Philosophy*." *Journal of Medicine and Philosophy* 4 (1979): 334–43.

Ebbesen, Sten. "Introduction." In *Sprachtheorien in Spätantike und Mittelalter,* edited by Sten Ebbesen, pp. xi–xx. Tübingen: Gunter Narr Verlag, 1995.

———. "The Semantics of the Trinity according to Stephen Langton and Andrew Sunesen." In GPC, pp. 401–35.

Eco, Umberto. *The Search for the Perfect Language.* Translated by James Fentress. Cambridge, MA: Blackwell, 1995.

Economou, George D. *The Goddess Natura in Medieval Literature.* Cambridge, MA: Harvard University Press, 1972.

Evans, Gillian R. *Alan of Lille: The Frontiers of Theology in the Later Twelfth Century.* Cambridge: Cambridge University Press, 1983.

———. "Boethian and Euclidean Axiomatic Method in the Theology of the Later Twelfth Century." *Archives internationales d'histoire des sciences* 30 (1980): 36–52.

———. *The Language and Logic of the Bible: The Earlier Middle Ages.* Cambridge: Cambridge University Press, 1984.

———. *The Mind of Saint Bernard of Clairvaux.* Oxford: Clarendon Press, 1983.

———. *Old Arts and New Theology: The Beginnings of Theology as an Academic Discipline.* Oxford: Oxford University Press, 1980.

———. "The Place of Peter the Chanter's *De tropis loquendi*," *Analecta Cisterciensia* 39 (1983): 231–53.

Ferguson, Chris. "Autobiography as Therapy: Guibert de Nogent, Peter Abelard, and the Making of Medieval Autobiography." *Journal of Medieval and Renaissance Studies* 13 (1983): 187–212.

Ferguson, Margaret W. "Saint Augustine's Region of Unlikeness: The Crossing of Exile and Language." *The Georgia Review* 29 (1975): 843–64.

Finke, Laurie A. "Truth's Treasure: Allegory and Meaning in *Piers Plowman*." In *Medieval Texts and Contemporary Readers,* edited by Laurie A. Finke and Martin B. Shichtman, pp. 51–68. Ithaca, NY: Cornell University Press, 1987.

Flood, Emmet. "The Narrative Structure of Augustine's *Confessions*: Time's Quest for Eternity." *International Philosophical Quarterly* 28 (1988): 141–62.

Fumagalli, Maria Teresa. *The Logic of Abelard*: Translated by Simon Pleasance. Dordrecht: D. Reidel, 1970.

Gandillac, Maurice de. "Intention et loi dans l'éthique d'Abélard." In PAPV, pp. 585–608.

———. "La nature chez Alain de Lille." In ALGCJG, pp. 61–75.

Georgianna, Linda. "Any Corner of Heaven: Heloise's Critique of Monasticism." *Mediaeval Studies* 49 (1987): 221–53.

Gersh, Stephen. *Middle Platonism and Neoplatonism: The Latin Tradition.* Vol. 2. Notre Dame, IN: Notre Dame University Press, 1986.

Ghellinck, J. de. *Le mouvement théologique du XIIe siècle.* Bruges: Éditions "De Tempel," 1948.

Gibson, Margaret T. "The Place of the *Glossa ordinaria* in Medieval Exegesis." In *Ad Litteram: Authoritative Texts and the Medieval Readers,* edited by Mark D. Jordan and Kent Emery Jr., pp. 5–27. Notre Dame: University of Notre Dame Press, 1992.

Gilbert of Poitiers. *The Commentaries on Boethius.* Edited by Nikolaus Häring. Toronto: Pontifical Institute of Mediaeval Studies, 1966.

Gilbert de Poitiers et ses contemporains: Aux origines de la "Logica Modernorum," Actes du 7e symposium européen d'histoire de la logique et sémantique médiévales, Poitiers, June 17–22, 1985. Edited by Jean Jolivet and Alain de Libera. Naples: Bibliopolis, 1987.

Gilson, Etienne. *Heloise and Abelard.* Translated by L. K. Shook. Chicago: Henry Regenery, 1951.

———. *Reason and Revelation in the Middle Ages.* New York: Scribner's Sons, 1951.

Grabmann, Martin. *Die Geschichte der Scholastischen Methode: nach gedruckten und ungedruckten Quellen.* Vol. 2. Freiburg: Herder, 1911.

Green, Richard Hamilton. "Alan of Lille's *Anticlaudianus*: Ascensus Mentis in Deum." *Annuale Mediaevale,* 8 (1967): 3–16.

———. "Alan of Lille's De planctu naturae." *Speculum* 31 (1956): 649–74.

Greenblatt, Stephen J. "Introduction." In *Allegory and Representation,* edited by Stephen Greenblatt. vii–xiii. Selected Papers from the English Institute 5. Baltimore: John Hopkins University Press, 1981.

Gregory the Great. *Moralia.* CCSL 143.

Gregory, Tullio. "Considerations sur *ratio* et *natura* chez Abélard." In PAPV, pp. 569–81.

Gruber, Joachim. *Kommentar zu Boethius De consolatione philosophiae.* New York: Walter de Gruyter, 1978.

Gurevich, Aaron. *The Origins of European Individualism.* Translated by Katharine Judelson. Cambridge, MA: Blackwell, 1995.

Hadot, Pierre. "Dieu comme acte d'être dans le néoplatonisme." In *Dieu et l'être,* edited by Paul Vignaux, pp. 57–63. Paris: Études Augustiniennes, 1978.

———. "La distinction de l'être et de l'étant dans le 'De hebdomadibus' de Boèce." *Miscellanea Mediaevalia* 2 (1963): 147–53.

———. *Philosophy as a Way of Life.* Edited by Arnold I. Davidson and translated by Michael Chase. Maldon, MA: Blackwell, 1995.

Häring, Nikolaus M. "Commentary and Hermeneutics." In *Renaissance and Renewal in the Twelfth Century,* edited by Robert L. Benson and Giles Constable, pp. 173–200. Cambridge, MA: Harvard University Press, 1982.

Herman, Gerald. "The 'Sin against Nature' and Its Echoes in Medieval French Literature." *Annuale Mediaevale* 17 (1976): 76–77.

Hodgkin, Thomas. *The Ostro-gothic Invasion*. In *Italy and Her Invaders*, 2nd edition. Vol. 3. Oxford: Clarendon Press, 1896.

Huizinga, J. *Über die Verknüpfung des Poetischen mit dem Theologischen bei Alanus de Insulis*. Amsterdam: Noord-Hollandsche uitgevers-maatschappij, 1932.

Hunt, R. W. "Studies on Priscian in the 11th and 12th Centuries I." In *Collected Papers on the History of Grammar in the Middle Ages*, edited by G. L. Bursill-Hall, pp. 1–38. Amsterdam: John Benjamins B. V., 1980.

Irvine, Martin. "Abelard and (Re)writing the Male Body: Castration, Identity, and Remasculinization." In *Becoming Male in the Middle Ages*, edited by Jeffrey J. Cohen and Bonnie Wheeler, pp. 87–106. New York: Garland Publishing, 1997.

Jacobi, Klaus. "Abelard and Frege: The Semantics of Words and Propositions." In *Atti del Convegno internazionale di storia della logica, San Gimignano, 4–8 dicembre 1982*, edited by V. M. Abrusci, E. Casari and M. Mugnai, pp. 92–93. Bologna: CLUEB, 1983.

——. "Peter's Abelard's Investigations into the Meaning and Functions of the Speech Sign 'Est.' " In *The Logic of Being*, edited by S. Knuuttila and J. Hintikka, pp. 145–80. Boston: D. Reidel, 1986.

——. "Sprache und Wirklichkeit: Theoriebildung über Sprache im frühen 12. Jahrhundert." In *Sprachtheorien in Spätantike und Mittelalter*, edited by Sten Ebbesen, pp. 77–108. Tübingen: Gunter Narr Verlag, 1995.

——. "Unpersönliche Aussagen in Abaelards Kommentar zur *Peri Hermeneias*." In *Mediaeval Semantics and Metaphysics*, edited by E. P. Bos, pp. 1–63. Nijmegen: Ingenium Publishers, 1985.

Jerome, *Epistulae*. CSEL 54; PL 22.

Jolivet, Jean. *Arts du langage et théologie chez Abélard*. Paris: J. Vrin, 1969.

——. *Aspects de la pensée médiévale: Abélard. Doctrines du langage*. Paris: J. Vrin, 1987.

——. "Non-réalisme et platonisme chez Abélard: Essai d'interprétation." In AST, pp. 175–95.

——. "Rhètorique et théologie dans une page de Gilbert de Poitiers." In GPC, pp. 183–97.

——. "Remarques sur les *Regulae theologicae* d'Alain de Lille." In ALGCJG, pp. 83–111.

Jordan, Mark D. *The Invention of Sodomy in Christian Theology*. Chicago: University of Chicago Press, 1997.

Kaiser, Erich. "Odyssee-Szenen als Topoi." *Museum Helvelticum* 21 (1964): 109–36, 197–224.

Kappelmacher, Alfred. "Der schriftstellerische Plan des Boethius." In B-FG, pp. 71–81. First published in *Wiener Studien* 46 (1928): 215–25.

Kaylor, Noel Harold. *The Medieval 'Consolation of Philosophy': An Annotated Bibliography*. New York: Garland Publishing, Inc., 1992.

Kearney, Eileen. "*Scientia and Sapientia*: Reading Sacred Scripture at the Paraclete." In *From Cloister to Classroom: Monastic and Scholastic Approaches to Truth*, edited by E. Rozanne Elder, pp. 111–29. Kalamazoo: Cistercian Publications, 1986.

Keiser, Elizabeth B. *Courtly Desire and Medieval Homophobia: The Legitimation of Sexual Pleasure in "Cleanness" and its Contexts*. New Haven: Yale University Press, 1997.

Kiang, Dawson. "Aristotle and Phyllis: Leonardo's Drawing of an Exemplum." *Accademia Leonardi da Vinci* 7 (1994): 75–80.

Klingner, Fritz. *De Boethii Consolatione Philosophiae.*" In *Philologische Untersuchungen.* Vol. 27. Berlin: Weidmann, 1921.

Kneepkens, Corneille Henri. "Suppositio and Supponere in 12th-Century Grammar." In GPC, pp. 325–51.

Knowles, David. *The Evolution of Medieval Thought.* Edited by D. E. Luscombe and C. N. L. Brooke. 2nd ed. New York: Longman Group Limited, 1988.

Kraft, Kent. "Modernism in the Twelfth Century." *Comparative Literature Studies* (1981): 287–95.

Kretzmann, Norman. "Aristotle on Spoken Sound Significant by Convention." In *Ancient Logic and its Modern Interpretation*, edited by J. Corcoran, pp. 3–21. Boston: Kluwer Academic Publishers, 1974.

——. "The Culmination of the Old Logic in Peter Abelard." In *Renaissance and Renewal in the Twelfth Century*, edited by R. L. Benson and G. Constable, pp. 488–511. Cambridge, MA: Harvard University Press, 1982.

Laurenzi, F. *Le poesie ritmiche de Pietro Abelardo.* Rome: Pustet, 1911.

Leclercq, Jean. *The Love of Learning and the Desire for God: A Study of Monastic Culture.* Translated by Catharine Misrahi. 3rd ed. New York: Fordham University Press, 1982.

Lerer, Seth. *Boethius and Dialogue: Literary Method in The Consolation of Philosophy.* Princeton: Princeton University Press, 1985.

Leupin, Alexandre. *Barbarolexis: Medieval Writing and Sexuality.* Cambridge, MA: Harvard University Press, 1989.

Lewis, C. S. *The Allegory of Love: A Study in Medieval Tradition.* Oxford: Oxford University Press, 1936.

Lewry, Osmund. "Boethian Logic in the Medieval West." In *Boethius: His Life, Thought, and Influence*, edited by Margaret Gibson, pp. 90–134. Oxford: Basil Blackwell, 1981.

Libera, Alain de. "A propos de quelques théories logiques de Maótre Eckhart: Exist-et-il une tradition médiévale de la logique néo-platonicienne?" *Revue de théologie et de philosophie* 113 (1981): 1–24.

Listening to Heloise: The Voice of a Twelfth Century Woman. Edited by Bonnie Wheeler. New York: St. Martin's Press, 2000.

Lluch-Baixauli, M. *Boezio. La ragione teologica.* Milan: Editoriale Jacabook, 1997.

Luscombe, D. E. "Peter Abelard." In *A History of Twelfth-Century Western Philosophy*, edited by Peter Dronke, pp. 279–307. Cambridge: Cambridge University Press, 1988.

——. "Peter Abelard and Twelfth-Century Ethics." In *Peter Abelard's Ethics*, edited by D. Luscombe, pp. xiii–xxxvii. Oxford: Clarendon Press, 1971.

——. "The *Ethics* of Abelard: Some Further Considerations." In PA, pp. 65–84.

——. "The Letters of Heloise and Abelard since 'Cluny 1972.'" In PAPWW, pp. 19–39.

Mackey, Louis. *Peregrinations of the Word.* Ann Arbor: University of Michigan Press, 1997.

Magee, John C. "The Boethian Wheels of Fortune and Fate." *Mediaeval Studies* 49 (1987): 533–42.

Maioli, B. *Teoria dell'essere e dell'esistente e classificazione delle scienze in M. S. Boezio.* Rome: Bulzoni, 1978.

Mâle, Émile. *Religious Art in France, the Thirteenth Century: A Study of Medieval Iconography and its Sources*. Princeton: Princeton University Press, 1984.

Marbod of Rennes. *De raptu Dinae*. PL 171.

Marenbon, John. "Authenticity Revisited." In LH, pp. 19–34.

——. *Boethius*. Oxford: Oxford University Press, 2003.

——. *Early Medieval Philosophy (480–1150): An Introduction*. Boston: Routledge and Kegan Paul, 1983.

——. "Gilbert of Poitiers." In *A History of Twelfth-Century Western Philosophy*, edited by Peter Dronke, pp. 328–57. New York: Cambridge University Press, 1988.

——. *The Philosophy of Peter Abelard*. Cambridge: Cambridge University Press, 1997.

Marshall, Linda E. "The Identity of the 'New Man' in the *Anticlaudianus* of Alan of Lille." *Viator* 10 (1979): 77–94.

Martin, Christopher J. "The Logic of Negation in Boethius," *Phronesis* 36, 3 (1991): 277–304.

Mazzeo, Joseph Anthony. "St. Augustine's Rhetoric of Silence." *Journal of the History of Ideas* 23 (1962): 175–96.

McCracken, Peggy. "The Curse of Eve: Female Bodies and Christian Bodies in Heloise's Third Letter." In LH, pp. 217–32.

McGregor, James H. "Ovid at School: From the Ninth to the Fifteenth Century." *Classical Folia* 32 (1978): 29–52.

McGuire, Brian. "Heloise and the Consolation of Friendship." In LH, pp. 303–21.

McInerny, Ralph. *Boethius and Aquinas*. Washington, DC: Catholic University of America Press, 1990.

McKeon, Richard. "Poetry and Philosophy in the Twelfth Century: The Renaissance of Rhetoric." In *Critics and Criticism, Ancient and Modern*, edited by R. S. Crane, pp. 297–318. Chicago: The University of Chicago Press, 1952.

McLaughlin, Mary. "Abelard as Autobiographer." *Speculum* 42 (1967): 463–88.

——. "Peter Abelard and the Dignity of Women: Twelfth-Century 'Feminism' in Theory and Practice." In PAPV, pp. 287–334.

McLaughlin, T. P. "Abelard's Rule for Religious Women." *Mediaeval Studies* 18 (1956): 241–92.

McTighe, Thomas P. "Eternity and Time in Boethius." *History of Philosophy in the Making*, edited by Linus J. Thro, pp. 35–62. Washington DC: University Press of America, 1982.

Mendell, Clarence. *Our Seneca*. New Haven: Yale University Press, 1947.

Merlan, Philip. "Ammonius Hermiae, Zacharias Scholasticus and Boethius." *Greek, Roman and Byzantine Studies* 9 (1968): 193–203.

Mews, Constant J. "Aspects of the Evolution of Peter Abaelard's Thought on Signification and Predication." In GPC, pp. 15–41.

——. "On Dating the Works of Peter Abelard," ADHLMA 52 (1985): 73–134.

——. "Peter Abelard's *Theologia christiana* and *Theologia 'scholarium'* Re-examined." *Recherches de théologie ancienne et médiévale* 52 (1985): 109–58.

——. *The Lost Love Letters of Heloise and Abelard: Perceptions of Dialogue in Twelfth-Century France*. New York: St. Martin's Press, 1999.

——. "The Development of the *Theologia* of Peter Abelard." In PAPWW, pp. 183–98.

Micaelli, Claudio. " 'Natura' et 'persona' nel *Contra Eutychen et Nestorium* di Boezio: Osservazioni su alcuni problemi filosofici e linguistici." In *Atti del Congresso internazionale di studi Boeziani*, edited by Luca Obertello, pp. 327–36. Rome: Herder, 1981.

Miller, J. Hillis. "The Two Allegories." In *Allegory, Myth and Symbol*, edited by Morton W. Bloomfield, pp. 355–70. Cambridge, MA: Harvard University Press, 1981.

Mohrmann, Christine. "Some Remarks on the Language of Boethius." In B-FG, pp. 302–310. First published in *Latin Script and Letters, A.D. 400–900*, edited by John J. O'Meara and Bernd Naumann, pp. 54–61. Leiden: E. J. Brill, 1976.

Momigliano, Arnaldo. "Cassiodorus and the Italian Culture of His Time." *Proceedings of the British Academy* 41 (1955): 207–45.

Monfrin, Jacques. "Le problème de l'authenticité de la correspondance d'Abélard et d'Héloïse." In PAPV, pp. 409–24.

Monson, Donald A. "*Auctoritas* and Intertextuality in Adreas Capellanus' *De amore*." In *Poetics of Love in the Middle Ages*, edited by Moshe Lazar and Norris J. Lacy, pp. 69–79. Lanham, MD: George Mason University Press, 1989.

Moos, Peter von. "Le silence d'Héloïse." In PAPV, pp. 425–468.

——. Mittelalterforschung und Ideologiekritik: Der Gelehrtenstreit um Heloise. *Kritische Information* 15. Munich: W. Fink Verlag, 1974.

Murrin, Michael. *The Allegorical Epic: Essays in its Rise and Decline*. Chicago: University of Chicago Press, 1980.

Nash-Marshall, Sioban. *Participation and the Good: A Study in Boethian Metaphysics*. New York: Herder and Herder, 2000.

Nédoncelle, Maurice. "Les variations de Boèce sur la personne," *Revue des sciences religieuses* 29 (1955): 201–38.

Newman, Barbara. "Authority, Authenticity, and the Repression of Heloise." *Journal of Medieval and Renaissance Studies* 22, 2 (1992): 121–57.

——. *God and the Goddesses: Vision, Poetry and Belief in the Middle Ages*. Philadelphia: University of Pennsylvania Press, 2003.

Nielsen, Lauge. "On the Doctrine of Logic and Language of Gilbert Porreta and His Followers." *Cahiers de l'institut du moyen âge grec et latin* 17 (1976): 40–69.

Nitzsch, F. *Das System des Boethius: und die ihm zugeschriebenen theologischen Schriften: eine kritische Untersuchung*. Berlin: Wiegandt und Grieben, 1860.

Obertello, Luca. "Boezio e la cosmogonia platonica." Appendice I in *Boezio. La consolazione della filosofia. Gli opusculi teologici*, edited by Luca Obertello, pp. 407–16. Milan: Rusconi, 1979.

——. "Proclus, Ammonius and Boethius on Divine Knowledge." *Dionysius* 5 (1981): 127–64.

——. *Severino Boezio*. Rome: Herder, 1981.

O'Daly, Gerard. *The Poetry of Boethius*. Chapel Hill, NC: University of North Carolina Press, 1991.

Olsen, Birger Munk. *I Classici nel canone scolastico altomedievale*. Spoleto: Centro italiano di studi sull'alto Medioevo, 1991.

Origen. *Homilia in Genesim*, PG 12.

Otten, Willemien. "Nature and Scripture: Demise of Medieval Analogy." *Harvard Theological Review* 88, 2 (1995): 257–84.

Otten, Willemien. *From Paradise to Pradigm: A Study of Twelfth-Century Humanism.* Leiden: E. J. Brill, 2004.

Payen, J. Ch. "L'utopie du contrat social dans l'*Anticlaudianus.*" In ALGCJG, pp. 125–34.

Pelikan, Jaroslav. *The Emergence of the Catholic Tradition. The Christian Tradition: A History of the Development of Doctrine.* Vol. 1. Chicago: University of Chicago Press, 1971.

Pessin, Sarah. "Boethius and the Neoplatonic Good: Hebdomads and the Nature of God in the *Quomodo Substantiae.*" *Carmina Philosophiae* 10 (2001): 51–71.

Peter Abelard, Proceedings of the International Conference, Louvain, May 10–12, 1971. Leuven, Belgium: Leuven University Press/The Hague: Martinus Nijhoff, 1974.

Petrus Abaelardus (1079–1142): Person, Werk, und Wirkung, edited by Rudolf Thomas et al. Trier Theologische Studien 38. Trier: Paulinus, 1980.

Pierre Abèlard—Pierre le Vénérable: Les courants philosophiques, littéraires et artistiques en occident au milieu du XIIe siècle, Abbaye de Cluny, July 2-9, 1972. Paris: Éditions du Centre National de la Recherche Scientifique, 1975.

Philo. *The Works of Philo.* Translated by C. D. Yonge. Peabody, MA: Hendrickson Publishers, 1993.

Powell, Morgan. "Listening to Heloise at the Paraclete: Of Scholarly Diversion and a Woman's 'Conversion.' " In LH, pp. 255–86.

Prepositinus, *De nominibus divinis: regule.* In Giuseppe Angelini, *L'Ortodossia e la grammatica: Analisi di struttura e deduzione storica della teologia trinitaria di Prepositino* (Rome: Università Gregoriana, 1972), pp. 199–303.

Prior, A. N. "The Logic of Negative Terms in Boethius." *Franciscan Studies* 13 (1953): 1–6.

Priscian. *Institutiones grammaticae.* In *Grammatici latini,* edited by Heinrich Keil. Vol. 4. Leipzig: B. G. Teubner, 1864, repr. Hildesheim: George Olms Verlag, 1961.

Pseudo-Dionysius, the Aeropagite. *The Celestial Hierarchy.* Translated by Colm Luibheid. Mahwah, NJ: Paulist Press, 1987.

———. *De divinibus nominibus,* PG 3.

Quilligan, Maureen. "Allegory, Allegoresis, and the Deallegorization of Language: The *Roman de la rose,* the *De planctu naturae,* and the *Parlement of Foules.*" In *Allegory, Myth, and Symbol,* edited by Morton W. Bloomfield, pp. 163–86. Cambridge, MA: Harvard University Press, 1981.

———. "Words and Sex: The Language of Allegory in the *De planctu naturae,* the *Roman de la Rose,* and Book III of *The Faerie Queene.*" *Allegorica* 2 (1977): 195–216.

Rahner, Hugo. *Griechische Mythen in christlicher Deutung.* Zurich: Rhein Verlag, 1957.

Rand, Edward Kennard. "On the Composition of Boethius' *Consolatio Philosophiae.*" In B-FG, pp. 249–77. First published in *Harvard Studies in Classical Philology* 15 (1904): 1–28.

———. *Founders of the Middle Ages.* New York: Dover, 1957.

Raynaud de Lage, Guy. *Alain de Lille: poète du XIIe siècle.* Montréal: Institut d'études médiévales, 1951.

Reed, Thomas. *Middle English Debate Poetry and the Aesthetics of Irresolution.* Columbia, MO: University of Missouri Press, 1990.

Reiss, Edmund. "The Fall of Boethius and the Fiction of the *Consolatio Philosophiae.*" *The Classical Journal* 77 (1981): 37–47.

Relihan, Joel. *Ancient Menippean Satire.* Baltimore: The Johns Hopkins University Press, 1993.

Richard of St. Victor. *Benjamin minor sive De gratia contemplationis* PL 196, 63–192.

——. *The Twelve Patriarchs; The Mystical Ark; Book Three of the Trinity.* Translated by Grover A. Zinn. New York: Paulist Press, 1979.

Rijk, L. M. de. "Boèce logicien et philosophe: Ses positions sémantiques et sa mètaphysique de l'être." In *Atti del Congresso internazionale di studi boeziani,* edited by Luca Obertello, pp. 141–56. Rome: Herder, 1981.

——. "Gilbert de Poitiers: Ses vues sémantiques et mètaphysiques." In GPC, pp. 147–71.

——. "La Signification de la proposition (*dictum propositionis*) chez Abélard." In PAPV, pp. 547–55.

——. "Martin M. Tweedale on Abailard: Some Criticisms of a Fascinating Venture." *Vivarium* 23, 2 (1985): 81–97.

——. "On Boethius's Notion of Being: A Chapter of Boethian Semantics." In *Meaning and Inference in Medieval Philosophy,* edited by Norman Kretzmann, pp. 1–29. Boston: Kluwer Academic Publishers, 1988.

——. "On the Chronology of Boethius' Works on Logic." *Vivarium* 2 (1964): 1–49, 125–62.

——. "Peter Abälard (1079–1142): Meister und Opfer der Scharfsinn." In PAPWW, pp. 125–38.

——. "Peter Abelard's Semantics and His Doctrine of Being." *Vivarium* 24, 2 (1986): 85–127.

——. "The Semantical Impact of Abailard's Solution of the Problem of Universals." In PAPWW, pp. 139–51.

Robertson, D. W. *Abelard and Heloise.* New York: The Dial Press, 1972.

Robins, R. H. *A Short History of Linguistics.* 2nd ed. New York: Longman, 1979.

Rohmer, J. "La finalité morale chez les théologiens de saint Augustin à Duns Scot." *Études de philosophie médiévale* 27 (1939): 31–49.

Roland-Gosselin, M.-D. *Le "De ente et essentia" de Saint Thomas d'Aquin.* Paris: Bibliothèque Thomiste, 1926.

Rosier, Irène. "Les acceptions du terme *substantia* chez Pierre Hèlie." In GPC, pp. 299–324. Naples: Bibliopolis, 1987.

——. "*Res significata* et *modus significandi*: Les implications d'une distinction médié-vale." In *Sprachtheorien in Spätantike und Mittelalter,* edited by Sten Ebbesen, pp. 135–68. Tübingen: Gunter Narr Verlag, 1995.

Rouse, Richard and Mary. "Biblical Distinctions in the Thirteenth Century." ADHDLMA 41 (1974): 27–37.

——. "*Statim invenire*: Schools, Preachers, and New Attitudes to the Page." In *Renaissance and Renewal in the Twelfth Century,* edited by Robert L. Benson and Giles Constable, pp. 201–25. Cambridge, MA: Harvard University Press, 1982.

226   BIBLIOGRAPHY

Rousseau, Philip. "The Death of Boethius: The Charge of *Maleficium*." *Studi medievali* 20 (1979): 871–89.

Ruys, Juanita Feros. "*Quae maternae immemor naturae*: The Rhetorical Struggle over the Meanings of Motherhood in the Writings of Heloise and Abelard." In LH, pp. 323–40.

Sarton, George. "Aristotle and Phyllis." *Isis* 14 (1930): 8–19.

Scanlon, Larry. "Unspeakable Pleasures: Alain de Lille, Sexual Regulation and the Priesthood of Genius." *Romantic Review* 86 (1995): 219–26.

Schibanoff, Susan. "Sodomy's Mark." In *Queering the Middle Ages*, edited by Glenn Burger and Steve F. Kruger, pp. 28–56. Minneapolis: University of Minnesota Press, 2001.

Schmid, Wolfgang. "Philosophisches und Medizinisches in der *Consolatio* des Boethius." In *Festschrift Bruno Snell*, pp. 113–44. Munich: Verlag C. H. Beck, 1956.

Schurr, V. *Die Trinitätslehre des Boethius im Lichte der 'Skythischen Kontroversen.'* Paderborn: F. Schöningh, 1935.

Scotus, Johannes. "Der Kommentar des Johannes Scotus zu den *Opuscula Sacra* des Boethius." In *Johannes Scotus*, edited by E. K. Rand, pp. 28–80. Munich: Quellen und Untersuchungen zur lateinischen Philologie des Mittelalters, 1906.

Seneca. *Agamemnon*. In *Tragedies*, edited by T. E. Page and translated by Frank J. Miller, pp. 1–87. Vol. 2. Loeb Classical Library. Cambridge, MA: Harvard University Press, 1953.

———. *De constantia sapientis*, In *Moral Essays*, translated by John W. Basore, pp. 48–105. Vol. 1. Loeb Classical Library. Cambridge, MA: Harvard University Press, 1928–1935.

———. *Hercules Furens*. In *Tragedies*, edited by G. P. Goold and translated by Frank J. Miller, pp. 1–121. Vol. 1. Loeb Classical Library. Cambridge, MA: Harvard University Press, 1979.

Sheil, James. "Boethius' Commentaries on Aristotle." *Mediaeval and Renaissance Studies* 4 (1958): 217–44.

Sikes, J. G. *Peter Abailard*. London: Cambridge University Press, 1932.

Silk, Edmund T. "Boethius's *Consolatio Philosophiae* as a Sequel to Augustine's *Dialogues* and *Soliloquia*." *Harvard Theological Review* 32 (1939): 19–39.

Simpson, James. *Sciences and the Self in Medieval Poetry*: Alan of Lille's *Anticlaudianus* and John Gower's *confessio amantis*. Cambridge: Cambridge University Press, 1995.

Smalley, Beryl. "*Prima Clavis Sapientiae*: Augustine and Abelard," in *Studies in Medieval Thought and Learning From Abelard to Wyclif*. London: The Hambledon Press, 1981.

———. *The Study of the Bible in the Middle Ages*. 2nd ed. Oxford: Blackwell, 1952.

Sorabji, Richard. "The Ancient Commentators on Aristotle." In *Aristotle Transformed: The Ancient Commentators and Their Influence*, edited by Richard Sorabji, pp. 1–27. New York: Cornell University Press, 1990.

Southern, R. W. *The Making of the Middle Ages*. New Haven: Yale University Press, 1983.

———. "The Schools of Paris and the School of Chartres." In *Renaissance and Renewal in the Twelfth Century*, edited by Robert L. Benson and Giles Constable, pp. 113–37. Cambridge, MA: Harvard University Press, 1982.

Steinen, Wolfram von den. "Die Planctus Abaelards—Jephthas Tochter," *Mittellateinisches Jahrbuch*, 4 (1967): 125–40.

Stevens, John. *Words and Music in the Middle Ages: Song, Narrative, Dance, and Drama, 1050—1350.* Cambridge: Cambridge University Press, 1986.

Stewart, H. F. and E. K. Rand. "Life of Boethius." In *The Theological Tractates, and The Consolation of Philosophy*, translated by H. F. Stewart, E. K. Rand and S. J. Tester, pp. xi–xv. Loeb Classical Library. Cambridge, MA: Harvard University Press, 1973.

Stock, Brian. *Augustine the Reader: Meditation, Self-Knowledge, and the Ethics of Interpretation.* Cambridge, MA: Harvard University Press, 1996.

——. *The Implications of Literacy: Written Language and Models of Interpretation in the Eleventh and Twelfth Centuries.* Princeton: Princeton University Press, 1983.

Stump, Eleonore. "Boethius' *In Ciceronis Topica* and Stoic Logic." In *Studies in Medieval Philosophy*, edited by John F. Wippel, pp. 1–22. Washington, DC: Catholic University of America Press, 1987.

——. "Boethius's Works on the Topics." *Vivarium* 12 (1974): 77–92.

——. "Logic in the Early Twelfth Century." In *Meaning and Inference in Medieval Philosophy: Studies in Memory of Jan Pinborg*, edited by Norman Kretzmann, pp. 31–55. Boston: Kluwer Academic Publishers, 1988.

Sweeney, Eileen C. "Hugh of St. Victor: The Augustinian Tradition of Sacred and Secular Reading Revised." In *Reading and Wisdom: The De doctrina christiana of Augustine in the Middle Ages*, edited by Edward D. English, pp. 61–83. Notre Dame, IN: University of Notre Dame Press, 1995.

——. Review of John Marenbon, *The Philosophy of Peter Abelard*, "Abelard's Progress: From Logic to Ethics." *International Philosophical Quarterly* 40 (September 2000): 367–76.

——. "Rewriting the Narrative of Scripture: Twelfth-Century Debates Over Reason and Theological Form." *Medieval Philosophy and Theology* 3 (1993): 1–34.

Taylor, Andrew. "A Second Ajax: Peter Abelard and the Violence of Dialectic." In *The Tongue of the Fathers: Gender and Ideology in Twelfth-Century Latin*, edited by David Townsend and Andrew Taylor, pp. 14–34. Philadelphia: University of Pennsylvania Press, 1998.

Taylor, Charles. *The Ethics of Authenticity.* Cambridge, MA: Harvard University Press, 1991.

Teräväinen, Juha. "Ultimate Reality and Meaning in 12th Century Logic." *Ultimate Reality and Meaning* 6 (1983): 22–31.

Thibodeau, Lucille Claire. *The Relation of Peter Abelard's "Planctus Dinae" to Biblical Sources and Exegetic Tradition: A Historical and Textual Study.* PhD diss. Harvard University, 1990. Ann Arbor, MI: UMI, 1990.

Thomas Aquinas, *Summa theologiae.* Translated by the Fathers of the English Dominican Province. New York: Benzinger Bros., 1947.

Tweedale, Martin M. *Abailard on Universals.* Amsterdam: North-Holland Publishing Co., 1976.

Tweedale, Martin M. "Logic: From the Late Eleventh Century to the Time of Abelard." In *A History of Twelfth-Century Western Philosophy*, edited by Peter Dronke, pp. 196–226. New York: Cambridge University Press, 1988.

Valente, Luisa. "Langage et théologie pendant la seconde moitié du XIIe siècle." In *Sprachtheorien in Spätantike und Mittelalter*, edited by Sten Ebbesen, pp. 33–54. Tübingen: Gunter Narr Verlag, 1995.

———. *Phantasia contrarietatis: Contradizzioni scritturali, discorso teologico et arti del linguaggio nel "De tropis loquendi" di Pietro Cantore (d. 1197)*. Florence, Olschki, 1997.

Vance, Eugene. *Mervelous Signals: Poetics and Sign Theory in the Middle Ages*. Lincoln: University of Nebraska Press, 1986.

Vecchi, G. *Pietro Abelardo, I "Planctus."* Modena: Societa Tipografica Modenese, 1951.

Vitz, Evelyn Birge. *Medieval Narrative and Modern Narratology*. New York: New York University Press, 1989.

Vogel, C. J. de. "Boethiana I." *Vivarium* 9 (1971): 77–93.

———. "Boethiana II." *Vivarium* 10 (1974): 17–26.

———. "The Problem of Philosophy and Christian Faith in Boethius' *Consolatio*." In *Romanitas et Christianitas*, edited by Jan Hendrik Waszink and Willem den Boer et al., pp. 357–70. Amsterdam: North-Holland Publishing Co., 1973.

Waddell, Chrysogonus. *The Paraclete Statutes Institutiones Nostrae*. Introduction, edition and commentary. Trappist, KY: Gethsemani Abbey, 1987.

Weinberger, Wilhelm. Introduction. *Ancii Manlii Severini Boethii philosophiae consolationis libri quinque* CSEL 67. Vienna: Hölder-Pichler-Tempsky,1938.

Weinrich, Lorenz. "Peter Abelard as Musician—I." *Musical Quarterly* 55 (1969): 295–312.

Wetherbee, Winthrop. *Platonism and Poetry in the Twelfth Century: The Literary Influence of the School of Chartres*. Princeton: Princeton University Press, 1972.

———. "The Function of Poetry in the *De planctu naturae* of Alain de Lille." *Traditio* 25 (1969): 86–125.

Wheeler, Bonnie. "Origenary Fantasies: Abelard's Castration and Confession." In *Becoming Male in the Middle Ages*, edited by Jeffrey Jerome Cohen and Bonnie Wheeler, pp. 107–28. New York: Garland Publishing, 1997.

Whitman, Jon. *Allegory: The Dynamics of an Ancient and Medieval Technique* Cambridge, MA: Harvard University Press, 1987.

Wielockx, Robert. "Le sentence de caritate et la discussion scolastique sur l'amour." *Ephemerides theologicae lovanienses* 58 (1982): 50–86, 334–56; 59 (1983): 26–45.

Williams, Paul. *The Moral Philosophy of Peter Abelard*. Lanham, MD: University Press of America, 1980.

Wilmart, André. "Note sur les plus anciens recueils de distinctions bibliques." In *Mémorial Lagrange. Cinquantenaire de l'École biblique et archéologique française de Jérusalem*, pp. 307–46. Paris: J. Gabalda, 1940.

Wilson, Katharina, and Glenda McCleon. "Textual Strategies in the Abelard/Heloise Correspondence." In LH, pp. 121–42.

Wolf, Christine. "Untersuchungen zum Krankheitsbild in des ersten Buch der Consolatio Philosophiae des Boethius." *Rivista di cultura classica e medioevale* 6 (1964): 213–23.

Wouters, Annelies. "Une larme pour Abner: Une lamentation de l'Ancien Testament remaniée par Pierre Abélard." In *Pierre Abélard: Colloque internationale de Nante*, edited by Jean Jolivet and Henri Habrias, pp. 295–306. Rennes: Presses Universitaires de Rennes, 2003.

Yearly, Janthia. *The Medieval Latin Planctus as a Genre.* 3 Vols. PhD diss. University of York, 1983.

———. "A Bibliography of *planctus*." *Journal of the Plainsong and Mediaeval Music Society* 4 (1981): 12–52.

Ziolkowski, Jan. *Alan of Lille's Grammar of Sex: The Meaning of Grammar to a Twelfth-Century Intellectual.* Cambridge, MA: Harvard University Press, 1985.

INDEX

Boethius—*continued*
  De hebdomadibus, 21, 26–33, 56, 130,
      138, 190 nn. 49, 50
  influence of, 2–3
  life of, 20, 40, 60, 191 n.62
  logical works, 9–20, 21, 180, 187 n.10
  perspectives, theme of, 7–8, 9, 11, 12,
      21, 34–35, 38, 39, 41, 42, 43, 50,
      57, 58, 60–61, 178, 180, 183
  plan to show consistency of Aristotle and
      Plato, 16, 60, 188 n.22
  theological tractates, 20–38, 180
  see also, Boethius, *Contra Eutychen et
      Nestorius*; *De hebdomadibus*; *De trinitate*
  De trinitate, 21, 33–38, 130, 132, 146
  see also disputation, in theology;
          esotericism; ethics; evil, problem of;
          faith an reason; fortune; future
          contingents; God, union with;
          Greek literature and myth in the
          Consolation; language; language,
          theological; logic; nature;
          Neoplatonism; paradox; poetry;
          providence, views on; rationalism;
          sin; spirituality; theology; universals,
          problem of; virtue
Bonaventure, 154
Brown, Catherine, 118
Burke, Kenneth, 139, 148
Burnett, Charles, 124
Buytaert, E. M., 87

Categories, *see* Aristotle, *Categories*
Chadwick, Henry, 18, 59
Chalcedon formula on Christology, 22, 25
chance, 18, 19, 56
Châtillon, Jean, 206 n.30
Chenu, M.-D., 155
Cicero, 9
Clanchy, M. T., 93, 94, 123, 202 n.107
Contra Eutychen et Nestorius, *see* Boethius,
      Contra Eutychen et Nestorius
"Confessio fidei ad Heloisam," *see* Abelard,
      "Confessio fidei ad Heloisam"
confession, in Abelard, 117
Confessions, *see* Augustine, *Confessions*
Colish, Marcia L., xi, 192 n.74
concepts, in Abelard, 69–70
consent, in Abelards' ethics, 115
Consolation of Philosophy, *see* Boethius,
      Consolation of Philosophy

Cottiaux, J., 90, 94
Crouse, Robert, 21, 26
Curley, Thomas F., III, 194 n.96

David, King, *see* Abelard, "Planctus David
      super Saul et Jonathan"; "Planctus
      David super Abner filio Ner quem
      Joab occidit"
Delhaye, Philippe, 211 n.89
Desire, figure of, in *De planctu naturae*, 160,
      164, 165
determinism, 17–18, 19
dicta, in Abelard, 77
dictionary, Alan of Lille's theological, *see*
      Alan of Lille, *Liber in distinctionibus
      dictionum theologicalium*
Dinah, *see* Abelard, individual planctus,
      "Planctus Dinae filae Jacob"
disputation, in theology
  in Abelard, 80, 81–82, 84, 93, 94
  in Alan of Lille, 140–42, 147, *see also* Alan
      of Lille, *Summa quoniam hominess*
  in Boethius, 25–26
  see also, theology, methods of
divine ideas, 12, 58, 70, 74
divine names, *see* language, theological
De doctrina christiana, *see* Augustine, *De
      doctrina Christiana*
Donatus, 159
Dronke, Peter, 96, 97, 103, 106, 107, 109,
      194 n.97, 200–1 n.89, 203 n.115

Ebbeson, Sten, 139
Eco, Umberto, 177
Epicureanism, 18
esotericism,
  in Abelard, 63
  in Alan of Lille, 129, 141–42, 150
  in Boethius, 22, 26, 31, 32, 33–34, 38,
      39, 59
esse, 28–29, 190 n.90
Ethica, *see* Abelard, *Ethica sive Scito teipsum*
ethics
  of Abelard, 91, 95, 118–20, 121, 195 n.6,
      202 n.107
  of Alan of Lille, 157, 170, 174, 211 n.89
  see also sin; virtue
Evans, Gillian R., 137, 148, 151, 156
evil, problem of,
  in Abelard, 89, 92
  in Boethius, 47, 49–51, 52